HURLING

America discovers an ancient Irish sport

By
Denis O'Brien

Copyright Information

Copyright © 2012 Denis O'Brien. All rights reserved worldwide.

No part of this document or the related files may be reproduced or transmitted in any form, by any means (electronic, photocopying, recording, or otherwise) without the prior written permission of the publisher.

A lot of hard work went into putting this book together. The information in this document is copyrighted. I would ask that you do not share this information with others - you purchased this book, and you have a right to use it on your system. Another person who has not purchased this book does not have that right.

Website: http://www.gaelicsportscast.com

Cover design Brandon Salfai.

Cover action photo by Sean T. Noonan.

Acknowledgement

Writing a book is a mammoth task. You discover this sooner than later. Helping me along the way with advice and encouragement have been several people to whom I owe a great deal of thanks.

Paul Darby provided timely feedback on early history segments of the book. His overall advice and encouragement have been of immense help.

I also would like to thank newspaper editor and hurler, John Simcoe for his early editing advice and help throughout the writing of this book.

I also would like to express my thanks to personal friends who provided continued support without question.

I would also like to thank Tim Flanagan, the North American GAA County Board PRO, who has always helped with facts and figures when requested. And also, to friend, author and Canada GAA Secretary, John O'Flynn for making available towards my research, sections of his own work on the GAA in Canada.

A huge thanks also must go to all the American Hurling Clubs that answered questions and took part in email interviews. I also thank them for the use of club images and photographs used in this book.

And to Aaron Ramponi for editing and proofing on short notice. And, to Brandon Salfai, who without hesitation, stepped in to help with readying the work for the ebook format and for providing a cover design. Both Aaron and Brandon have been pivotal and I can't thank them enough.

Introduction

There is a new sport on the horizon in America. Its legacy is ancient. Its birthplace – that mystic green island across the Atlantic Ocean. The sport is called the fastest game on grass, and today, America is falling under its spell. This sport is Hurling.

Americans are beginning to discover hurling's power and grace. This book tells you about the sport that is hooking Americans young and not so young.

Readers follow a trail of discovery from hurling's ancient roots, to the byways of hurling's history on the Emerald Isle, to its arrival in America, to its meaning for Irish immigrants, and of its growing presence on campuses and American public parks.

Along the way we explore how and why Americans, on seeing hurling for the first time, are simply 'blown away'. How and why Americans are getting hooked on the game and in the most unlikely of places.

Hurling's magic is reaching out beyond the confines of Irish immigrant life and grabbing hold of Americans in ever increasing number. Its warrior-like power has even inspired members of the U.S. Armed Force. Hurling speaks to them directly, it has changed their lives.

This book also examines why discovery has taken so long and what the sport's growing presence across America could mean.

Taking in a local St. Patrick's Day Parade for one day in the year, America gets to wear 'the green', savor Irish dance and music, and no doubt, sup from the fountain of Ireland's finest whiskeys and ales.

As Americans line the festive thoroughfares of the country, notice may be taken of the local hurling club marching behind a banner with players kitted out in team colors, 'pucking' a baseball-like ball to and fro. But amidst the colorful floats, pipe bands, drill teams, horse teams, cheer leaders, uniformed groups, and the various organizations, that weird stick ball sighting can be readily forgotten. It is put aside as a curiosity. After all, the important stuff is 'the wearing of the green', the dancing, the music, the merry making …. isn't it?

America and Irish America have been missing out on an integral part of Irish culture for many, many, generations … Hurling.

Introduction

The sport of hurling is as intrinsic for the Irish as baseball is for Americans. Its ancient link is treasured. Its place held sacred.

Irish America isn't aware of hurling's significance, its importance. It is necessary to look at that marching hurling club with new eyes. It is necessary to freeze frame the moment and paint in hurling's lost American memory.

Research for this book was conducted over a three year period. It draws from scholarly works, books, papers, magazine articles, organization reports, letters, newspaper archives, email and Facebook interviews, first-hand accounts, and my own reporting while in America.

It also draws on the podcast called GaelicSportsCast which I produce and publish. The podcast reports on Gaelic Sports – Hurling, Mens and Ladies Gaelic Football and Camogie (ladies hurling) news around the globe since late 2009.

Gaelic Sports are played in Ireland and by Irish ex-pats around the globe. The sports are little known outside Ireland.

It is time to bring the story of Gaelic sport's oldest and greatest game... Hurling...out from the shadows of obscurity and into the light.

That is why this book is written.

Denis O'Brien

Table of Contents

Copyright Information.. 2
Acknowledgement 3
Introduction 4
Table of Contents 6
Chapter 1 .... Made for Americans 7
Chapter 2 .... The Sport 14
Chapter 3 .... Ancient Game 32
Chapter 4 .... Early American Hurling 50
Chapter 5 .... Hurling Revolution 75
Chapter 6 .... The Barley House Wolves – Warrior Hurlers 130
Chapter 7 .... College Wildfire 154
Chapter 8 .... The Big Picture 179
References 210
About the Author 219
The Rules of Hurling 220
Map of Ireland 233

Chapter 1

Made for Americans

Americans were born to play the sport of Hurling. Once a hurley stick is placed into an American hand something magical happens. It is an instant hook.

Hurling is the national sport of Ireland. It is one of the oldest team sports in the world and called the fastest game on grass.

Its roots go back to antiquity with earliest texts telling how hurling was played in Ireland over 1000 years before the Christian era. Today the sport is weaving its way into American hearts as all across the United States people are starting to take a hurley into their hand and 'puck' a baseball-like ball around their local green.

Hurling is not to be confused with curling – a kind of shuffleboard on ice. It couldn't be any more different as the Irish sport is an entirely different animal all together. It could though be called a cousin of ice hockey. Some think it's more a parent than a cousin of that great Winter game. Some even think that Baseball has its roots steeped in hurling.

Hurling has been played in America for over a century and a half, but the thing is, nobody has ever heard about it. Americans are only really beginning to find out about the game now.

Ironically, the U.S. might have come to know and love the sport before this if only ESPN had continued its experiment. However, the man who made TV sport what it is today might agree that hurling is made for Americans.

Roone Arledge, that icon of televised sports, might also tell you that America's newest sporting discovery could make super TV entertainment. In reality, it would have taken a guy like Arledge to recognize the game's potential as a sports and entertainment product in America.

Roone Arledge, when starting with ABC Sport in 1960, became the producer of NCAA football coverage at the tender age of 29. From that very first ABC presentation of their initial NCAA game that season, Roone revolutionized how sport is televised.

Before Arledge, a football game on TV was presented straight-up with fixed overview shots in a once-off time line. What you see is what you get. But Arledge changed all that.

He introduced more cameras, more shot angles. He used hand-held cameras, cameras on mic booms, elevated cameras, and was the first to employ instant replay and slow motion in sports.

Every time you think of the instant replay, and slow motion camera angle shots of New York Giants Mario Mannigham's brilliant sideline catch in the recent 2012 Super Bowl, think Roone Arledge. Arledge was all about capturing the moment, capturing the drama.

For Giants fans it was ecstasy, for Patriots, agony. He is said to have coined ABC Sports line: 'The Thrill of Victory, the agony of defeat'.

He would go on to become a legend – personally in charge of production for 10 Olympic Games, the creator of Monday Night Football and the maestro behind ABC's legendary, Wide World of Sports.

TV sports coverage has had a big bearing on popularizing sports in the U.S. Stanley J. Baran in an article entitled 'The Industrial Benefits of Televised Sports' for the Museum of Broadcast Communications website, outlines how TV influenced the modern evolution of sport in America. During the 1950s sports like professional and college football prospered as TV promoted the sports to local, regional and national audiences. Interest in a sport was enhanced through the medium of television and of course TV rights meant greater economic benefits for the respective sporting organization.

Arledge saw the potential that sport offered as an entertainment medium. Similarly, in hurling, he would have recognized a fast paced, tough tackling, high energy, high scoring game. He would have recognized it as having all the ingredients necessary to create TV drama.

In an internal memo – referencing football – he said, he would 'take the viewer to the game'. This notion was to apply equally to both sports and casual viewer.

But if only Arledge, or some visionary like him, had been around ESPN when the channel first set up shop on Sept 7, 1979. Why? Well, on the very first weekend that ESPN went on air that September, they showed the sport of hurling to America.

Yes, in the flesh. Ireland's national game on U.S. TV, a sport that nobody had ever heard about before. ESPN shone the spotlight on hurling but it was a straight-up presentation and produced by Irish TV for an Irish audience.

Wrote Megan Gwynne Mullen in her book,'Television in the multichannel age: A brief history of cable television':

> "[F]irst at 7 a.m. Saturday, September 8, there was Munster hurling. Two million Americans [compared to over 100 million subscribers alone today in the U.S.] had ESPN on their cable system, and probably only a handful of them knew what they were watching early this morning."

Besides little appreciation for the sport, the program wasn't packaged for an American audience and this may have contributed to ESPN discontinuing the series.

This author recalls the period when ESPN showed the Munster Hurling Championship from Ireland. Living in New York in the early 1980s, a flick through the channels one evening and there it was hurling in the flesh. Thunderstruck understates the sighting. It had an Irish commentary for an Irish audience and Americans would have been lost tuning in. However, there are Americans out there who remember the program. One of them is Irish American James Tierney, who lives in Portland, Maine with his wife and three kids.

When James was 10 years old, he had seen the ESPN show and something about the game stayed with him. Then one fine day, 28 years later in the summer of 2007, his memory got rebooted.

James remembered the sport he had seen on ESPN when he got wind of someone at work trying to start off a hurling club in Portland. It all came back to him and the next thing you know he was eagerly trying to find out everything he could about the sport.

In an interview in 2011 for the podcast GaelicSportsCast – reports on hurling and other Gaelic Sports (mens and ladies Gaelic football, camogie – hurling for ladies) worldwide – Tierney said the memory of ESPN's program got things started:

> "That's literally what triggered it and something sound[ed] familiar about it. So I went on You Tube and looked it [hurling] up. I saw a bunch of different clips and I said, well you know, this is going to be interesting. Not sure if my wife will approve, or, my three kids."

James Tierney was 38 when he first picked up a hurley and though he found the game tough at the start he stuck with it, and now years later, is loving it:

> "[I was] really fascinated by it. I had been a cyclist for a long time. I got there for my first practice with hurling and the next day I could

barely move. I decided that something makes me hurt this bad, I had at least give it a try.

"So yeah, am now in my fourth year and love the sport!

I've managed to go through four full years almost without getting hurt too badly but I do wish I had found it earlier in life.

Maine has a fairly large Irish population, and you know, it's just a shame that the sport never spread north of Boston for the longest time, but we're trying to change that right now."

In the past hurling had been known and played only by Irish immigrants, and from time to time by a minority of their descendants.

Down through the years some efforts had been made by the local Irish Diaspora and the game's governing body in Ireland, the Gaelic Athletic Association (GAA), to popularize the game but such efforts fell through the cracks of time and the sport never became a popular pastime in the U.S. Although, during the late 19th century and the early 20th century, many mainstream newspaper hacks reporting on the game in cities such as New York and Boston, thought that it would only be a matter of time before hurling became popular with Americans. But it didn't.

Yet today, Americans are beginning to rediscover the fascination for the game and are helping sprout fledgling clubs all across the country. From Maine to Oregon, American adults are signing up in droves and seemingly they can't get enough of the sport. And, they're not just Irish American adults but Americans of all backgrounds.

If you happen to be an Irish American reader, you could be forgiven for scratching your head a little at this juncture. '... HURLING ... what the heck is that?? Nobody in the family ever told me about this. I mean I heard about Irish traditional music, Irish dancing, Irish beer and whiskey and that, but HURLING ... a sport? Never heard of it.' But you're not alone, as many people and sports fans around America and the world, haven't a notion it exists either.

So then, why should the sport be a fit for American athletes? Why should it be made for Americans? Well because, it's the game Americans were always meant to play.

Take the batting and catching elements of baseball, mix in a little football physicality, agility and strategy, add a dash of ice hockey stick-work, and a sprinkling of Lacrosse finesse, and you have a game that's perfect for Americans. Hurling has all these elements.

It is fast paced, has oodles of skills and plays. It is high scoring. All the things that Americans love in outdoor sport. And, though it's not like anything anyone has ever seen before ... It's made for Americans! Tailor made. However, Americans didn't know and still don't know the sport exists. A mystery sport for sure.

It was hidden away out of sight within the Irish immigrant community, mainstream America never got exposed to the sport. It remained unseen. It never became a household name.

Over the past 150 years, the organization and operation of the sport has been dependent on Irish immigrants and their descendants. The sport stayed in the shadows and for various reasons never really got its day in the sun like football and baseball.

The organizational model relied, and still does, on Irish immigrants and short term Irish students who make up the playing numbers for summer leagues in places where there are lots of native Irish, like New York, Boston, Chicago and San Francisco.

But there also existed a mindset that as you had plenty of immigrants ready to play, you didn't need to recruit locally. Parallel to this line of thinking was the mindset that only the Irish, who grew up with the sport, could play it and that you were wasting your time if you tried to teach the sport to others, like American adults. However, American hurlers are beginning to discover that this ancient sport is beginning to speak to them in ways that other sports never could. They are finding that hurling's unique facets are engaging. They like executing its multiple plays.

Such as: make yardage with ball in hand; make a shoulder tackle; bat up field; score a point (over bar and between uprights) from a 70 yard distance; score a goal (under-cross) – and there's no such thing as offside, ever; kick the ball; palm it; strike off the ground, bat when in the air; bat gingerly; bat fiercely; scoop up with hurley; roll-up with hurley (more on that in a bit); prevent attack from in front and behind; catch a falling ball; catch a speeding ball; catch a bouncing ball; catch a pass from in front or from behind; side step with ball; hop ball off ground with bat, hop ball on hurl and balance the ball on the hurl while running.

When a spectator witnesses an exciting game it's akin to experiencing something raw, yet beautiful. Something electric, yet ancient. There's something about hurling that goes beyond other sports.

It has unbelievable skill but it also possesses physicality. It has sublime moments. It has continued frenzy. Power is expressed but so is grace.

Football, baseball, basketball and ice hockey, in their own unique way, of course posses similar qualities but there is something about the Irish sport of hurling that can leave you breathless. It is a force of nature.

It is different to anything anybody has ever seen before, yet somehow, one knows instinctively that it always existed.

Once you put a hurl into your hand and bat the ball down-field 100 yards, that feeling that you always knew this game existed, comes to life. A feeling that it was always meant to be played. From there you begin to live it.

Hurling has a way about it which players come to recognize once they get into the game. The feel and tempo of the sport gets clearer with every scrimmage. Spectators, once they grasp the simple rules of engagement, will not be able to take their eyes off the field.

American Mike Statz, General Manager of the all American player Hurling Club of Madison in Wisconsin, got introduced to hurling by a friend who told him that this might be the game for him.

Mike was a swimmer at high school and he gave hurling a try in June of 2008. He found that the game was right for him:

> "I went down there and it was love at first sight. You know it was really right up my alley. It kept me active. It has that finesse factor and you got to be fit to play it, and it's a lot of fun," Mike told GaelicSportsCast in October of 2010.

Madison Public Relations Officer, and fellow American Michael Stapleton in the same interview, was upfront about how the sport takes a bit of getting used to when learning from scratch:

> "It was definitely an interesting experience to say the least. It's a unique game and it's very skillful and trying to get used to that or trying to get into the mentality of what it takes to play hurling was a transition.
>
> It's not like any game we play here you know. I played basketball in high school and I grew up playing baseball and it takes a whole different mentality to wrap your head around hurling's skills."

The idea of the sport fitting Americans like a glove is also seen when the newly formed Orlando Hurling Club decided to promote the sport at the 2010 Central Florida Highland Games.

Club founder, American Scott Graves, spoke of the game's immediate connection with Americans in an email communication. "When we put hurleys in peoples hands, they absolutely loved it. They were both receptive to it and you know it seemed to strike a chord with a lot of Americans."

And, it's not just adults that are getting 'hooked', the younger generation is also beginning to find something very attractive about the sport as college athletes from Connecticut to California are organizing hurling clubs on University campuses at astonishing frequency.

Younger students are also getting in on the act as youth development programs are attracting high school kids. And, the game could soon spread throughout the defense forces as a bunch of U.S. soldiers have recently started to play the sport. In fact, in Irish mythology, war and hurling have had a close relationship as all seemed to be intertwined.

John W. Hurley in his book, 'Shillelagh: The Irish Fighting Stick', figured that you played hurling in time of peace to prepare for battle in time of war.

Perhaps some in Charlie Company in Baghdad circa 2004 – who today serve in the New Hampshire National Guard – are finding the modern version of the game very useful in keeping alert, keen, and united.

Many Americans are getting hooked on the sport of hurling but some are dumbfounded as to why it hasn't already caught on. They are also perplexed by attitudes that only a chosen few can play. One American describes such elitism as 'hogwash'.

But how is the sport actually played? What are its rules? And what exactly is it about the game that hooks?

Chapter 2

The Sport

This chapter was written to introduce the game to those who've never heard of hurling or seen it played.

Hurling has similarities with other sports but there are many differences that a newcomer will notice immediately.

Each section includes a few key aspects of the sport, which can also be applied to camogie, the woman's version of the game that shares most of the same rules.

THE BASICS

Hurling is a team sport and has 15 players on opposing sides. It is similar to lacrosse and field hockey but uses a shorter curved wooden stick called a hurley (caman in Gaelic) to strike a small ball. The hurley stick is made from ash wood and is wider and more rounded at the bottom than both ice hockey and field hockey sticks, and doesn't have any netting as in lacrosse.

Image 1: Hurley and Ball .(Photo courtesy of P. O'Kane Hurls)

When the game was modernized by the Gaelic Athletic Association (GAA – the sport's governing body) in Ireland in 1884, early images of teams show that the hurleys used then were narrower than those of today and were rather similar to the modern ice hockey stick. The ball or sliotar (pronounced 'slitter') is similar in size to a baseball but not as hard and dense or smooth surfaced. It is made from a cork core that is covered by two strips of raised leather stitching.

Image 2: Balls or Sliotars.(Photo courtesy of P. O'Kane Hurls)

SCORING

One of the main differences between hurling, hockey and lacrosse is that any player can catch the ball and after tossing it in the air they can then bat it with the hurl from their hand. The scoring system is much different as well. The high scoring is one element of a hurling match that attracts Americans to the sport.

There are two main types of scores – one is a goal: striking the ball with the hurl or even boot across the opposing goal line and under the crossbar for three points, while the other is striking the ball over the crossbar and between uprights for a single point.

If a game finished with Team A ending on 4 goals and 15 points, written as 4-15 and Team B finished with 3 goals and 17 points, it would mean that A wins by a single point 27 to 26 points.

> **4-15 is 4 x 3 = 12 plus 15 = 27 points total**
>
> **3-17 is 3 x 3 = 9 plus   17 = 26 points total**

As long as you remember that one goal equals three points you can work out the totals.... "4-15" is 4 x 3 = 12 + 15 = 27 points total, while "3-17" scoreline is 3 x 3 = 9 + 17 = 26.

One can score a goal or a point from open play, or through a free strike. But a team may also get a point from a sideline "free-take," called a cut-in or sideline ball.

When the ball goes over the sideline in football, the play goes to the hash-marks and a huddle, or is a throw-in in soccer. In hurling, a free strike of the ball on the ground either directed forwards or even backwards to a team-mate, is awarded to the opposing team after the other side hits the ball across the sidelines.

Executing this sideline cut-in requires exceptional skill, particularly if trying to score one point. The ball is placed on the ground next to the line and the player has to hit the ball in such a way as to get enough elevation, and the desired amount of accuracy. It's a bit like using a hurl to make a 30-40 yard chip in golf, but instead of aiming at the pin on the green, you have to place the ball between the uprights. Witnessing this piece of skill is, to say the least, an eye-opener.

SKILLS

Hurling is a highly robust game but also possesses very high skill level on a par with any major international sport. Some of these skills have never been witnessed by Americans. When a person sees the elements of the game live – at an Irish festival or while on vacation in Ireland – first time viewers are simply blown away.

One of these skills is the scooping of the ball with the hurley off the grass at speed.

Illustration 3: American hurlers of the Indy Hurling Club ready for a scooping drill Jan. 31, 2012, at the Super Bowl Village in Indianapolis.(Photo Kyle Keesling)

Another skill is running freely, again at top speed, with the ball balanced on the widened bottom of the hurl as if it were stuck to it. This is called the Solo Run. Or, there is the scoring skill of a hurler tossing the ball and striking it from an acute angle between the uprights.

Because it is a territorial game with uprights at either end of the playing field, players get to bat the ball far up the field on a regular basis. For a baseball player it would be like hitting a home run every time at bat. For a footballer, it would mean getting the opportunity to blast through multiple downs in a matter of seconds.

One recent convert to hurling is Stanford University student, Chris Stucky. He caught the hurling bug like others in universities throughout California. In a 2009 video on You Tube, he talks about his passion for the sport and its many skills. "I love the game. It's fantastic. Ever since I started playing I have just fallen in love with it. It's an amazing game. It's fast paced [and] it has all these different aspects of a variety of sports."

The sport has all the excitement of typical American sports, but when you add in the free-scoring of points from general play when the ball is struck between the uprights, the game becomes a very high scoring spectacle and as a result a very attractive form of entertainment.

SPEED & GRIP

Illustration 4: Batting and Grip (Photo by Peter Marney)

As in any sport, one usually doesn't get a "free touch" or play without coming under pressure from an opponent and this is especially so in hurling.

The fast pace of the game dictates that when in possession of the ball you "make yardage" by striking or batting the ball either off the ground or from the hand.

When batting the ball, the grip employed is also a major difference to other stick sports. In hurling, the dominant hand is beneath the non-dominant hand while holding the hurley.

In baseball, ice hockey, lacrosse, field hockey, golf and cricket, it is the reverse with the dominant hand (if right-handed) below.

This grip change especially for baseball and ice hockey players can be an issue in the short term but rookies eventually adjust.

Before tossing to bat the ball down-field you can also evade an incoming tackle and side-step or move forward but you are only allowed four steps with the ball in hand before off-loading.

When in possession you can also head for a gap and go on a solo run. For speedsters, the solo run can be deployed as a yardage mechanism. The player employing this strategy can be very useful for an offense to get open as the opposing team's defensive lines will have to try and stop the runner penetrating deeper and close to goals.

Defensive lines can be split wide open if the solo runner is allowed to go straight through the middle of the defense.

Of course said speedster might have to carefully spread such solos throughout the 70-minute, 35 minute halves or tired legs could arrive quicker than wished.

In relation to the solo run, there is a tried and well-tested saying in hurling – instead of your legs doing the running (making yardage this way) it's best that the ball does that. A bit like in football where the quarterback - given the law of averages - makes the most yardage when he throws the ball instead of running it himself.

DEFENSE

In hurling, an opponent has a range of defensive options against a player striking the ball.

He or she can hook an opponent's hurl from behind with their own, when the opponent swings to strike or bat the ball. Or, perform the braver option of a frontal defensive play with the hurl at close range or at a slightly further distance to actually block a player from striking the ball.

Illustration 5: Frontal block technique by player on right (Boston Cork) on player striking ball (Boston Tipperary) - venue Canton Gaelic Park, MA (Photo Denis O'Brien)

HAND TOSS

When in possession and you get surrounded by opponents – without being pushed, pulled or dragged (all of which are offenses that will draw a penalty) – and you are not able to get rid of the ball by striking it, you are allowed to make a hand-pass to a teammate. To do this you simply toss the ball slightly – a few inches from your hand – and then strike the ball with the palm of your hand to a colleague.

Confused about all the above?

Well, when seeing hurling for the first time, the game kind of explains itself as there's so much going on with multiple skill factors from puck-out – kick-off or face-off – to scoring, that the viewer and player will get a feel for it after a while. It's a bit like a baseball fan instinctively knowing where the strike zone is and if a ball's a strike or not. And on that note, when wondering how to judge if a speedy player takes more than four steps with ball in hand, well the baseball strike-zone analogy applies here also.

CATCHES

One of the greatest skills in hurling is the catching of the ball out of the air, or, on the fly. A goalkeeper will hit a "puck-out" after a score or a wide – when the ball goes either side of uprights.

The keeper drives the ball 80-100 yards down the field to gain as much territory as is possible. Or, he could also hit it closer, to a loose teammate, if free, in order his team keeps possession.

Illustration 6: Catching a high ball (Photo courtesy of Indy HC)

Unlike American football, there is no single player chosen or allowed to field the ball, as gaining possession is literally up for grabs.

A group of players will bunch under the dropping ball in order to take possession. The "grab" part happens when one of the players in the bunch gains possession by catching the ball on the fly. This means that should a player decide that this puck-out ball is his to catch, he will have to bravely put up his hand to grab it as other players try to keep it away from him.

Others may even try to hit the ball on the fly with their hurl, catch it for themselves or make a defensive swat to bat the ball away from the pack.

When executed cleanly it is an amazing sight to see a player jump and fetch a ball among a throng of opponents.

Because of the possibility of sustaining a head injury, especially when trying to catch the ball from a puck-out, helmets were introduced by the Irish governing body, the GAA in the 1970s with an option for players at senior grade to disregard them if they so choose. While rules had already been imposed for lower-level players to wear helmets with protective wire face guards, a rule from January 2010 mandated helmets for the top tier players at senior Inter County level in Ireland having to wear such protective headgear.

Illustration 7: Hurling Helmet (Photo courtesy of Fox River HC)

LEAGUES

What is "Inter County" competition? The answer brings us to the area of competition formats in Ireland.

This necessitates explaining how the Gaelic Athletic Association (GAA) in Ireland structures the format of the different competitions and playing levels. There are different formats in America also.

First off, hurling is not a professional sport, it is amateur. Some might think the word "amateur" implies unskilled or a low grade but nothing could be further from the truth. The performance level at Inter County Hurling competition is very high and in many ways is similar to professional sports. Amateur purely means that the players are not paid for playing even though 'Inter County' is the premier level of competition.

For many American players who have taken up the game in the last 5-10 years, this aspect of an amateur ethos attracts them to hurling as it brings things back to basics. Sports are played for the love of playing rather than for the money.

While you have counties of course in each state in the U.S. the county system in Ireland is more akin to the Federal state system.

In Ireland each of the 32 counties acts like a state from both political and cultural standpoints where each county also has its own hurling or Gaelic football team.

Within counties you have either hurling or Gaelic football clubs (latter game similar to Australian Rules). These clubs are affiliated through a hierarchical system: a County Board, a Provincial Board, and lastly, to the GAA at national level. Headquarters of hurling and Gaelic Sports is at Croke Park stadium in Dublin, Ireland's capital.

Each county has their own club championship each year, and the best club players are then selected to represent the county or, in American terminology, a "state" team. When counties play each other, this is called Inter-County and it is the highest level where the best hurlers in the country compete. The sports premier competition is the All Ireland Championship and it is played during the summer period.

In the U.S. since 1959, the North American County Board (NACB) – an odd title for sure – founded by Irish natives, has been the traditional body organizing the sport on a national level. The NACB does not include the Greater New York City region as it runs a separate organization, New York GAA. Both entities are affiliated with the parent body, the GAA in Ireland.

While the majority of hurling clubs in America are affiliated to the NACB and therefore, the GAA in Ireland, this does not mean of course that you can't start a club and have no affiliation to the aforementioned bodies. Or, for that matter start off one's own governing organization and structures.

The North American GAA is structured by a division system with nine across the country. They are: the Northwest, Boston/Northeast, Chicago/Central, Philadelphia, Mid Atlantic, Midwest, Southwest, San Francisco/Western and Southeast. Each Division acts as the parent or governing body for affiliated clubs in the region, but many clubs run their own independent competitions as well.

The main competition run by the NACB is the annual North American GAA National Finals. This has traditionally been run in a different location each year on Labor Day weekend, and is growing in popularity each season.

The three cities of Boston, Chicago and San Francisco run large league type competitions – where the vast majority of clubs are dependent on Irish summer students for players and the winners of the respective leagues qualify for the National Finals. Clubs outside of these cities – mostly all-American player clubs – also have league style competitions but it is largely left up to the individual clubs if they want to send teams to the National Championship each year.

One of those young American hurling organizations is the Milwaukee Hurling Club (MHC) of Wisconsin. This club runs its own 10-team league summer competition and over a short period of time has grown to become the largest hurling club in America.

The Milwaukee HC has become something of a phenomenon within the U.S. sporting landscape. Before the club began, hurling was unknown to the state that is home to the American football team the Green Bay Packers. No one had ever heard of the game, ever! But 17 years ago, Americans Dave Olson, a former baseball player, and Cory Johnson changed all that. They started a club and today with 300 members and 10 adult teams it's now the single biggest hurling club in the country.

Former club Administrative Coordinator and American player, Karen Fink, MHC is also co-ed, says that hurling has many attractions particularly for rookies wishing to take up the game:

> "We have found that the sport appeals to anyone that puts a hurl in their hand, if even for 10 minutes. What our members have liked is that there are so many skills, you are bound to be able to at least do a few. And with some hard work, you can get good at many of the skills. If you like being challenged hurling will deliver," Fink told this author in a 2009 email interview.

When you consider that this is coming from an American, and not an Irish person, it indicates the potential of the game to become more popular in the U.S.

Hurling is also cropping up in other states and cities, which like Milwaukee, don't have large Irish communities and had no clue that the game even existed.

Take the state of Oregon for example. Hurling had never been played in the state until recently.

Each year a large gathering of Irish Americans make their way to the fields at Sheldon High School in Eugene for the annual Irish Festival. In March of 2009, patrons saw something they hadn't seen or heard before. What the festival goers witnessed was "Hurling 101."

At the festival a crowd gathered around as two members of the recently formed Columbia Red Branch Hurling Club from Portland, explained the basics of the game. One of these, American Todd Brothers, was a medieval

Irish history student at Washington State University. He discovered the game in the course of his studies where at a medieval festival, he saw the game being played. He got hooked. But Todd's enthusiasm didn't end there as he proceeded to dig much deeper. "I made my own sticks, I made my own ball and I made my friends play," was what he told Nat Levy, who was reporting on the festival for The Register-Guard newspaper.

To explain things a little further to the 'hurling class', the Red Branch and another new club, Benton Brigade, from Corvalis, had a scrimmage to show how to play the game.

Levy said that though score trackers fell behind, it mattered little as everybody seemed to be enjoying the spectacle:

> "During the game, scorekeepers lost the count, but it didn't really matter. The match showed a new twist on the idea that it's not whether you win or lose, it's how you play the game. This time, it was just about the game."

Milwaukee has its own summer league competitions, while other smaller clubs band together for small regional tournaments often at Irish festivals. Local Winter Indoor Leagues are also proving to be very popular with newer clubs.

THE PITCH

Hurling offers plenty of room to maneuver as the game is played on a rather large field area of 137 meters in length (149 yards) and 82 meters (90 yards) in width.

Contrast this with the official size of an NFL football field and you just begin to see some of the differences. An NFL field length from end-zone to end-zone is 120 yards (109m) and just over 53 yards (48.76 m) in width.

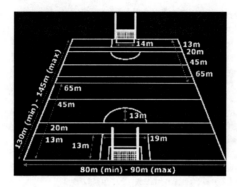

Illustration 8: Hurling Pitch Dimensions

Soccer by comparison has a much smaller playing area. In fact there is no hard and fast rule as to what exact dimensions a soccer field should be as a pitch can be any size, however, it must be between 100 yards (90m) and 130 yards (120m) in length and the width should not be less than 50 yards (45m) and not more than 100 yards (90m).

A rugby field is 109.36 yards (100m) from upright to upright with a further 22 meters back to the dead ball line at each end. Its width is 76.55 yards (70m).

The goals at each end of the field consist of two uprights 6 meters high (6.56 yards), 7 yards apart and connected by a crossbar 8 feet above the ground. A net hangs from the crossbar to the back of the lower goal posts.

In hurling, there is plenty of room for long distance ball striking and plays, hence 15-a-side is not as many as might seem.

THE PLAYERS

Teams line up with a goalkeeper, six in defense, six in attack and two midfielders. Teams are allowed five substitutes over the course of the 70 minutes.

The defense is broken down into three fullbacks in front of the goalkeeper: one corner back on the right, a fullback in the center and another corner-back on the left. Then in front of the fullbacks you have the halfbacks taking up similar center and wing positions.

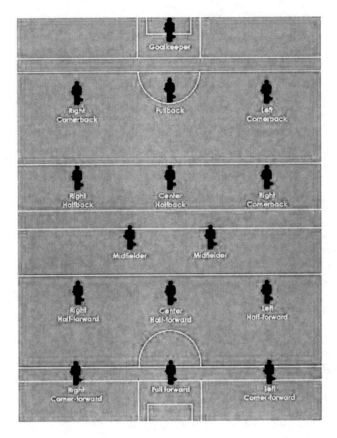

Illustration 9: Hurling Team Positions

Next we have two midfielders. These guys are usually very versatile hurlers and good all-rounders. They will see a lot of possession time and will have to be fit and highly mobile.

The offense then sees three half forwards and three full forwards and unlike in soccer, where marking can be non-existent, in hurling every player has another on the opposing team to shadow.

The fullback will be marking the opposing team's full forward, or in another scenario, the right half back will be marking the other team's left half forward.

This element of marking a man, where a tight defender will literally be breathing down the back of his marker's neck, sets hurling apart because there's no place to hide. Usually one's direct opponent will be the first to highlight deficiencies.

Football corner-backs do their best to keep track of wide receivers, but in hurling each player is either marking a specific man or is being marked.

Penalties

1. A player can not run for more than four steps with the ball in hand.
2. The ball may not be thrown; the correct hand-pass technique must be used.
3. The ball may not be picked directly off the ground; the roll or jab-lift must be used.
4. A player who is in possession may not score with his/her hand.
5. A player cannot throw the hurley.
6. Square ball: A player cannot be in the small square at the moment the ball enters.
7. A player may not handle the ball more than twice.

PENALTIES

An offense or foul in hurling against an opponent constitutes pushing, pulling, grabbing a shirt, and, generally dragging down a player. You can't place a hand on a player's back; you can't high tackle a player with hurl or arm and you can't trip.

In a crowd of players trying to gain possession of the ball on the ground, a wild swing by a player in such a scenario is most definitely a penalty – a free hit – and a bookable offense for dangerous play.

The referee might decide to give a warning or increase the sentence to a yellow card, and yes, two of these and a player is off.

A straight red card could be for very dangerous play, striking a player either with your leg, hand, elbow, head or hurl. Red cards also carry future time/match playing bans.

Hurling is fast paced with the ball being sent up and down the field on a regular basis. In the heat of battle, play can continue for several minutes or longer before a break in action occurs. Supporters get involved in the game and are regularly off their seats for one reason or another.

One difference between say soccer and hurling as regards the crowd, is that in the latter, the fans of the different teams are interspersed through the stadium randomly. There is no sectioning of one set of supporters from the other in hurling.

CONTESTS

As with the high stakes of a Super Bowl, so to is hurling's greatest prize, the All Ireland Hurling Final.

Intensity levels both on and off the field are usually at fever pitch in a final that celebrates the best hurling county in Ireland.

An All Ireland final is not only the premier sporting event of the season but it has special cultural significance for the nation.

Before the start of the game, the teams line up in front of the Hogan Stand and the President of Ireland gets to wish the players the best of luck.

Then one of the most exciting and colorful sights in all of sports takes place as the two teams, in military formation, follow after a brass band, the Artane Boys Band (always the same band) around Croke Park.

The parade is unique in world sports and is a great spectacle with 82,000 cheering fans roaring on their county in one last rush of emotion before battle. The atmosphere is rarely duplicated worldwide.

TRUE HEROES

In professional sports today, very high-paid players may seem far removed from the ordinary supporter in the terraces.

Team supporters rarely ever get to meet or know a player. The media are the only ones with unique access to the players, and to the average supporter, a high paid player may seem as remote as a distant star. In hurling, it is different.

The fact that players are amateurs means that no high priced salary tag is attached to their shirt and there is a purity about them playing for the love of the game. Of late in Ireland, the trials of having to come home from work and train for two, three or four nights a week, is beginning to affect players' commitment to the sport. With economic hard times in Ireland, it's getting harder and harder for players to commit so much energy and time to a sport like hurling.

However, players still love to play and this factor supersedes all others. Being amateur can also bring rich social and cultural reward as players are seen as local heroes. They are held in very high esteem.

Hurlers allegiance is to their native county and fans know and love this. Players are people's next-door neighbors. It means also that supporters can be teammates at local club level; former underage brothers and opponents, friends, fellow workers as well as the people from the community of which the player grew up.

To a large extent, the player and the county team become extensions of the county and its people. Each county hurler is indeed a local hero.

STATUS

In 2006, the U.S. media outlet, *Men's Fitness* Magazine got to witness a hurler as mythical hero when visiting Ireland to check out the sport.

The magazine put it like this: "In Ireland, it's hurlers – not firemen or astronauts – whom every young boy grows up admiring."

For an article on the sport, writer Joe Gould sank himself into the culture. He went to games, attended training sessions and spoke with players. One of those was charismatic former County Clare goalkeeper, Davy Fitzgerald, – as of 2012 – the team's new manager.

As a player he was an inspirational part of the team. Just before a game began he used to bang his hurley off his goal's crossbar ... a kind of ritualistic call to battle.

As a boy Fitzgerald liked to watch his county's goalkeeper's every move. He dreamed of the day when he would be pulling off a great save for Clare. "I remember standing behind the goalkeeper, studying his every move and saying that someday I'm going to be him. It was my dream. It was all I ever wanted to do," said Fitzgerald.

The Men's Fitness writer was also impressed with how players – as amateurs – prepared themselves for a game as they put the same amount of effort into training as any sport's professional. "Despite day jobs, mortgages, and children, the guys on Ireland's hurling teams still find time to train just as hard as any pro."

After having seen County Clare in action, Gould would miss their next game but mused wilfully about the day and its meaning:

> "The weather promises another soggy day. But no matter – even with a misty veil over the field, there will be plenty of time-honored grunts plus the smack of hurley against hurley. From the stands, it'll be difficult to identify the players through the bitch of a mist. But even in the fog two things remain clear, just as they have for thousands of years: the power and purity of sport played purely for sport's sake."

Hurling holds a special place in Irish people's hearts. Its unbroken link to the ancients is a source of pride.

Chapter 3

Ancient Game

So where did the sport of hurling find its beginning?

In search of hurling's origin, scholars find themselves traveling a land of mystery with no clear path to follow. No one knows hurling's exact origin.

Talk of the sport's beginnings may lead one to suggest that it is a close relative of ancient stick games akin to hockey. Some think that hurling evolved from hockey like games, while others say it's the reverse.

In his book, the 'Sports of Ancient times', Nigel B. Crowther goes back 6,000 years before Christ to Mesopotamia, the purported cradle of western civilization, to trace the evolution of sports.

He says that sports flourished even at this time. In the southern tip of Sumeria, now modern day southern Iraq, games such as wrestling, boxing, acrobatics, archery, and running as well as stick ball games took place, "The Sumerians played a game with a ball and stick, like field hockey or hurling."

Later during the time of the Pharaohs in Ancient Egypt, Crowther describes how a relief in the temple of Hatshepsut, in the fifteenth century (BCE), shows Tithmosis III holding a bent stick in one hand and a ball, the "size of a softball in the other. It also portrays two priests with raised arms to catch the ball. The hieroglyphic text reads, 'batting the ball for Hathor'" as in a ritual ball game. Scholars have made references to the similarities with baseball.

The author also notes that a painting from the tomb of Kehti at Beni Hasan, around 2000 (BCE), depicts two males holding sticks with curved ends and using a hoop in a bully-off position that some have compared to hockey, but he adds that latest research says that this is a game for children and not adults.

Crowther also points to the fact that the ancient Greeks may also have played a form of a field ball game. A 5th century (BCE) image (known as the 'hockey relief') on the base of an artifact, shows six figures of teams of three on each side with five sticks and a ball in the middle.

He also notes that from illustrations and literary reference in Europe during the Middle Ages there is a similar type of game called la soule or la choule with similar curved sticks where the object of the game was to hit the ball as far as possible into the opponent's territory, something similar to the old form of hurling.

The sport of hurling is also mentioned in Irish manuscripts dating to the 13th century with suggestions that it is Europe's oldest field game. Others have pointed to variations of the game played throughout Europe and beyond, and think that the Irish may have been responsible for bringing hurling to Scotland where it evolved into "shinty or shinny" writes Andrew Leibs.

The author of "Sports and Games of the Renaissance" also paints a picture of a range of hurling-like stick games across Europe and references the first signs of similar games in North America:

> "The game['s] was also played in England as 'cambuca' or 'bandy', in France as 'jeu de mail' and in the Netherlands as 'het kulven'. Early European settlers saw the game played by numerous Indian tribes throughout North America."

Looking more closely at the roots of hurling, and its close cousin, Shinty – which is still played today in Scotland – we notice that hurling's influence on shinty was considerable.

The Scots, like the Irish, descended from the Celts and preserve with pride their Gaelic heritage. Nearly 2000 years ago, Irish missionaries arriving in Scotland not only brought with them their religion but seemingly also brought their love for the game of hurling. Scottish scholar, Hugh Dan MacLennan in his article 'Shinty's place and space in world sport' writes that:

> "Shinty – iomain or camanachd in Scottish Gaelic – was introduced to Scotland along with Christianity and the Gaelic language nearly two thousand years ago by Irish missionaries.
>
> Indeed, it is worth noting, 1,400 years after St Columba's death, that the venerable Saint is said to have arrived on these shores as a result of a little local difficulty at an Irish hurling match."

Speaking to hurling's origin MacLennan says that, "It has such a distant ancestry that it is impossible to pin down its origins."

In relation to shinty he adds that:

> "The earliest written reference to shinty or 'schynnie'" is in 1589, in the Kirk Session Records of Glasgow. The Club of True Highlanders, regarded shinty as being: 'undoubtedly the oldest known Keltic sport' or pastime. The game is also called Cluich bhall, shinnie, shinty,

bandy, hurling, hockey, and at one time was a universal and favorite game of the whole of Keltland."

U.S. sports scholar Stephen Hardy, in looking at ice hockey's history in his article, 'Polo at the Rinks: Shaping Markets for Ice Hockey in America, 1880-1900,' talks about hockey's purpose and indeed naming and suggests a common theme on how to play these type of early stick-ball games. "'Hockey' was an English name for a game that required players to drive a ball (or similar object) into a goal, or simply to keeping the ball away from opponents."

Hardy adds that 'Bandy' was another English name for a similar game and:

> "The Irish version was called hurling or hurly; the Scots played shinty. The English game was probably named after the short stick used for play.
>
> The Oxford English Dictionary explains that the name 'hockey' was of 'uncertain origin,' but most likely it 'originally belonged to the hooked stick'. Of [Old French] hoquet 'shepherd's staff crook' suits form and sense.' It was also popular among schoolboys."

In peeling away at early hockey-like games history, Hardy references a story of what a visiting English man sees when traveling to Ireland in the late 17th century. "An Englishman visiting Ireland in 1673 refers to the common people as playing bandy (hurling) with balls and crooked stick much after our play at stow-ball."

(The Sports Historian (became Sport in History in 2003), by David Terry. 2000 May Vol. 20 No. 1 p. 33-43. THE SEVENTEENTH CENTURY GAME OF CRICKET: A RECONSTRUCTION OF THE GAME by David Terry.)

Another American scholar, A.J. Sandy, in his book, 'The Continuing Saga of Ice Hockey's Origins, suggests common name usages between hockey and hurling. "'Shinty', 'bandy', shinny', 'wicket' and 'hurling' are all forms of early hockey games. Early hockey sticks were called "hockies" and early hurling sticks were called 'hurlies'."

Hurling's role as a forerunner of ice-hockey is seen when looking at the winter game's origins in Canada.

In his book, "The History of the Gaelic Athletic Association in Canada," Canadian born GAA Secretary, John O'Flynn, finds references to suggest that hurling's legacy in the New World is far older than that created by the arrival of mass Irish immigration.

Even the legend of voyager, St. Brendan – who is said to have first discovered North America even before a certain Christopher Columbus laid eyes on the new world – might have been a keen hurling fan.

St. Brendan himself is not a legendary figure as he was born in the south west of Ireland in County Kerry (c. 484 AD – c. 577AD) – locals would call it the next parish to America – and set up both local and foreign missions in his travels.

Mr Flynn reports that:

> "Early map makers and explorers give credence to the legend that St. Brendan the Navigator, with seventeen 'hurling monks', reached Terra Repromissionis Sanctorum (The Land Promised the Saints) in the early days of the sixth century."

He adds that the story of their voyage in a leather-hulled Curragh is told in an old Irish saga, 'The voyage of St. Brendan, the Abbot.'

Flynn says that there have been reports of Irish settlements in the St. Laurence Valley between 875 – 900 AD, and suggests, "How else might one explain lacrosse, akin to hurling, witnessed by the early French explorers being played along the banks of the St. Laurence by the Mic Mac Amerindians and other tribes?"

He also points to historical evidence that the, "Mic Macs wore crosses on their playing tunics". Flynn stresses the connection when stating, "Isn't, 'Mic Mac' the Gaelic inverse of 'Mac Mic,' meaning the son of the son?'"

Had St. Brendan reached North America? Did his monks spread the gospel and the game of hurling, which evolved into lacrosse? Is lacrosse a direct descendant of hurling?

The Mic Mac were the dominant tribe in the Canadian Maritime and since the 1794 Jay Treaty between Great Britain and the United States, the Mic Mac have had the right to move freely back-and forth across the border, and today are one of the largest Native American tribes in New England.

This free movement might explain the eventual spread of a stick ball game like Lacrosse to America's Northeast where it eventually took hold in places like Baltimore, New England, and New York.

The earliest written record of the Irish and trade between Ireland and Newfoundland in Canada, goes back to 1595. By 1731, the majority of men in Newfoundland were Irish Catholics.

O'Flynn notes that some of the earliest games of hurling in North America occurred in St. Johns in 1788 on a piece of land called the Barrens. By the year 1845, there was a considerable Irish population in the Sillery, a Quebec suburb, and many took to neighborhood hurling games on the streets. However, not everyone was thrilled with this turn of events the author noted:

> "The number of Irish playing their native games in the city soon led to the authorities passing a by-law in 1845 that forbade hurling to be played in the narrow streets. There must have been some severe window damage happening for a by-law to be passed!"

Just as stick-ball may have challenged the best-made windows in American neighborhoods 50 years later, Canadian streets suffered the same wrath from sliotars.

John O'Flynn also points out possible Mic Mac language connections where there are distinct similarities and cross-over between Gaelic names, ice hockey and hurling. "The word puck is derived from the Irish word 'poc', which is the action of striking the ball with a hurley."

Around 1875, ice hockey was played in Montreal not by French speakers but by mostly Irish Catholic students from McGill University. Many of the Irish would go on to star with the two-time Stanley Cup winning ice hockey team, the Montreal Shamrocks. That name would later be adopted by a Gaelic sports team that still exists today.

But of course, Ireland too has its own tales and texts passed down from generation to generation telling of hurling's mystic beginnings.

Ireland sees the game as being some 3,000 years old, where the basis for such a position is found in Irish legend.

The earliest historical evidence regarding the stick-and-ball games of Ireland is found in an Irish document dating to the twelfth century. The tale references the pastimes of legendary figures from Irish mythology. The story, the 'Táin Bó Cúalnge' (The Cattle-Raid of Cooley) is found in the Book of Leinster.

It is a story about one of Ireland's greatest mythical heroes, Cuchulainn. There a reference to hurling or 'caman' in Gaelic is clearly noted.

Cuchulainn is said to have loved the game of hurling as a youth and was master of all its skills. As a boy he was known as 'Setanta' and raised in the court of the King of Ulster, Conor mac Nessa.

TW Rolleston, in his work, 'Celtic Myths and Legends' recounts the tale. The king and his nobles were invited one evening to the house of a wealthy smith named Cullan, who had a fierce hound protect his house. Setanta was to accompany them but decided to follow on later as he was in the midst of playing a hurling match with his young friends. When he later followed, he met with the hound, which he slew when striking his hurling ball into the hound's mouth.

But in Irish mythology, hurling is not just seen as sport for boys but it had a much more serious side to it as it was also played by men of war.

Some 1,300 years before Christ, a famous battle is said to have taken place in Ireland, the 'Battle of Moytura' at Cross near Cong, County Mayo, in the west in 1272 BC (Bronze Age).

Irish Archaeologist, Colm Moriarty in his blog 'Irish Archeology' talks about the story being referenced in the romantic tale, 'Cath Mhaigh Tuireadh Chunga' (The Battle of the Boastful Death). This particular story to this day has inspired active U.S. soldiers.

The battle was between the native Fir Bolg and the invading Tuatha de Danaan who were demanding half the country. In preparation for the battle, a hurling match was played between members of the opposing armies.

Indeed this connection of hurling with war and battle would resurface again during the turbulent times of the late nineteenth and early twentieth-century in Ireland, when nationalist passions were high during British continued occupation. Hurling was seen as a sport that identified with the ideals and dream of an unoccupied country, as players would parade with their hurls over their shoulders as if they were rifles.

Michael L. Mullan writing in the Journal of Sport History in his work, "Ethnicity and Sport: The Wapato Nippons and Pre-World War II Japanese American Baseball," described direct linkages between nationalism, hurling and the military:

> "Hurling matches 'assumed all the pageantry of a nationalist rally' complete with banners, bands playing revolutionary tunes, and players who marched to the playing field with their hurley sticks sloped in military formation."

At the Moytura battle, the hurling match took place between the best 27 players from each camp. Hugh Dan MacLennan recounts the detail of the mythological war game:

> "'Many a blow was felt on legs and arms 'till their bones were broken and bruised and they fell outstretched on the turf and the match ended.
>
> The Fir Bolg won the match and then proceeded to 'fall upon their opponents, and slew them'."

Ireland too has its own historical motifs of hurling as archaeologist Colm Moriarty suggests to possible references of the game on two crosses:

> "Possible representations of hurling are also found on two high crosses from Kells [County Meath] and Monasterboice, County Louth which date from 9th/10th centuries. On each of these crosses a biblical panel is depicted which illustrates David killing a lion with what appears to be a curved stick and ball. The killing instrument should in fact be a sling, but it appears that a hurley was chosen instead as it may have been more familiar to an Irish audience."

Moriarty goes on to tell of another hurling artifact which can be found in the Northwest of Ireland where "a 16th century Galloglass's grave slab from County Donegal clearly depicts a sword, hurley and sliotar."

Taking into account other historical references to hurling's past, one must consider the ancient Irish sporting festival, the Tailteann Games. This event tantalizes the imagination for its longevity but amazingly little, if anything at all, is known about it.

Said to predate the Olympics games of Greece, the Tailteann Games are believed to have lasted for as long as 1,800 years and would have seen stick-ball games if not hurling itself. Aberdeen University's Hugh Dan MacLennan explains, "We know that the Tailteann Games, said to be the oldest recorded organized sports in the world.....Stick-and-ball games would have been central to their performance."

The Games were said to have originated around 632 B.C. at the behest of King Luaghaidh Lamhfáda in honor of his foster mother's death, Queen Tailté. The festival, which began on August 1, lasted for a week and was attended by kings, chieftains and nobles from across Ireland.

Cathal Brennan, in his excellent online article documenting efforts to revitalize the ancient games during the 1920s (that revival ended in 1936), recounted how the last ancient games were held in the early part of the 12th century and then came to an abrupt halt:

> "In 1169, the last traditional Tailteann Games were held under Rory O'Connor, the final High King of Ireland. The date was significant as

this was the year Ireland was invaded by the Normans, and as the program [revised 1920 Games Program] stated, 'A foreign power now held sway in Ireland and the games, with the other national gatherings, were heard of no more.'"

Ancient Irish law known as Brehon Law, so named because a Judge back then was known as a Brehon, has frequent references to hurling.

According to The Seanchás Mór texts on Brehon Law, it describes how the son of a Rí (local king) could have his hurley hooped in bronze while others were only allowed to use copper. Brehon Law is also known to have made provision for compensation to the families of those injured while playing hurling.

From an invader's perspective, hurling was seen as something else, as noted by Irish author Seamus King in his work a, 'History of Hurling in Ireland.' He tells that during the 13th century the Norman Statute of Kilkenny outlawed hurling on account of excessive violence. But still the sport persisted and is mentioned in a law of 1527 and in the Sunday Observance Act of 1695.

During the 18th century, John T. Koch, in his 'Celtic culture: a historical encyclopedia' says hurling remained popular and in 1755 the lord lieutenant attended an Inter-County match.

In Ireland at the time, there was two different versions of hurling being played. One was a winter game akin to Scotland's shinty called, 'Commons'. It forbade taking the ball in hand and the ball was made of wood and interestingly was played with a narrow blade of a crooked stick. This game was played mostly in the north of Ireland in the counties of Derry, Antrim and Donegal and players were from differing religious backgrounds, often Catholic and Presbyterian.

The other form of hurling was called 'Baire' or Iomán and was played in the south during the summertime. The ball was made of animal hair, softer and called a 'sliothar'.

Kevin Whelan in his article in The Cambridge Companion to Modern Irish Culture, entitled, "The Cultural Effects of the Famine," describes how in the south the landed gentry supported the summer game and popularized it:

> "Unlike 'Commons', this sport was extensively patronized by the landed gentry or landlord as a spectator and gambling sport.
>
> The gentry formed and captained the teams, issued the challenges, supplied the hurling greens and supervised the matches. The gentry's

hurlers were especially active in Cork, Tipperary, Kilkenny, Wexford and Galway.

This game required well drained pitches of the type especially found in limestone areas which also produced abundant ash, the best material for making hurls."

The gentry's support of the southern game was essential for its continued success, however, the author points to outside influences from seemingly the most unlikely of linkages that would interfere with hurling's fortunes. Oddly, the landscape of hurling was about to be changed by the hand of the French Revolution.

This dramatic event shifted the cultural and political landscape as it "sharpened class and political divides and the spread of metropolitan behavioral norms, eroded the landlords' local loyalties."

With the landlord class withdrawing their support for the sport towards the end of the 18th century, hurling fell on hard times and became more and more marginalized. Still the early part of the 19th century saw hurling still very much part of the cultural fabric of Ireland and it was particularly loved in rural areas.

A clearer image of the game's particular importance for the rural population of the country comes to focus when one reads of an English couple's intriguing experiences while traveling in Ireland between 1825 and 1841.

In that 16-year period, Mr. and Mrs. Samuel Carter Hall made five holiday visits to Ireland, and they wrote down their recollections of their trips in a fascinating three-volume work.

Extracts from their observations of Irish life was published in the "Encyclopedia of Irish History and Culture" and recounted in detail Irish life just before the Potato Famine of the late 1840s. That event would be what triggered a mass emigration from the country.

In one of their trips between 1841-1843, they visit the south and the County Kerry region and give a firsthand picture of life in rural Ireland at the time. The same county that gave birth to St. Brendan.

The Halls come across a peasant wedding and get to experience a full-on hurling match between two neighboring villages; not for the faint of heart, and they noted every move and happening.

Ancient Game

To get a sense of the time and place it is necessary to include a large extract from the Hall's observations as they traveled by horse-drawn jaunting car along the highways and byways of the south west of Ireland:

> "The entrance to the county of Kerry ("the kingdom of Kerry," as it was anciently called), from that of Cork, is through a tunnel, of about two hundred yards in length; a very short distance from which there are two others of much more limited extent. They have been cut through rocks — peaks to the mountain we have described as overlooking Glengariff.
>
> As the traveler emerges from comparative darkness, a scene of striking magnificence bursts upon him — very opposite in character to that which he leaves immediately behind; for while his eye retains the rich and cultivated beauty of the wooded and watered "glen," he is startled by the contrast of barren and frightful precipices, along the brinks of which he is riding, and gazes with a shudder down into the far off valley, where a broad and angry stream is diminished by distance into a mere line of white. Nothing can exceed the wild grandeur of the prospect; it extends miles upon miles; scattered through the vale and among the hill slopes, are many cottages, white always and generally slated; while to several of them are attached the picturesque lime-kilns; so numerous in all parts of the country. . .
>
> We had scarcely passed the tunnel, and entered the county of Kerry, when we encountered a group that interested us greatly; on inquiry we learned that a wedding had taken place at a cottage pointed out to us, in a little glen among the mountains, and that the husband was bringing home his bride. She was mounted on a white pony, guided by as smart looking and well dressed a youth as we had seen in the country; his face was absolutely radiant with joy; the parents of the bride and bridegroom followed; and a little girl clung to the dress of a staid and sober matron — whom we at once knew to be the mother of the bride, for her aspect was pensive, almost to sorrow; her daughter was quitting for another home the cottage in which she had been reared — to become a wife. . .
>
> Postponing, for a while, our descriptive details of the wildest but perhaps most picturesque of the Irish counties, we shall take some note of the games in favor with the peasants of the county . . .
>
> But the great game in Kerry, and indeed throughout the South, is the game of "Hurley" — a game rather rare, although not unknown in England. It is a fine manly exercise, with sufficient of danger to produce excitement; and is indeed, par excellence, the game of the

peasantry of Ireland. To be an expert hurler, a man must possess athletic powers of no ordinary character; he must have a quick eye, a ready hand, and a strong arm; he must be a good runner, a skillful wrestler, and withal patient as well as resolute. . .

The forms of the game are these: — The players, sometimes to the number of fifty or sixty, being chosen for each side, they are arranged (usually bare-foot) in two opposing ranks, with their hurleys crossed, to await the tossing up of the ball, the wickets or goals being previously fixed at the extremities of the hurling-green, which, from the nature of the play, is required to be a level extensive plain. . . . A person is chosen to throw up the ball, which is done as straight as possible, when the whole party, withdrawing their hurleys, stand with them elevated, to receive and strike it in its descent; now comes the crash of mimic war, hurleys rattle against hurleys — the ball is struck and re-struck, often for several minutes, without advancing much nearer to either goal; and when some one is lucky enough to get a clear "puck" at it, it is sent flying over the field. It is now followed by the entire party at their utmost speed; the men grapple, wrestle, and toss each other with amazing agility, neither victor nor vanquished waiting to take breath, but following the course of the rolling and flying prize; the best runners watch each other, and keep almost shoulder to shoulder through the play, and the best wrestlers keep as close on them as possible, to arrest or impede their progress.

The ball must not be taken from the ground by the hand; and the tact and skill shown in taking it on the point of the hurley, and running with it half the length of the field, and when too closely pressed, striking it towards the goal, is a matter of astonishment to those who are but slightly acquainted with the play. At the goal, is the chief brunt of the battle. The goal-keepers receive the prize, and are opposed by those set over them; the struggle is tremendous, — every power of strength and skill is exerted; while the parties from opposite sides of the field run at full speed to support their men engaged in the conflict; then the tossing and straining is at its height; the men often lying in dozens side by side on the grass, while the ball is returned by some strong arm again, flying above their heads, towards the other goal. Thus for hours has the contention been carried on, and frequently the darkness of night arrests the game without giving victory to either side. It is often attended with dangerous, and sometimes with fatal, results. . . "

We learn from this eyewitness account of hurling in the early 1840s that the game is a much different animal to today's codified affair. Now there are 15 players on each side while back then up to 60 players could line out for a team or indeed, village.

When the governing body of hurling, the Gaelic Athletic Association (GAA) codified the game at the organization's founding in 1884, it allowed 14-21 players aside. A year later the number of players on a team was reduced to 17 before it was again changed in 1915 to 15. Since that time, there has been no further changes to player numbers in Ireland, although most of America – excluding New York and Milwaukee – play 13 players a team today.

The sport in the mid 19th century in Ireland must have been a very physical affair as players played in their bare feet. With the ball in close proximity, and hurleys flying, a blow to the ankles and toes must have been a distinct possibility. While no mention is made of exact game duration, they were known, as stated, to last hours but could also go on for days. We notice also from the account that the game at the time used wrestling techniques or man blocking plays.

The Halls found the action around the goals area particularly exciting and were quite amazed with the skill of running with the ball on the stick – the solo run. It is interesting also to note that the game though rare in their own country, was still played and was "not unknown in England."

Indeed hurling may have had similarities with a game played in England during the early part of the 17th century. This sport was one was one of many games enjoyed by Englishmen on Feast Days and the Sabbath.

According to Richard Carew in his 'Survey of Cornwall' (1602) hurling matches were of a similar nature as in Ireland where whole villages and regions participated in the ancient sport and were played over several miles with village landmarks and houses filling in as the goalposts.

While there is no reference to hitting a ball with sticks, there is certainly mention of the word 'hurlers' as players in the game. Here is a description by Carew of a game taking place:

> "Some two or more Gentlemen doe commonly make this match, appointing that on such a holyday, they will bring to such an indifferent rent place, two, three or more parishes of the East or South quarter, to hurle against so many other, of the West or North. Their goals are either those Gentlemen's houses, or some towns or villages, three or four miles asunder of which either side maketh choice after the neernesse to their dwellings...A silver ball is cast up

and that company, which can catch, and carry it by force, or sleight to their place assigned gaineth the ball and victory.

> Whosoever getteth seizure of the ball, findith himself generally pursued by the adverse party; neither will they leave till...he be laid on Gods deare earth ...The Hurlers take their next way over hills, dales, hedges, ditches, yea, and thorow bushes, briers, mires, plashes and rivers whatsoever; so as you shall see 20 or 30 lie tugging together in the water, scrambling and scratching for the ball.'" (Qtd. in Gorn and Goldstein, 'A Brief History of American Sports').

Apart from being a forerunner to modern hurling, such matches may have been the antecedents of football in Britain. All things been equal, this game sounds very much like a football ball-carrying territorial game and no doubt a distant relation of American football.

Back in Ireland things would get worse for hurling as the middle of the 1840s brought that tragic black period of Irish history – the deadly potato famine.

To make matters worse, Kevin Whelan argues that a more affluent Catholic middle class moved away from hurling as a past embarrassment. But there were other causes that fought at keeping hurling from being played. The Catholic church also played its part in marginalizing the sport as anglicized priests demonized the game and lawmakers feared crowds gathering at matches and what that might bring.

Hurling's downfall says Whelan was directly proportional to the ideological assumptions of the time and things seemed to change overnight for the sport:

> "The rapid Anglicization of Irish culture in the second quarter of the 19th century, which saw the catholic middle classes engaging in a precipitate retreat from vernacular cultural forms, a retreat conducted at a break-neck speed unprecedented in nineteenth century Europe."

Hurling was attacked on all sides by the landlord, clergy and lawmaker, and that it wasn't just a question of it dying out but more of it being "killed."

By the early 19th century, the game was played only in isolated pockets, however it survived, and by the early 1880s we see the drive for revival and organization take place in Dublin. On January 1883, the Dublin Hurling Club was founded with one Michael Cusack drawing up rules that included a call for a wider bottom hurley.

Scrimmages were held in the Phoenix Park in Dublin and though the club folded soon after, players resurfaced when Cusack again – who also played cricket and rugby – tried and succeeded to generate interest in the game in the city. Hurling spread throughout Dublin and eventually led Cusack and others to found the Gaelic Athletic Organization (GAA) in Thurles, County Tipperary a year later.

The GAA saw its aims as the revival and strengthening of Irish identity through the promotion of Irish cultural pastimes – including hurling, Gaelic football and athletics.

The chief mechanism to achieve such a goal was through the establishment of clubs that would be in charge of organizing games in each county. The new organization introduced codified rules and the size of playing fields was regulated. The rapid spread of clubs saw hurling's fortunes once more blossom and three years later, the GAA initiated the All Ireland championships in 1887.

Sports historian and author Dr. Paul Rouse in a lecture at Dublin in 2010, speaks of Cusack's and Dublin's influence in reviving hurling:

> "Such was the importance of Dublin in taking the ancient game of hurling and squeezing it onto a modern playing field that it might be considered that Dublin was the crucible of the modern game of hurling.
>
> While Thurles was the formal birthplace of the GAA, the idea of the association was forged on the grass of the Phoenix Park in Dublin. It was there, after all, that Michael Cusack had fixed the revival of hurling even before he founded the GAA."

Before the codification of the game, there existed a code of honor associated with the sport. The game of hurling carried the honor of village or those living in the countryside and despite games being of a rough and tumble nature, there still existed a sense of fair play and a sportsman-like conduct was becoming.

Outing Magazine, a late-nineteenth and early twentieth-century American publication covering various sports, carried an article by one Robert T. Walsh who reminisces about an old Irish fair he witnessed as a child in 1876. Such fairs would have been forerunners or had similarities to 'Picnic Days' held by Irish immigrants in New York and Boston leading up to the turn of the 20th century. Hurling was a regular occurrence at 'Picnic Days'.

The Irish fair took place at a place called Camphill, near the old town of Kinsale, County Cork (neighbor of Kerry) in the southwest of Ireland. Walsh, who saw his article published in Outing in 1891, describes various activities at the fair including an account of a hurling match in progress. He later describes another game he witnessed that intriguingly appeared similar to baseball:

> "And the hurlers played a game of games. Ballinspittle was three goals ahead in the first half, and the Courcies country people were jubilant. But the turn came, and the Innoshannon and Shipool contingent 'put their first foot foremost.' After a terrific tussle, during which noses and faces and chests and shins peeled off their bark, and colored the players for the honor of their country sides, the umpire — almost at the risk of his life — declared 'time up, and the game a draw. Pandemonium reigned a while. But finally, beneath the shade of the "Rakes of Mallow," and not having the historical beech tree to fulfill Virgil's line, the combatants made merry over the fact that 'one was as good a man, or better, than the other.' And in this way do all hurling matches — those which are inter-parish — take place, determination to win at the cost of much exercise of brawn and loss of strength being first factors, and jollity and good-humored acceptance of defeat or victory being the second. The battles are fought with a peculiar earnestness — the honor of the parish depends on it; but the simplicity of character of the players always prevents bad feeling, and losers and victors alike celebrate the result good humoredly... .....And despite the attempt to crush out the manhood of Ireland by forbidding their use of weapons, the common people established the "old fair," the last of which died out in 1876.
>
> Then for a time the game of hurling died out, and it was not until the establishment of the Gaelic Athletic Association, during the present decade [1880s] that it began to revive.
>
> Now branches of that association exist in nearly every parish in Ireland, and on Sundays it is not unusual to find ten or twelve thousand people watching an exciting game with all the pleasure that did their forefathers and mothers watch the contests at the annual festivals or at the old fairs."

Robert T. Walsh goes on to refer to the early hurling years in America and how the birth of the Gaelic Athletic Association had influenced immigrant life especially along the east coast of the U.S.

According to his understanding of the numbers involved in hurling clubs in America, he tells that the sport was much sought out and was popular in the late 1880s:

> "I believe there are in all forty-nine hurling clubs in the United States. And it is pleasant now and then to climb the heights of Hoboken [New Jersey] and watch the young Irish-Americans emulating the Fioinea [Fianna] of sixteen hundred years ago in their wielding of the hurley."

The Fianna, an elite warrior group who lived by a strict code of honor, protected the High King of Ireland from within and from invaders without. There are several accounts of them enjoying the playing of hurling.

Rather intriguingly, Walsh then goes on to give an account of another game played during that time in the late 19th century in Ireland and very similar to America's beloved game, Baseball. He saw the game being played once in Kerry and gives this fascinating account – the similarities to baseball are indeed apparent.

The game that he witnessed was called 'Trap' and drew thousands of people and it is fitting to reproduce his observations in full here:

> "There was another game played at the olden festivals and fairs of Ireland that reminds me curiously of baseball. It is called 'trap,' and as it so closely resembles America's national game and was practiced in Ireland more than one thousand years ago, I shall describe it here. The last game I saw played was at a place close to Ventry harbor, in the county of Kerry. It was during an annual celebration of the 17th of March. –
>
> In a great field were thousands of the peasantry and people from Dingle, and even from Killarney and Listowel and Limerick. At a signal the entire concourse moved toward the hill where I was standing with a friend, and there remained on the battlefield only fifty men. These were the players, and this is how the game was played: A captain for each side being selected, the forty-eight players stand in a row, and from them the captains alternately call each twenty-four men. Then they toss for innings and the game begins. It is played with a hurley and a ball of horsehair and leather formed like a double cone. This is placed on the ground near to a hole, which answers the purpose of the baseball homeplate; under it is a spoon-shaped piece of wood called a kippeen.
>
> This the batsman strikes and the ball rises in the air when he hits at it. Should he miss three strokes, he is out. If he fails to drive it forty

hurley lengths (about ninety feet) he also loses his innings." And he scores nothing unless the ball is driven at least the distance of fifty hurley lengths.

Behind the batsman is the captain of the opposing team, and his twenty-four men are arranged in a semicircle on the field, about fifty yards from the batsman.

At a line distant from the hole about twenty hurley lengths are stationed two men of the in side, and their duty is a strange one. When the ball is struck the fielders endeavor to catch it on the fly or after one hop, and should they succeed in doing this, with one hand, the man is out. If they do not catch it they throw it toward the hole. And then comes the business of the two men who stand on this "twenty-hurley line." It is their duty to prevent the ball getting within that line and they are permitted to strike it as it is thrown, and so increase the score of their friend. Should they miss three times, then the batsman is out, as though it was he himself who had made the false hits.

If the ball is thrown behind the player the opposing captain endeavors to so strike it that it goes within the twenty hurley line, in which event also the batsman relinquishes his hurley. The score is counted by distance only. For instance, nothing counts until after the ball has been struck fifty hurleys' lengths, and after that each length counts one, the length of the game being usually five hundred.

Or sometimes it is decided by the aggregate of the innings. It seems to me that this game is a more scientific one than baseball. It requires greater skill in handling the bat and infinitely more strength, and certes the work of the fielders is more difficult and requires absolute skill in the determination of the throw toward the hole. Of course it is not precisely similar to baseball— for instance, there is no pitcher— but the mode is not so very dissimilar that one cannot trace a close resemblance.

This game continues to be played in many parts of Ireland, particularly in the West and Southwest; and so great is the interest taken in it in the parishes where it is played that all country sides turn out to watch this picturesque test of the strength and skill of their athletic young friends. In the days of the old fairs this game rivalled hurling. But that olden celebration is no more. An' more's the pity."

The game described certainly had similarities to baseball, though notably, no pitcher would have been a big departure from the much-loved American game. Robert T. Walsh's account, written in the late 1880s, also suggests that the game of 'trap' he witnessed and that resembled baseball was 'practiced in Ireland for more than one thousand years.' He gives no evidence for such uttering – perhaps he is mixing in some ancient hurling lore – but if true that 'Trap' had such an old lineage one could definitely say that historically baseball has a strong connection to Ireland.

Robert T. Walsh's article on the game of 'Trap' appears to have made an impression at the time as apart from the Outing Magazine publication, the piece was carried also on the front page of The Louisiana Democrat, April 19, 1891.

The sport of rounders is also similar to baseball and is believed to have its roots in this game called Trap.

When mass emigration arrived during the mid part of the 19th century for thousands upon thousands of Irish, many took their love of the sport of hurling with them.

Hurling now arrives in America.

Chapter 4

Early American hurling

In 'Sports and games of the Renaissance,' Andrew Liebs explained how various forms of hurling were carried on throughout England and Europe. At the same time, stick games were also very popular in the New World. Liebs finds early European settlers reported such games being played by many Native American tribes throughout North America.

The Wichita of Oklahoma, the Omahas of Nebraska, and the Makah of Washington State had their own version of a stick game similar to hockey. The game was played with hockey-like sticks and took place on varying size of grounds:

> "They used a three-foot length sticks that were curved at the end along with a hardball three inches in diameter carved from knots in wood or by stuffing leather pouches tightly with animal fur.
>
> Play took place in an area of ground up to 40 yards wide and 400 yards long, but could also stretch to a mile with the aim being to drive the ball between 3 to 6 foot wooden goal posts at each end of the field. Sometimes just one post was erected with the goal then being to hit that post."

The Creek, Choctaw and Cherokee had their own variety of stick-ball games. In the Cherokee game one could scoop the ball off the ground with a stick and into one's hand then head for goal - two stakes two meters wide – while the opposition tries to pry it from one's grasp using any necessary means. This Native American variety appears to have similarities with hurling at Irish Fairs.

An early reference to hurling in America is briefly suggested in the Journal of American History (1997) where Thomas. L Atherr in his overview of a book by Nancy. L Struna entitled "People of Prowess: Sport Leisure and Labor in Early Anglo America" notes her research of how, "Irish immigrants established hurling clubs in New York by the 1780s," but there is no further mention in the article about the sport in that epoch.

By the early 1800s, European settlers continued to arrive in the new world and with them they brought their customs and sporting games. At this time, most of the population of the young country lived in rural areas. In contrast, urban areas had 5% of the population and sport was a rarity.

But the American landscape, both from a population dynamic and a sporting one, would undergo a cataclysmic shift over the next 50 years.

In his work 'City Games: The Evolution of American Urban Society and the Rise of Sports', Steven A. Riess talks of the changes to life in the new world that would forever alter the rather tranquil sporting landscape.

The main sports in 1820 were outdoor activities such as traditional field and stream, blood sports and contests of strength and skill. It was rare to have horse races while team sports were virtually unknown – most had yet to be created. But all that would change within half a century as the growth of urban centers saw sport becoming a focal element of social life in cities.

Between 1820-1870, the percentage of the population that lived in cities multiplied four-fold. New York alone saw huge increases in a three decade period between 1830-1860.

Reiss outlines how the growth of cities was driven by industrial and capital investment which led to better transport and communication networks. Political institutions, social and ethnic organizations were also established and together set the foundations for a modern society where the evolution of sporting subcultures could be born.

But in cities, along with wealth, you also found overcrowding, crime and poverty, with little if any real sense of community spirit.

Organized sport emerged out of the city cauldron as a means of keeping a more traditional way, as the way of life for most residents had changed radically. "Communities of people who shared the same values and culture sought distance from men unlike themselves by organizing ethnic and class sport clubs," unlike those in rural, close-knit communities, noted Reiss.

The relative small size of cities allowed people to access sports from both within and around urban centers. Blossoming sporting fraternities were largely patronized by the working class. This male-dominated world sought solace from the mundane nature of the industrial-era workday, as well as need to steer clear of the feminine world and domestic life.

One of the reasons for the rise in city populations, particularly along the East Coast, was influenced by an influx of Irish immigrants. Apart from industry and technological advances driving people to urban centers, a major contributory factor to the growth of East Coast city populations, particularly New York and Boston, was the horrific Irish Potato Famine 1846-1850.

During a four-year period disease and starvation killed more than a million people and drove a further million from Ireland's shores.

The influx into New York City alone over a 40-year time-line saw the Irish immigrant population rise to extraordinary numbers. By the middle of the century, 133,760 or some 26% of the New York population was Irish. Towards the end of the century in 1890, Irish Americans numbered almost half a million and had grown to over a third of the population of the city.

The Irish who arrived in New York and Boston were largely unskilled and illiterate. Coming from rural upbringings, adjusting to big city life was difficult and it wasn't made easier at the hands of anti-Irish discrimination. They had to make do with the jobs that nobody else wanted and lived in the worst slums.

Sports meanwhile, during the middle part of the 1800s, was confined to indoor activity, namely in bars.

Riess said that the tavern was the principle locus of the sporting fraternity, and as in the past, publicans were important "promoters and facilitators of sport recognizing its value in attracting thirsty customers."

As well as this, there simply was no room for outdoor sports in crowded city neighborhoods that had yet to adopt extensive park and public grounds areas. Billiards, cock fighting and boxing matches were the most popular indoor sporting practices at the time. Boxing in particular thrived among the poor working class districts of New York, Boston, Philadelphia, Baltimore, and Irish immigrants participated as both fighter and spectator. In New York City between 1840-1860, over half of the city's boxers were Irish.

During that period only cities such as Boston and Philadelphia had open public parks where people could picnic and come together for any type of outdoor sporting activity.

After the Civil War a movement had begun to create open public spaces for people to enjoy, not only from a health and exercise perspective but also as a means of escaping, if only for awhile, the confines of the crowded slums.

During the 1850s, the cities of St Louis in Missouri, Hartford and New Haven in Connecticut, Providence in Rhode Island, Baltimore in Maryland, Cincinnati in Ohio, New Orleans in Louisiana, and San Francisco in California created public parks. By 1858 a design was put forth for Central Park in New York and the movement towards public parks encouraged people to get out of the inner confines of city tenements and catch a breath of air.

William Joseph Baker in his book, 'Sports in the Western world,' said that parks offered, "crowded tenement dwellers to turn out to walk, picnic, hold footraces, kick footballs, play cricket, and baseball games, and, ice-skate in winter."

Not only did public parks bring a better quality of life to the individual, they also paved the way for sporting groups to form and as a result allowed for sporting events and their organization to prosper. Together with improved and cheaper mass transit systems, city streets became less congested with sporting activity as people could now go to the park. "Instead of clogging narrow neighborhood streets with games of stick-ball ... young players took advantage of the many fields in playgrounds and larger parks." The New York City Department of Parks & Recreation said in their historical, 'Bat Sports in Parks.'

Meanwhile, English immigrants fared well in America as they spoke the language, had skills as in the weaving and textile industry and were more in tune with the culture. They introduced their game of cricket around the 1830s with many textile workers taking up the sport, and later, English merchants organized teams in the cities of Philadelphia, New York and Boston.

The game grew beyond the borders of the English communities and by the mid 1800s, it had become the most popular sport with intercity games a norm. Meanwhile, the Scottish organized themselves with picnic days featuring their native Highland Games. Purses or prize money was awarded for the various weight throwing activities and these became very popular events during the 1870s. Stephen A. Reiss in his book reported that the Caledonian Scottish events attracted the biggest crowds.

The Irish too began to organize themselves similarly in relation to outdoor sporting activities and entertainment.

Picnic field-day events sprung up throughout the major urban centers. Irish Societies, groups and newly formed athletic clubs began to sponsor athletics and various games at popular 'Field Days' or 'Picnic Days'. Politicians and businessmen took on the job of nurturing the fledgling clubs and eventually these athletic organizations sponsored games grew in popularity around the turn of the century in Irish communities and later were copied by other ethnic groups. In many respects 'Picnic Day' events on a Sunday were a throwback to the old fair day back in Ireland.

In Boston organizations such as the Irish Athletic Club of Boston (IACB) formed in 1879 by first generation Irish Americans – was the forerunner of the organization of hurling and Gaelic football.

Northern Ireland sports scholar Paul Darby in his article 'Irish Diaspora in Boston 1879-90', says that often an IACB Field Day ended with a hurling match.

The playing of hurling had been going on before that in various guises with regular games taking place across the Hudson River from Manhattan in Hoboken, New Jersey. Robert T. Walsh saw hurling played there in the late 1880s but before that Hoboken had been a frequent venue for many years.

The Hoboken Guards Hurling Club – recently formed American club (Irish and mostly Americans players) – in their research on hurling, found evidence to suggest that matches were being played on a regular basis between clubs in Manhattan and Hoboken.

During the 1880s the Kenmare Guards hurling team, who lived in New York's notorious 'Five Points' area, played hurling in Hoboken. The Hoboken Guards – who took the name of the older club – cite a report of a game played by the Kenmare Guards in 1858 on the Elysian Fields in Hoboken and believe it to be the first ever hurling match played in America. "As it stands, that St. Patrick's Day inner-squad match in Hoboken was the first reported hurling match in America, though not under GAA rules, as the GAA was formed three decades later."

Picnic and Field Days proved to be very popular and the Fourth of July celebrations of 1880 in Boston saw Irish people from all over the region descend on the city's famous old park in the center, Boston Common.

In the Boston Daily Globe (now Boston Globe), July 6, one of the many reports on the various activities throughout the "Great and Glorious" day, heard of a huge crowd at a hurling match on the Common early in the morning. The column head, read: "Irish Games" with the sub head: "the famous old game of hurling on the Common".

The first paragraph gives an insight into their thoughts on the time on hurling's influence on other sports, and sports at a very early stage. "The exhibition of the famous old Irish sport of hurling, from which comes the modern school game of hockey, on the Common at 10am., was witnessed by 10,000 or 15,000 people, who stayed as long as the playing was kept up, and then cried for more."

The beginnings of clubs was in evidence at the time as the two teams playing on the day were selected from the newly formed Boston Hurling Club with two captains, J.C Looney and Francis Fitzpatrick picking sides. Looney's wore white caps and Fitzpatrick's green. An American and Irish flag at either end served as goals.

The report cites 'judges' and a referee present. At 10 a.m. sharp, the ball was thrown in with a, "series of five games: Looney's with 2 wins, Fitzpatrick's 1 and 2 draws before play ended at 11.30."

The writer thought that the last game was the best he had witnessed and was impressed with the skill levels:

> "This was the most hotly contested of the series, and the skill which some of the men showed in scooping the ball from the ground and batting it over the heads of their opponents was admired by the crowd."

In 1882 in Boston there is another detailed and rather interesting Boston Globe (Sept 7, 1882) report of a game between the Boston Hurling Club and the South Boston Hurling Club.

A big crowd gathered for the match at Beacon Park, September 6 in the afternoon. There was payment to view the game with the gate money, which was deemed to be "considerable," going to the match winners with each side contributing $300 to the pot.

In those days playing for a purse in the U.S. was the norm, even though two years later the new governing body of Irish Gaelic sports in Ireland, the Gaelic Athletic Association (GAA) created an amateur sporting organization.

The match was much anticipated as the two city rivals previous meetings had ended controversially, "without the satisfaction to all concerned".

Two 16 a-side teams took to the field and the report names all the players on either side and with a team to win two-games-out-of-three declared winner. Stakes at either end were used as goals and would have been connected approximately six feet from the ground across the top. It is not clear if scoring over the bar is allowed and this matter becomes a hot topic after the game.

After a late start, due to the referee not showing up, another was selected and the ball was thrown in at "3.10pm". The game was, "from the first one of the hottest and most exciting. Members of both sides showed excellent playing."

The reporter picks out good skills by various players. "Crowley made some remarkable runs" with the ball going up and down the field, then South Boston struck for a goal. "At 3.53, a surprising bit by T.F Lynch put the ball between the stakes for the South Boston's."

After a short break, Boston Hurling Club came back to level the game with a score when "Mike O'Sullivan put it between the sticks," and with the scores level, the next goal would be a winner and the excitement increased with that anticipation.

Money exchanged hands amongst the crowd at a frenzied rate, observed the reporter:

> "betting was heavy, and the adherents of both sides were confident of victory." But then a quick score arrived catching many off guard. At 4.10 the ball was again thrown. The result was as sudden and unlooked for as before. Luke Corrigan for the Bostons, in the midst of the tussle knocked the ball well into the air and it passed beyond the stakes. There was a general cry of victory for the Boston's and congratulations were showered upon them."

The reporter like many others must have felt that the game had come to a satisfactory conclusion, however, other voices declared not so and doubt on the outcome of a game once again resurfaced:

> "Stakeholders began to reach for their money when the assertion was made and repeated that the ball went over the flags and not between. There was much dispute upon this point and as the referee left the ground without making any definite decision the matter was left in a very unsatisfactory state."

The reporter duly noted, "The Bostons declared themselves winners, the South Boston's disagreed the validity of the claim with the referee yet to speak on who was the proper winner."

Despite this the reporter described the game in a very positive light. "Whoever is declared the winner, one thing is for certain, the game was a most interesting one and exciting while it lasted."

Later a letter to the Boston Daily Globe dated Sept 17 from the South Boston HC, looks for the Boston HC to honor rules they quote as saying that the ball must go under the upright. No further information is available on the outcome.

Other Boston clubs like the William O'Briens, the Emmets and Worcester, formed and a Boston Championship began. Other cities like New York had their clubs and champions as well.

Scholar, Steven Reiss says that hurling at the time had a strong presence within the Irish American community and popular among second and third generation who played for teams like the Irish Athletic Club, the South

Boston AC, and the Shamrock Hurling Club. But a change was already underway.

While hurling remained popular among the Irish, things had already been changing for working class Irish in American cities as a need for increased assimilation into the new culture and the lure of stable income, saw many young Irish Americans move away from hurling and Irish sports to other games such as baseball. Soon greater importance was placed on "American sports" such as baseball.

From its beginnings in the 1840s as a city and regional inter-social club activity, baseball's popularity spread fast.

In New York, the widespread increase of 'Baseball Fever' during the 1850s saw more and more clubs forming, and soon the game began to grow nationally and by the early part of the 1870s the sport enters the era of professionalism. Now a national pastime, baseball's influence on the American psyche also stirred young Irish Americans. Irish men flocked in their thousands to games. Not only that, but when taking up baseball, the Irish excelled at the game so much so that one correspondent of the Sporting News claimed in 1872 that one-third of major league players were of Irish extraction.

Benjamin Rader in his book, "Baseball, A History of America's Game," quotes former Brooklyn Dodgers bat-boy and later iconic baseball historian, Harold Seymour, on how the Irish influenced baseball in the 1890s, and "'that some thought they had a special talent for ball playing.'"

Irish American Hall of Fame, cites such greats as Michael "King" Kelly, Roger Connor – the home run king before Babe Ruth – all-time ERA leader Big Ed Walsh, and N.Y. Giants manager John McGraw, were some of the early greats of baseball.

The game of hurling was moving also in a changing environment as the mid 1880s brought rules changes with the birth of the governing body the GAA in Ireland in 1884.

Change also beckoned courtesy of a visit to the U.S. of an elite group of Irish hurlers and athletes labeled, the 'American Invasion'. This amounted to a 10-city tour and according to the Encyclopedia of Ethnicity and Sports in the United States "helped to start a new era for hurling in the US."

The GAA in Ireland had laid down a new code of rules and a regulation size of field for hurling and Gaelic football. Irish immigrants had brought both sports traditions with them on their arrival. The 'American Invasion' tour however, introduced the new codified rules and greatly influenced the progress of the game locally.

The first port of call by the Irish touring party was to that iconic haven for Irish immigrants, New York City.

THE IRISH INVASION

The tour caused quite a stir at the time not only among the Irish community but it also caught the widespread attention of the city.

From the Irish tour's perspective, the main focus was of a fund-raising nature to garner interest, support and finance for the revival in Ireland of the ancient, Tailteann Games. The modern version of the Tailteann Games, was open to all of Irish birth or ancestry, and didn't eventually get going until 1924 with participants from England, Scotland, Wales, Canada, South Africa, Australia and the United States.

A further tour objective was to try and promote Irish sports such as hurling to a wider American audience.

The Irish party arrived by the steamship 'Wisconsin' on September 25, 1888. The group comprised of 53 athletes and hurlers along with GAA President Morris Davin, for an athletics tour series that included exhibitions games of hurling over a six week period.

Newspapers in New York and Boston labelled this first ever GAA tour of America as the 'Irish Invasion'.

The New York Times of Sept 26, recalled the moment when the athletes and hurlers disembarked from the boat:

> "They carried big blackthorn sticks and hurling clubs in their hands. Their sticks commanded universal respect, and a big policeman eyes them with special interest and his own locust under his coat. The curved hurling or shinny sticks of hard wood carefully polished looked formidable, but in the hands of the muscular athletes they were as [s]witches."

The tour fulfilled dates around New York City before traveling on to Trenton and Newark in New Jersey, to Lowell and Boston in Massachusetts, as well as to Philadelphia and Providence, Rhode Island.

Signaling the close ties of Gaelic sport and athletic organizations in U.S. urban cities at the time, the first exhibition took place at the Manhattan Athletic Club.

The game apparently caught the imagination of the spectators and a journalist reporting for the Boston Daily Globe (Sept 30, 1888):

> "The visitors today gave an exhibition of hurling on the grounds of the Manhattan Athletic Club ... The spectators, who for the most part had never seen the game played before, grew wild with excitement, and the result must have been exceedingly gratifying to the players, though the grounds are far too small for the purpose."

At the time, the number on a hurling team was 21 with the size of the playing field 110 yards by 196 yards. The report mentions that there were two umpires and a referee officiating for the exhibition. The reporter detailed the positions on the field and the dress of the players, "one back, two quarterbacks, two half backs, three forwards, two sides on left, two sides on right and nine centers:

> "The teams wore different color jerseys, a crest of a harp embroidered on the jersey, a cap of the same color, brown corduroy knee breeches, brown stockings (other team black) and russet leather shoes and both teams had GAA written across the front of their jerseys."

Was the new Irish organization trying its hand at some early-day branding? There is no doubt that the game left an impression with the Boston Globe scribe, who wrote:

> "The game reminded the American boys of the old-time shinny only it was reduced to a science. At times the ball was kept in the air for the space of five minutes and the players hustled and jostled each other from one end of the ground to the other."

The program of events also included a complete list of track and field events with medals awarded to the winners. Later in the week the tour traveled to Boston to compete against New England athletes for an afternoon of sports at Beacon Park.

When they arrived in Boston they were received by the city's Mayor Hugh O'Brien (himself a member of an athletic club), who said it was the first time ever the city had the pleasure of entertaining a visiting group of Irish athletes.

The mayor showed them the city as they visited Deer Island and there was a banquet for the visitors at Parker House. The mayor employed some political gusto in his address to locals and the touring party when sounding all the right notes:

> "He said that if the visitors at any time meet defeat in America it would be at the hands of their own countrymen, for in this country the best fighters, the best baseball players, and the best athletes are Irishmen (applause)." Reported the Boston Daily Globe, October 4 1888.

Morris Davin, the GAA President in Ireland, told of their efforts to revive the old ancient Irish games and stressed the need for rules for the games. The secretary of the GAA, John Callinan, thanked America for all the assistance it had given Ireland and added that he hoped that Americans would be pleased with the old games they would show on their trip.

The games on that sunny October afternoon had drawn a crowd of 6,000 people and the Boston Daily Globe, gave full coverage with the headline "Enthusiastic thousands cheer the men from Ireland."

By all accounts the large Irish American crowd was more than what the police could handle as they invaded the 'track' at intervals:

> "The Irish citizens of Boston with a love for athletics, and there are few Irish men in which the trait is not developed, made the reception of the strangers a duty and the only fault to be found was their zeal for defying all efforts at restraint, they crowded on the track and the efforts of a handful of policemen were utterly lost against the surging mass of humanity."

The article shows illustrations of the hurling teams lined up ready for the game to begin. The hurling exhibition took place after the athletic contests and was said to have been a "rattling" affair with "clean good natured, though sharp play characterized the game and as an exhibition it was a decided success."

They also competed a second day in athletics on Oct 5, 1888 at Beacon Park and at the end of the athletics program there was another hurling match exhibition. However, there was less enthusiasm as none of the local hurling clubs could get a game going against the visiting Irish teams because of the amateur status of the visitors.

Professional sports like baseball had already begun to influence the local Irish sporting culture where Irish Americans saw sports as a means of earning a fixed income and garnering increased social and cultural mobility. Before the visitors arrived, hurling in American cities was organized by athletic clubs and played for considerable sums of money with betting transactions in the crowd also a perfectly normal practice. But when the Irish visitors arrived, everything is done at an amateur level, and so full participation by local teams was limited and attendance suffered.

Overall, despite good attendance in Boston and Philadelphia, the tour from an Irish and GAA perspective was labeled a failure in regard to securing monies for the Tailteann Games the following year.

Conversely, the tour was seen as having a positive effect for clubs in America says scholar Paul Darby in his book, 'Gaelic Games, Nationalism and the Irish Diaspora in the United States':

> "The 'Gaelic Invasion' has generally been written off on the basis that it failed to attract the type of interest and gate receipts that the GAA had hoped for and, as a consequence, did not generate sufficient funds for the Tailteann games to occur in 1889 as originally intended.... it is difficult to classify the tour as anything other than a resounding success when considering its impact on the development of Gaelic sport in the U.S."

Darby also points out that some 17 of the touring party did not return to Ireland and their presence immediately boosted the local clubs they joined. Boston particularly benefited with the addition of Young Ireland's hurling club the following year joining existing clubs like the Wolfe Tones, Emmets, and Redmonds. The tour's game-playing format also saw the local clubs get a feel for the new rules of the game.

HURLING MEDIA FOCUS

When comparing American press coverage on the sport of hurling in today's media with that of the era shortly before the turn of the 20th century, and into the early part of the first decade, one finds little if any resemblance.

It's important to remember that hurling and Gaelic sports reporting from a century ago was carried on by mainstream U.S. newspapers and on a regular weekly basis. Nowadays, you'll have mostly Irish American indigenous papers like the Irish Immigrant in Boston or the Irish Voice in New York, report on hurling and Gaelic sports action within the Irish diaspora community in the immediate area.

In the past, local Irish American papers also covered the games but unlike the modern era, American mainstream papers were very interested in what was going on at these picnic days and at early organized championships and leagues. However, long gone are the days when the likes of the Boston Globe or the New York Times send reporters out on a weekend assignment to cover hurling at Canton outside Boston, or at Gaelic Park in the Bronx, N.Y.

Less and less is mentioned in the press from 1910 onwards. From the Great Depression through to World War II, we see little or no coverage with only the rare mention in mainstream newspapers. Sporadic features crop up here and there during the 1960s and again in the 1980s, and in the early part of the new millennium when the Irish began to migrate away from American shores once more.

However, the trend during 2011, and over the past few years with the Irish economy once more falling into decline, sees a resurgence of Irish coming to America. With the rise in immigration there is an upswing in hurling and Gaelic sports in America.

Since shortly after the turn of the 20th century, hurling's fortunes have been tied to the immigration-migration axis, where one invariably affected the other. With less and less first-and second-generation Irish Americans taking up the sport of their fathers, the new arrivals from across the ocean were counted on to backbone the sport and club. Over the years, this Irish immigration player model persisted and remains dominant today.

Following the exploits of immigrants, mainstream newspapers' hurling coverage, for decades was confined to once-off St. Patrick's Day features and the like. But over the past six years their collective eye has refocused, often without the need to hook a story on the holiday.

Now the U.S. mainstream press has started to take note of Gaelic sports, and hurling in particular because for the first time in the history of the game in the U.S., Americans are starting to play and with little need for that native Irish backbone support. Out of the blue, more and more Americans have started to form new clubs all across the country.

The scope of this new revolution is breathtaking given that there is absolutely no TV marketing of the sport through American broadcast TV networks and cable providers. While the annual hurling championship in Ireland can be picked up on various pay per view channels like Premium Sports, there is no mainstream free-to-air broadcasting of the games in the U.S. Despite this, interest among Americans has increased, and often people new to the sport stumble across hurling by accident.

Over the past few years, such interest has been largely driven by social media sites such as YouTube, Twitter, Blogs and of late, Facebook.

Before going into what exactly is happening today on the ground, we return to the past to examine other factors that have played a part as to why hurling declined in coverage in the U.S. media and faded as a potential popular mainstream sport for Americans.

Ten years before the end of the 19th century and one year after the Irish hurling tour of 1888, the mainstream press, despite some negative coverage as regards to the roughness of the sport – though they were forced to address the dangers of early college football when players lost their lives – the press of the day was still very impressed with hurling. Many assumed it was going to make it as an All-American sport.

In 1889, the Boston Daily Globe did a major exposé about hurling, complete with sketches. They asked that given the amount of Irish immigrants living in America: why hadn't hurling caught the American public's imagination. "When the number of Irishmen who have made their homes in this country is considered, it is a bit surprising that their national game has not become Americanized."

The 'Globe went as far as to say that the game of baseball wasn't as imbedded in the social psyche of America as the sport of hurling was in Ireland and that there didn't seem to be any effort taking place in the U.S. to put an organizational structure in place. "Baseball is not better known and more appreciated here than is hurling in Ireland, and yet until this winter there has been no systematic effort to introduce the game to this continent."

The newspaper said that in light of the previous year's athletic and hurling match exhibitions, interest in hurling had been aroused and that several athletes had stayed behind such as JJ Cullen. He was described by the Globe as the "champion individual hurler in Ireland" and having become a member of the Gaelic Society in New York, his purpose would be to act as an American hurling instructor.

Still there was hope that the game would catch on, as under the guidance of Cullen, hurling games were played every "pleasant Sunday and by reason of the open winter, the game has taken a good start."

Despite past mainstream media reports allowing for greater exposure than that of today, hurling was still little understood in America at the time and in an interview with Mr Cullen the paper goes into detail about the game. It describes the size of the hurling field, the shape of hurley and the kind of ball, the rules, and how the game is played.

A sketch of two players of the previous year with the caption a 'Bruised Shin' suggests to the American reader that the game is not for the faint of heart and that injuries occur. When asked if it has 'rough play' Cullen answers that 'maybe it does' and proceeded to rattle off rules that are there to prevent roughhouse tactics. He told the reporter that hurling wasn't dangerous but admitted that in the excitement of the game some shins will be bruised but this is due in most cases to unskilled players use of the hurley.

Cullen talked about the amateur status of the sport in Ireland and at the time it was played all over the country by adults and children and that in the Gaelic Athletic Association (GAA) there was 1700 clubs of which 35,000 members played hurling.

The Boston Daily Globe's article went on to say that contrary to hurling's amateur status in Ireland, it was carried on in Boston on a "semi-professional" basis where teams play for a "stake or purse offered by some organization."

At the time, The Boston's and The Shamrocks were the most prominent teams in the city of Boston and in 1888 on America's national holiday July 4th, they played in the center of the city at The Common before thousands of spectators. One of the leading players and well-known figures in hurling circles in the city at the time was a certain Captain McCarthy. During the time of the touring party he reckoned that if either of the Bostons or the Shamrocks played the visitors that they would have beaten them.

In the Globe's feature he is asked that if there were such teams in Boston why wasn't the sport more popular. According to McCarthy, the reason for the failure of hurling to make an American impact was put down to clubs not having "convenient" places or facilities on which to train and "therefore only the men likely to play in a match took enough interest to turn out." However the paper perhaps felt that there was more to the argument for the game not becoming more mainstream as it did attract a following:

> "That the general public took interest in the sport was evinced by the throngs of people who watch the game whenever a match is played, and at many of the summer picnics hurling is one of the most attractive points."

Perhaps it wasn't quite as simple as putting it down to playing facilities. Perhaps there were other factors that prevented hurling flourishing as a sport.

While a clear set of rules was introduced following the formation of the GAA in 1884 in Ireland, and the subsequent tour's presentation of those rules in exhibition matches, the idea of hurling as a rough game was certainly one that prevailed during the late 19th century with American newspapers.

Reporting on hurling games, as well as the other GAA code Gaelic football (a mix of Australian Rules, rugby, basketball and soccer), papers like The New York Times often gave unflattering reports on games. No doubt some justified and others perhaps not. But there is no doubting that some reporters came away from matches with a negative viewpoint on the game. Negative press wouldn't have helped market the sport outside the Irish community.

An example of such coverage is seen when the New York Times, December 19, 1892, reported on a hurling match played at Ridgewood Park, Long Island, as being more like a brawl at an Irish Fair than a game of sport. The paper reported that 300 people were on hand for a hurling match where, "broken heads are common incidents of these games...and there was one of these old fashioned hurling matches yesterday."

Apparently there was a bitter rivalry between the two teams in question, the Irish-Americans and the Wolfe Tones, who were said to be members of the Gaelic Association of America. This is one of the earliest references to efforts of any type of organization of Gaelic games in America at the time.

The Times reporter describing the nature of the game noted several incidents. One of which was how arguments broke out on the field and at one end of the field fists went flying resembling "a veritable Donnybrook Fair." Another aspect was on the scars of battle and the indifference of the players to such slights:

> "Maxwell, one of the players on the Irish-American team, was struck a terrible blow with a hurley and a hole half an inch in diameter stove in his forehead but a little thing like that did not affect him and after wetting a piece over the wound he went into the field again."

But while there had been both negative and positive pieces in the press on hurling, violent scenes reported at hurling matches paled in comparison to that of American football.

Player deaths and high injury rates were a common feature of early college football competition. The sport's future was under threat. By 1905 football was getting all the wrong headlines as an article in the Richmond Times Dispatch of that October painted a sobering picture. "The Record of Football Awful'" was the head with the subhead "Forty-five deaths and Hundred of serious injuries in five years past."

Mass plays and 'unnecessary roughness' were the main culprits. New rules by the Intercollegiate Football Committee were brought in by 1910 to make the sport safer with the prohibition of the flying tackle and other changes to stop mass plays. Meanwhile, the stigma of hurling as being a rough and dangerous sport has remained stuck in the American media psyche ever since.

Roughness is often defined according to American romantic projections of Irishness, however at the same time there is nothing romantic about the continuing fatal injuries in football today. There is commentary in American media about crippling injuries to high school footballers but when commenting (if infrequently) about a sport like hurling, the dangers can often be highlighted without paralleling the continuing injury crisis in American football.

A report entitled, the 'Annual Survey of Football Injury Research' was initiated in 1931 to make football a safer sport. The report is commissioned by The American Football Coaches Association, the NCAA, and National Federation of State High School Associations. In the 2008 report, it showed seven fatalities directly related to football during the 2008 football season. All seven fatalities were in "high school football."

At the turn of the 19th century in Boston hurling continued to thrive around the city and region, as there was hurling clubs in Cambridge, Roxbury, and Fall River. The July 4th celebrations of 1893 attracted thousands to see local clubs compete for a cash prize. The Boston Globe reported of how two teams, the Shamrock hurling club of Boston and the William O'Brien club of Cambridge played at the Boston Common in the morning for the $100 purse offered by the city government. "Nearly 10,000 persons witnessed the game, which was exciting," recalled the newspaper.

However yet again, the game ended unsatisfactorily as the reporter noted that the, referee or the umpire, as was commonly called at the time, was for whatever reason unable to give a definitive result of the outcome of the match.

The seeming regular inability to determine winners at such events would not have endeared potential young Irish American players who were already looking to more organized and stable fare in baseball, and with that, a good American future. No doubt, with undecided endings, hurling's supporters would have begun to slowly drift away especially if betting monies were unsatisfactorily lost.

Another in-depth article on hurling in The New York Sun appeared in March 12, 1893. It told of the sport's roots in Ireland and where it was played and by whom and the different type of hurleys used by the different counties in Ireland. Artist's impressions of the various shapes from several counties is presented in the feature.

The article speculated that another possible 'invasion' of Irish athletes, similar to the one that took place nine years prior, would take place again. It had been rumored that a particularly strong hurling team would be on tour that would be visiting Chicago for the World's Fair and would be taking on the best in America.

"Hurling has always been known as one of the national sports of Ireland," said the Sun.

In the past, the game was known to the American media and the public in a general sense, judging from the U.S. national newspapers' coverage of the local Gaelic sports games in urban centers. In contrast, today's American media know little or nothing about its existence and portray it as an oddity, correspondingly the public are not aware hurling exists.

But at the turn of the century there was a much greater awareness about the game in general. Inter-city games were beginning to be organized where hurling and Gaelic football teams from Boston and New York competed at the Congress Street grounds in Boston. Newspapers of the day were providing coverage on hurling games every weekend and were familiar with the teams, the players and the club rivalries.

It is also noteworthy in that The New York Sun, March 12 article, had a viewpoint that hurling might enjoy a more favorable future in America than its "little brother," Gaelic football. "The advent of the Irish hurlers will add to the interest in the games which promises to equal if not excel Gaelic football in America."

According to The Sun at the time (1893), Gaelic sports first found support in Chicago where there was 12 prosperous clubs (all with hurling teams). It doesn't give a year as to when the clubs were formed. The paper mentions about hurling clubs elsewhere with five clubs in St. Louis and with others in Philadelphia, New York and Boston.

In Chicago, hurling was played regularly at 37th Street and Indiana Avenue, and it was in the city that the first attempts at greater organization began with the founding of the Gaelic Athletic Association of Illinois in 1892.

WEST COAST

On the West Coast, Gaelic sports were also popular among the Irish, despite the fact that Irish emigration wasn't as strong as it was on the East Coast. Paul Darby alludes to the fact that San Francisco was already up and running with Gaelic sports taking place each week.

While San Francisco had a history of Gaelic sports going back to the mid 1850s, it wasn't until January of 1888 that the formal organization of games would take place. The GAA of San Francisco was created at a meeting in the Knights of the Red Branch hall with games to be played on grounds in the Mission district and at other venues in the city.

Darby in his article, "Without the Aid of a Sporting Safety Net?': the Gaelic Athletic Association and the Irish Émigré in San Francisco (1888-c.1938)', printed in the International Journal of the History of Sport, outlines the early days of Irish sports in the city:

> "By the early 1890s, the formally constituted San Francisco GAA was organizing a regular program of league matches, typically during the winter months, at various locales around the city, including the U.S. Army parade grounds at the Presidio and Golden Gate Park. That said, the number of clubs involved by the start of the 1892 season was modest in comparison to numbers elsewhere in the United States."

There was five Gaelic football clubs at the time, and as for hurling, after continued difficulties associated with getting hurling equipment shipped to the west coast, three hurling clubs, the Wolfe Tones, the Geraldines and Columbia were in place by 1896 and later on, came the Independents, Young Irelands, Emmets and Davitts. The games grew within the Irish community and by the early part of the 20th century more clubs were founded outside San Francisco in places such as Oakland, Port Costa, San Jose, Richmond and Crocket.

In one of the first instances to get young Irish Americans taking up hurling, the MacBrides club of Crockett was very prominent in this regard writes Darby. "This latter club was particularly significant and took great strides in promoting the game among young first- and second-generation Irish."

Darby uncovers of how, the Leader - a prominent Irish-American newspaper - in its coverage of the establishment of this club, commended the commitment of the founders and suggested that, "'Their enthusiasm has aroused the entire youth of the neighborhood, with the result that baseball has been discarded and every boy provided with a self-made caman [hurley]'".

It is not clear how this youth venture fared with hurling and Gaelic sports undergoing various ups and downs in the city over the years – the downs due to interest waning and the organization having difficulties, to better times when a new Gaelic Athletic Association of California was formed in February of 1903.

Attendance at games ebbed and flowed with club numbers dwindling and with the start of World War I in 1914, the area saw no league organization, apart from intermittent field day activities. Hurling suffered greatly during the war era, but after the war Darby reports that there was a revival of interest in Gaelic sports in the San Francisco area with regular competition and with further growth through the early 1920s.

A significant boost was the arrival of the first ever All-Ireland winning team visit by Tipperary to the U.S. in 1926. The team toured New York, Boston, Chicago, and Buffalo. In San Francisco, the visitors defeated a select California team at the leased Kezar Stadium in front of the largest ever crowd of 15,000 for a game of hurling in San Francisco.

Another noteworthy development took place a few years later when if it had taken hold could have had seen hurling become an everyday sport in America.

What was started then has been resurrected today in California and is the one of most exciting developments taking place today in hurling in the U.S. We are talking here about U.S. college hurling. Unheard of in the history of Gaelic sports in America, in 2009 the sport of hurling found its way onto California college campuses at Berkeley, Stanford and more recently at UC Davis. Hurling has also reached out to the vast Midwest college community and is spreading like wildfire at present.

Back in 1933, the forerunner of hurling at California colleges began when the sport was played at St. Mary's College, Moraga, Oakland.

A diocesan college for Catholic boys, St. Mary's College had cultivated a strong American football pedigree during the late 1920s. The dean of the college, Tipperary native Brother James Shanahan, introduced the sport of hurling to the college in 1933, a move that was greatly appreciated by the region's Gaelic sports enthusiasts.

The team was comprised of faculty and students, most of Irish descent, along with Irish natives as well. Their play on the field quickly got attention and the following year saw them competing in the senior league and in their first game beat the reigning Pacific Coast champions, Cork. The college was delighted with the college's new sporting star status but things would take a drastic turn.

St. Mary's College second game versus Clare was a very rough affair ending with several of the Christian Brother faculty requiring medical attention. This wasn't looked upon kindly by college management and despite the best efforts of Dean Shanahan, the college decided to end its affair with hurling. The decision was a hammer blow to the future fortunes of the game in the region.

Darby notes that maybe a chance had been lost when referencing Patrick J. Dowling in his book, 'Irish Californians: Historic, Benevolent, Romantic' on the college's departure from hurling:

> "One can only assume that if hurling had been adopted by St. Mary's on a permanent basis, other Catholic colleges would have followed, and Ireland's national game would have become an integral part of American sports."

An assumption, yes, but hardly too wide of the posts given that a sport such as American football got its start on U.S. college campuses.

With the onset of the Great Depression with low immigration rates and poor attendances, games in the San Francisco area went into decline once more and would not be revived until after the second World War. While the likes of New York, and Boston had seen greater levels of Irish immigration than San Francisco, nevertheless the road that Gaelic sports followed in the east is largely similar to the west coast pattern up to the end of World War II.

EQUIPMENT AND VENUES

The cost of playing is another factor that mitigated against the development of hurling in America. Hurling demanded that not only did a player require boots, and gear, it also called for a player to possess a hurley.

The hurley made from the ash tree was generally hard to come by and had to be imported at some expense from Ireland. The Boston and New England Gaelic Athletic Association in 1984 alluded to footballs (Gaelic) popularity at the time and hurley supply problems when compiling a 100-year history of the local organization (1884-1984):

> "Football was the main attraction in both the number of teams playing and followers. Hurling was slower in gaining a hold, possibly because of the additional skill required and the difficulty of securing

an adequate supply of hurleys," wrote a research team for the organization.

Finding suitable playing locations in urban centers like New York was also an ongoing problem.

From the mid 1920s onwards, Innisfail Park in the Bronx took over from Celtic Park in Queens, to become the home of Gaelic Sports in New York. It would later become known as Gaelic Park in the 1950s and to this day is still the mecca for New York enthusiasts of the sports.

Another problem for the development of hurling and Gaelic sports would arise this time in the guise of war and economic woe. With America's entry into the First World War in 1917, all Gaelic Sports activity practically stopped in America up until the 1920s.

Players, instead of marching off to play hurling each weekend, now found themselves in the fields of France with a gun in their hand rather than a hurl. The ceasing of Irish immigration into America during the war years also contributed to Gaelic sports' decline. All the while young Irish Americans were becoming less concerned about their Irish cultural heritage and more focused on their more immediate American life. Going to battle for one's country, more than anything else, solidified this in one's mind.

Things did pick up after World War I and at Boston in 1923 we see the need for greater organization in the creation of the Massachusetts Gaelic Athletic Association. Over the next 10 years, some nine hurling clubs and 15 football clubs would affiliate with the new organization.

In New York control of hurling and Gaelic sports was moving away from athletic organizations like the Irish-American Athletic Association and later the Irish Counties Athletic Union, noted former and recent NY GAA Chairman, Larry McCarthy. In his article, "Irish Americans in Sports: The Twentieth Century' (2009) he talks of a new era taking hold with the foundation of The New York Gaelic Athletic Association in 1914.

In 1926, thirty eight years after the 'Irish Invasion' of 1888, All Ireland Hurling Champions Tipperary arrived in the Big Apple for the New York leg of their tour. Such was the expectation surrounding the event, that Celtic Park and any of the other GAA sites, were deemed too small for the potential crowd size, so the event was moved to New York's Polo Grounds.

The visitors took on NY Offaly, the champions of New York at the time, (and champions also in 2010-2011). The New York Times reported that the game was played before a capacity crowd of 30,000. Unfortunately for the home side, they were well beaten as Tipperary who won by 11 goals and 4 points (37) to NY Offaly's 2 goals and 2 points (8).

Other tours would follow, including visits in 1927, 1931 and 1933 by All-Ireland football champions, Kerry, while Kilkenny and Tipperary hurlers would also return in that period with large crowds in attendance at venues such as Yankee Stadium and Madison Square Garden.

Yet despite big numbers attending tour events in New York and local clubs bolstered by such visits, the level of interest had dropped off since the first tour of 1926, due to another tragic event in American history -- the Great Depression of the '30s.

Survival, rather than sports, was top priority during the Depression era as one in every four Americans was out of work. Breadlines were a common feature of everyday life in cities across the nation.

Some 13 million Americans, more than a quarter of the work force, were unemployed and the economic turmoil was passed on to professionals sports. Attendances at boxing, baseball, and American football plummeted. With the likes of an up-and-coming sport like hurling struggling to survive in such hard times, tours from Ireland were seen as vital to keeping club finances and American interest alive.

But tougher times followed as noted by the Boston and North East Gaelic Athletic Association report where a strictly enforced immigration ban saw hurling and Gaelic sports decline further, and as if things weren't bad enough, the outbreak of World War II brought the sports to a standstill yet again.

After the war participation started to pick up again for the sport of hurling, as the country saw increased Irish immigration to America. However, a dependency on immigration to bolster club numbers did little to develop hurling but instead kept it squarely confined to the Irish immigrant community.

On an organizational front, a movement was afoot to try and bring all the Gaelic sports associations in the various cities together under the one governing body and so it was agreed, that in conjunction with the GAA in Ireland, the National Council GAA of the United States was setup in 1950.

The new body saw the U.S. divided into three zones where New York was Zone 1, the Mid-West Zone 2, and New England Zone 3, with competitions to take place between each zone. Following the format of the GAA in Ireland, each zone would be regarded as another province attached to the parent body.

But the experiment was short lived as according to the Boston Northeast GAA's manual 'A Century of Boston GAA,' the new organization had financial difficulties and saw New York depart:

> "New York withdrew from the organization thus dealing the Inter-Zonal competition a mortal blow. The Zones were a failure partly because of the financial difficulties of transporting players and teams such vast distances but mainly because of the withdrawal of New York, who regarded the Zones as a burdensome imposition."

Through the 1950s hurling and Gaelic sports were in a relatively healthy position with many clubs being formed in cities but there would be growing acrimony between New York and Ireland over the coming years – one that has lasted until recently as there has been something of new and positive relationship of late.

At GAA headquarters in Croke Park stadium in Ireland, something of a milestone for the association came about in the modern era when the GAA allowed the playing of 'foreign games' on their pitch between 2006 - 2010. This was for a temporary bases while rugby and soccer organization's joint home facility was being replaced with a new stadium. A ban on sports played on the GAA's own pitches had been in place (and still is with exception of Croke Park on special permission). However in 1953, an American Football game was played at Croke Park with two teams from the U.S. Air Force in action. The New York Times reported on the event in an October 3, 1953 article with the headline, 'Irish Allow US game'.

Back in the states during the latter part of that decade, there was a further effort to organize Gaelic sports on a national level and so in Philadelphia in 1959 the North American County Board was born. The new organization affiliated to the GAA in Ireland, and, by its very naming, the organization followed an Irish world view of how things should proceed.

Notably, New York and New Jersey stayed outside of the new organization, though affiliation with Ireland would take-place. Canada was included in the new association at the time – hence the 'North American' designation – but later formed its own body, Canada GAA.

Though things were starting to get more organized – the game of rugby in America would not see a national organization until 1975 – the Immigration Act of 1965 severely hindered Irish immigration to America which had a detrimental effect for hurling and Gaelic sports club numbers.

The immigration swing-pattern continues through today, as Irish immigrants move to and out of the U.S. in pursuit of economic fortune, and accordingly clubs and player numbers decrease and increase in an endless cycle.

Looking back over the past 100 years and the last 50 in particular, there is one huge difference between the U.S. Gaelic sports scene of yesteryear and today and that is that Americans are now beginning to play the sports, and particularly so with hurling.

Hurling clubs are sprouting across the country. They are formed and run by Americans. They are taking root in cities that have no history of Irish immigration and in towns that never heard of the sport of hurling.

Chapter 5

Hurling Revolution

In 1984 the Boston and New England Gaelic Athletic Association, in their 100-year history compilation, noted that a factor which saw Gaelic football more popular than hurling was on account of the "additional skill" needed in order to play hurling.

It has long been considered a doctrine among traditional hurling clubs across America, as well as those in Ireland, that you can't really teach hurling to an adult and that only through practice from a young age can you really take up the game. The definition of success in teaching hurling to an adult was predicated on them having to reach a certain perceived level of mastery in order for the experiment to be deemed worthwhile. However, in America's recently formed and largest hurling club, the Milwaukee Hurling Club – whose players are all American – success is perceived differently.

Other newly formed clubs across the country, who are also primarily comprised of American players – and that includes a squad of U.S. soldiers – will also tell you the same thing.

Often the more traditional clubs in the U.S. and those across Ireland place greater emphasis on playing the sport at its highest possible grade as opposed to a very basic adult learning level. Their idea was that you learned the sport as a child and that if you didn't you had no real business learning it as an adult. If you didn't master it when young, forget about playing it later on. It is like telling a person new to golf to forget it as it'll never work out. Unless you're going to become the next Tiger Woods, don't bother.

The idea that someone might enjoy a new sport in and of itself seemed strange and bazaar. This has been the prevailing theme over the years among the more traditional Irish clubs in the big cities in America: You can't really teach it to someone who hasn't been brought up with it and so why would you bother.

A clear example of such thinking can be seen in the History Page of the website of the Connecticut Irish Festival. The site provides a good overall picture of the Irish in the state over the past 150 years and even says that hurling was played there as far back as the 1860s. "As early as 1866, Connecticut newspapers reported "hurley" matches among Irish factory hands."

The website goes on to talk of hurling teams in the 1920s and 1930s, but the sport declined with the coming of WWII. The sport enjoyed renewal after the war and increased immigration until the late 1970s. During the 1980s:

> "The number of hurlers from Connecticut dwindled and games were fewer and fewer. There is widespread belief that hurling is a game more suited to native Irishmen who learn to play as youngsters: it is difficult to teach and dangerous for the unskilled."

The negative attitudes are changing, nevertheless, the skill and "only Irish play" thinking is still prevalent among clubs. Instead of reaching out to promote hurling as a new sport that can be enjoyed at one's own level, many clubs turn to Ireland to keep themselves in existence. It is a system that has failed in the past and continues to fail hurling to this day.

American John Simcoe, a new hurler and journalist in the Baltimore area, frowns upon the thought of hurling as a sport that's perceived as too hard to learn. Over the past couple of years he has created a blog, 'Hurley to Rise', in his spare time. It is purely dedicated to the promotion of hurling in America.

In his article 'Hurling should be fun first', he writes that the joy and fun of playing should be paramount to the game's development:

> "Here in America, when hurling enthusiasts get together, we talk about how great the sport is and how we can make it grow. We want to show everyone we meet how great the game is. We want them on the field and having some fun."

This is a viewpoint of many people taking up the sport for the first time in this country but he contrasts this with the more traditional ideas about the game that he finds in Ireland.

"The Sports Desk" blog of the Irish Examiner newspaper does a good job in summing up the constant drumbeat of angst:

> "The fact is hurling is elitist. There should be no shame in that. It's an art-form, something that can only be performed by a minority because it takes years upon years of mastering. That's why it's such a treasure. It's a fanciful thought to believe every boy and girl in the country is going to puck a ball. It should be that way but hurling can't and will never be that game simply because it's so difficult to play. Not enough people have the patience to pass on or absorb the skills."

That observation from one of Ireland's national dailies leaves Simcoe, the American news editor with the York Dispatch in Pennsylvania, a tad uneasy. He writes:

> "Such talk continues on to complain that hurling is a sport that will be continually dominated by just a few regions because no one else can even consider catching up — Kilkenny and Tipperary counties are just too good to even bother stepping on the pitch when they're your opponent.
>
> That dominance, they say, is what's killing the sport. People aren't interested in watching the game, and they certainly aren't interested in learning the almost-cryptic skills needed to play. These issues are draining the life right out of the game, they say.
>
> Hogwash, I say.
>
> Here in America, we are just playing hurling for the fun of it. Someday, we might have clubs to rival the greats. But until then, we just play because it's an incredible way to spend an afternoon."

The hurler/journalist doesn't like being so readily dismissed and robbed of his new-found love for a sport that just happens to be hurling.

> "We may not have even a sliver of the skills of the Kilkenny Cats or Tipp's [Tipperary] Blue and Gold squad, but as long as we're having a good time, we're gonna keep having a go at it.
>
> I would suggest the Irish naysayers do the same. Just get out there. Get better at the game and keep the sport alive.
>
> You don't need to win a championship to play a sport. You just need to be willing to walk out on the field."

Simcoe's second last line of, "You don't need to win a championship to play a sport" sums things up nicely as its exact opposite has been the mantra of the traditional Irish clubs in America, and for that matter, in Ireland.

This type of thinking is at the heart of why the sport never really got off the ground in the U.S.

However, while depressions, war, immigration decline, equipment and land shortage have also played a role in hurling's hidden status in America, there is still another factor to consider.

The sport's official parent body in Ireland, the GAA, isn't quite sure how to be a world organization. We return to this important issue towards the end of the book.

Since the mid 1990s, Americans such as Simcoe have increasingly become hooked on the sport. They play for the joy and fun aspects the game brings. Americans like Hurling Club of Madison's Mike Statz find the sport suits them to a tee.

Over the past five years the growth of new clubs is revolutionary in comparison to what has gone before.

At present there are approximately 54 hurling clubs in America (does not include college) with at least 3-6 more in development. Roughly 75% of these have a strong American player base mixed with some Irish natives, with the other 25% operating as the traditional Irish modeled club relying on the summer player from Ireland.

Before the mid-1990s the situation would have seen many more traditional bodies but without any American players or clubs. Now the American clubs in just a short space of time are in the ascendancy. This is a totally new development in the history of hurling in the country.

Hurling clubs have been springing up all over the place and what makes this really interesting for the sport is that the new clubs are not found in traditional Irish diaspora enclaves like New York, Boston, Chicago, Philadelphia and San Francisco. Instead new clubs are starting in cities that have little or no background of Irish immigration such as places like Milwaukee, Wisconsin; Atlanta, Georgia; Indianapolis, Indiana; Augusta, Georgia; Seattle, Washington; Concord, New Hampshire; Portland, Maine; Eugene, Oregon and many more.

This in itself is a major step forward for the sport.

Hurling is now spreading beyond the Irish immigrant communities but what is noteworthy is the type of new club. Up to now Irish immigrants and some of their off-spring – in the early days at least – were the only ones playing hurling. Today it is Americans that are taking up the game and founding clubs by themselves. From Florida to Oregon, Americans are getting 'hooked' on the sport with many of them having no affiliation whatsoever to Irish cultural traits and pastimes.

Americans are drawn to the sport because of the uniqueness of how the game looks, its many skills, the game's speed, its physical nature and high scoring. U.S. Hurling, while coming out of the shadows of past mistakes and lingering problems, is by no means in the same penetration category as lacrosse, one of the fastest growing sports in America. But even lacrosse is barely a blip on the sports radar of the U.S. when compared to the likes of American football, baseball, basketball, ice hockey, golf and auto racing.

Lacrosse is played in high school, college and at youth level as well as in post-college leagues where currently 75 teams compete as amateurs as part of the American Lacrosse League, run by US Lacrosse. There are also two professional leagues: Major League Lacrosse, an outdoor league began in 2001, and the older indoor, National Lacrosse League, which was founded in 1987. While the colleges and university circuit alone has hundreds of teams run by various collegiate organizing bodies, there is also Men's and Women's National teams. The men's team compete every four years in the Lacrosse World Championships last held in 2010 in Manchester, UK.

In America over the past decade, media attention on lacrosse has grown with Fox, CBS and ESPN regularly showing a schedule of games. Lacrosse of course is native to America and with increased TV coverage the sport is primed for growth. The sport is an exciting, high-scoring sport and Yahoo Voices writer Kaitlyn Joseph thinks that with increased TV coverage and promotion the sport will continue to prosper:

> "Why is this sport taking off? It is a full contact sport and it seems like a mix of hockey, soccer, and football. Some games can be very high-scoring which makes it exciting for fans. Colleges are promoting their lacrosse teams more and more, which has really helped put this sport out in the open. College students are soaking this sport up and definitely taking it to the next level. This sport will continue to get more television time and continue to get kids involved in lacrosse."

Compare this to hurling's recent rise.

For starters hurling is not native to America, isn't officially and culturally embedded in the school and college systems and doesn't enjoy any weekly mainstream newspaper reporting and U.S. TV national coverage. If hurling (from Ireland to begin) enjoyed national TV coverage with a very basic annual schedule the effect of such exposure would likely result in a dramatic increase in both adults and young people seeking out local clubs. The steady growth of Americans taking up the sport and forming clubs, along with seeds been sown for the first time on college campuses, suggests there is no reason to believe, with time and exposure, that hurling cannot follow a similar path as lacrosse.

When it comes to how Americans discover hurling, there are many different stories to be heard: hearing about the sport as a child, to American tourists seeing the game played in Ireland, to students finding the sport on study abroad programs, to hearing about it in the local watering hole and investigating, and to others who happen upon the sport by complete accident.

From a playing perspective, a common denominator seems to be that once a hurley is put in the hands of an American, instinct and athleticism take over and a passion for the game ignites.

Despite the surname, Matt Schwertfeger, new chairman of the all American born Michael Cusack Hurling Club, Chicago, does have some Irish background but it wasn't this aspect alone that brought him to the sport, he declared in response to a questionnaire back in 2009:

> "I chose hurling for three reasons. First, I had heard about hurling growing up as a child. I had family from Ireland and stories of the sport were in the air. But, as a kid I was more into baseball.
>
> I picked up hurling in college. Baseball wasn't really an option for me in college, and, having just returned from a term at UCG [University College Galway, Ireland], hurling really caught my interest and I needed to do something to keep myself in shape."

Schwertfeger, a former student at Purdue University and who helped found a hurling club at the college a number of years ago, describes his passion in the following terms:

> "My favorite thing is the quickness and the physical aspect of the sport. Most of our players enjoy the action, that play is continuous, the physical aspect as well, and there are a few glory hogs out there that simply love being on top of the scoring chart."

Indeed his former Purdue colleagues' interest go along the lines of cultural backgrounds and the attraction of an exciting new sport. "Most of the guys who play and have played with us generally fall into two categories: (1) have Irish heritage or have been to Ireland or (2) looking to keep active and thought hurling looked interesting."

When Matt graduated from Purdue, he chose to stick with hurling. He joined a young club in Chicago, Michael Cusack Hurling Club (named after the founder of the GAA in Ireland) and in late 2009 helped form a new organizing body for hurling at colleges in the mid-west called the Midwest Collegiate Hurling Association (MCHA).

The Michael Cusack HC is an example of one of the new clubs that recently got its start with American players in the thick of the action over the past few years. The club participates in the hurling league of the Gaelic Athletic Association of Chicago with games played at Gaelic Park in the south side of the city and is comprised of Americans who have taken up the sport in the last two years.

In the Spring of 2011 an intriguing effort to promote the sport to other Americans living in the Chicago area was initiated.

This saw informal hurling scrimmages take place in a prominent green location in the city on Sunday afternoons on the Lakefront at Montrose Harbor. Several new recruits joined the club as a result with Irish born hurler and newly appointed GAA Games Development Administrator (GDA) for the Midwest, Tom Sheehy, one of the principal promoters of the event:

> "'We were looking into promoting it in the city, to expose more people to the game," says Sheehy. "'We hoped that people would pass by and take up the game. The idea has been a success in attracting six or seven new players to the league," he told Newcity.com.

The GDA program initiated by the GAA in Ireland – with the fiscal support of the Irish government over the past three years – is a new approach to the promotion of Gaelic Sports in America.

There are six part time paid GDA's operating throughout the U.S. – each of them attached to hubs like New York, Boston, Chicago, and San Francisco. They have responsibility for conducting coaching clinics for schools and adult clubs, as well as aiding in the organization of youth leagues programs and schedules.

North America GAA or NACB (North American County Board) has some 112 Gaelic Sports clubs with 15 of these youth league clubs spread across the country.

The hurling numbers and competitions according to a new hurling development committee – formed in 2010 - is growing each year. The Hurling Development Committee (HDC of NAGAA) in a March 2011 report states, "The HDC has identified a huge increase in games played outside of the NACB Playoffs. Many tournaments are played throughout the year and are much more prevalent in hurling than Gaelic football."

One of the goals of this committee is to help young clubs get going and it is hoped that 10 new clubs can be assisted over the next three years.

But driving this growth is the emergence of the American hurler and he or she is getting involved in setting up and running new clubs.

With the growing number of Americans one club stands out in particular as one of the most interesting developments ever to take place in the history of Gaelic sports in the U.S.

MILWAUKEE HURLING CLUB

The Milwaukee Hurling Club is all-American out of the Dairyland state of Wisconsin. Milwaukee HC is the oldest all-American hurling organization in existence and is also the largest hurling club in the country.

This is particularly noteworthy given that the club with some 220 adults and 70-80 youth players dwarfs any of the traditional Irish immigrant-fueled hurling clubs in New York and Boston, and anywhere else in the country. When you consider that this growth only happened over a time-span of 17 years it is an incredible achievement, especially given the zero national TV exposure of hurling.

In comparison, some of the traditional Irish clubs – who depend largely on summer players from Ireland to keep things going – have been around in various forms for well over 50 years.

This describes a sharp contrast in how an all-American club is operated and how an Irish traditional club is run. And, ultimately may point to how the sport of hurling may evolve in the U.S. in the future.

How did Milwaukee grow so quickly, and in a city that had no major history of Irish immigration? No one had ever heard of the sport of hurling in Milwaukee but today all that has changed.

In an article in Milwaukee Magazine in 2009, writer Sowmya Bhagavatula doesn't hold back in her introduction when talking about the sport's growing popularity in the city:

> "One of the hottest sports on Milwaukee's lakefront originated in Ireland more than 2,000 years ago. Called the fastest game on grass, hurling is a fusion of lacrosse, field hockey and soccer.
>
> Though played in America for more than a century, the sport has seen its popularity soar in recent years, with the country's largest club found in Milwaukee. Starting with just 25 players in 1995, the Milwaukee Hurling Club now includes more than 200 hurlers."

The piece goes on to describe how Americans with the club, who have a passion for the sport, are beginning to take hurling to a level never seen before in the country. Former administrative coordinator with Milwaukee HC,

American player Karen Fink (the club is co-ed) told the Magazine of how the sport could spread beyond the traditional Irish immigrant context:

> "An end to Irish domination of the sport could make it more popular in America," says Karen Fink, administrative coordinator for the club. "We are a multi-ethnic society," she says. "It's important that it represents this."

Another female, and club player, writing in her blog athleticgals.com points to the qualities of the Milwaukee HC in linking to Irish traditions of the past but at the same time introducing fresh new perspectives on club format. "The club's growth is an amazing success story summed up nicely in its motto. 'Is Fui Agus Is Feidir' [Gaelic] loosely translates to, 'It is important and it is worth doing.'"

One other very special aspect of Milwaukee's hurling club is that it is purposefully Co-Ed. Says the blog writer:

> "It's the only club we know of where the women can play with the men. [More clubs are co-ed now]. Yep. Traditional hurling is a men's only endeavor. Women usually play camogie, same game but no men allowed. In the Milwaukee Hurling Club, women can play camogie, hurling, or both....There's also a thriving youth league."

The blogger joined the club in 2006 and though into other American sports, heard about the game through a friend and since then has become one of those hooked Americans:

> "This is my third year playing. A friend of a friend suggested it (knowing that I've been in love with playing ice hockey for years now) and I'm finding hurling to be wonderfully addictive as well. I'm also finding Milwaukee's club to be outstanding at welcoming rookies and providing good instruction, practice opportunities, and a truly warm family atmosphere.
>
> It's a close knit group though it keeps expanding. It seems that everybody knows everybody though there are more everybodies to know every year which is exactly as it should be."

She ends by trying to reach out to possible converts when saying, "Come on out and see what it is I'm talking about."

This type of thinking and promotional effort has never been in the mindset of the Irish immigrant who runs traditional Irish immigrant model clubs. Until recently they wouldn't dream of reaching out to local Americans because they could depend on their resident immigrant and summer sanctioned Irish player to keep their clubs and leagues ticking over.

But just how did the MHC manage to become so successful is a question worth exploring in depth as many new all-American clubs like Atlanta HC, St. Louis HC, Akron HC and Hurling Club of Madison, are adopting the Milwaukee HC model.

Milwaukee Hurling Club was founded in 1995 by two Americans, Cory Johnson and Dave Olson. Both had no Irish connection and had never heard of the sport of hurling.

Dave Olson, whose efforts have been central to the success of the MHC, had grown up with baseball. He loved baseball, it was his sport. He couldn't get enough of it and he didn't see the need to change to anything else. But he did:

> "Baseball was, and is dear and true to my heart. When I was younger I played a lot and had my shot at a couple of professional tryouts and had my chance; played it for as long as I could [and then] hurling kind of got in the way."

He explained in an interview for the podcast, GaelicSportsCast in 2010:

> "It all started with one Tommy Knowles who worked in The Black Shamrock pub in downtown, Milwaukee. On a visit to Ireland he discovered the game of hurling. Then a young man by the name of Danny Quigley from County Tipperary in Ireland, also worked in the pub and he started 'talking the sport up.'"

Olson's wife, who has some Irish blood, was often present when Tommy and Danny tried to get Dave into hurling and start a club. However, her husband's familiar response was, "I play baseball. Why would I want to play this game that I've never even heard about ... What are you, mad?!"

But they kept at it until a camping trip. Danny came along and it resulted in the Irish man producing a pair of hurley sticks and sliotar (hurling ball in Gaelic) and so the two of them found an open space and started 'a puck around'. Dave decided 'let's see what happens.' "Went out, found a field and started hitting that ball around and it was like ... it was like it was always been there in the hand." So they decided to try starting off a hurling club.

There was few at first then another few until about 25 members made up the new sporting organization in the city. Olson said that at the very start the club was always about 'working together' and at the end of 1995 the founders thought that this actually could work.

Everybody he said "was mad in love with the game" and after consuming as much literature and videos of the game as they could muster, the second year saw them doubling in size and already able to create a phenomenal four teams with 18-20 on the roster with only three Irish players.

The club liked the idea of going co-ed from the very start and felt because of the 15 a side nature of the sport, there was a position for every player and this fed into the "inclusiveness, family and camaraderie which is the beginnings of everything," Olson insisted.

The club operates out of several county parks, specifically Brown Deer Park, north of the city. In those early years, the young club sought videos in order to get a basic understanding of how to play the sport and from there began close drills and then created their own hybrid drills. Ultimately, the best drills and training systems were formulated and so American players slowly began to acquaint themselves with their new sport.

Dave Olson like Matt Schwertfeger has similar views on why Americans who take up the game love it so much. "It's an easy sport to fall in love with; it's fast, it's non-stop. If you have a background in baseball, lacrosse or hockey, even tennis ... you can bring something to the table... when you join a hurling club."

The club keeps on drawing in new American players and back in 2009 they broke all previous records for recruiting adult rookies with 54 new players signed up.

Such a phenomenon of introducing adult hurling rookies was and still is completely foreign to the traditional U.S. Irish hurling clubs who stubbornly feel that relying on immigrants and summer Irish players will somehow sustain clubs. This despite the fact the story of Gaelic sports in America shows that if you tie your existence to the Irish immigration model, your club will eventually exhaust itself and die once immigration dries up.

The Milwaukee hurling club caters to younger generations of American hurlers and from every conceivable background with programmes for U7, U12 and U15s. Irish clubs in America too have been looking to the younger generation in setting up youth programs and over the past number of years some resident immigrants are trying to break the sole Irish adult player model. There are many former Irish players who have helped start off clubs and look to recruit rookie players, but still the majority of traditionally run Irish clubs don't appear to have any interest in starting off adult rookie recruiting programs. MHC has a different approach.

Olson feels that, while it's important to commence youth programs, it's essential to get hurling adult rookies playing the sport and to build community around the new sport. This way the sport develops a foothold and a growing following. It spreads out from there in a new country without the parameters and often constraints of the Irish hurling culture getting in its way. And, Olson believes that the sport of hurling will take off in America:

> "The game as we say in America is a gimme. You see it and you can't help but fall in love with this game. There's too many positive things. You know, and as much as I love American football and baseball, it is as molasses when it comes to hurling!"

Helping to grow the game locally, MHC has come up with some unique approaches to promotion.

Three distinct Milwaukee ways of doing things are seen in (1) introducing a second referee onto the pitch (2) a unique draft system within their league each Spring and (3) a co-ed format to their games. The latter may have taken place by accident and lack of knowledge of how games were organized in Ireland but the other two approaches are distinctly new. They seem to be working and making a real impact with other new American clubs as well.

The club from the very outset decided that "hand picking teams" wasn't going to cut it. They were looking to perhaps introduce an American way of doing things to get a new sport off the ground in Milwaukee. The results have been phenomenal. This new approach was the introduction of a draft system which came into being from the beginning.

In order to make the draft system run smoothly another new system was initiated in that there would be two captains of each team with a distinct off-the-field role for each:

> "The captains aren't in the traditional sense as in Ireland. The captains are team managers, motivators, referees, everything, the jack-of-trades. We [the club administrators] get together and we go through the captains every year and if anybody is stepping out [as in], the previous year's captains.
>
> We look for the highlights in the people out there who are showing leadership and invite them to be a captain." A player ratings system is then introduced with captains responsible for giving each player a rank. This is achieved by means of roughly a six week window of pre-season drills, and a special skill number rating system is established.

"So the captains run the sessions, watch the people and then we get together at the end of the pre-season and we rank every player in the league. In the early days we had 1 to 10 or 1 to 12 [skill rankings] we're up to 1 to 25 now on a grading scale."

From here the club came up with innovative methods of ranking players so that equity amongst teams is paramount and thus a competitive league can begin:

"We sit down for six or maybe 10 hours ranking everybody. Then we go into what we call 'Specialties' – the top offensive players and the top defensive players. Then we have what we call 'Line-to-Line' people who are individuals that per se are the runners who would be like a Midfielder who can move all day long.

We have a specialize Goalie, as all the goalies in the league are ranked also. When we get done with all this – we are on our second generation of computer program – we feed all the rankings into the computer and each captain is ranked also.

The computer starts doing its work and starts spitting out teams like last year [2009] was nine team segments and we start with a series of maybe 10 spreadsheets of 9 teams and then we start voting with all the captains of which of these sections is going to be the most competitive for us as a league."

After an exhaustive period of going through all the various team scenarios, whether a particular captain is happy or not with the outcome, teams are formulated based on the skill ranking points system where "every team on paper is equal!"

The success of this ranking and draft model has worked wonders for the club in promoting the sport in the city as 2011 saw another bumper year where the Milwaukee Hurling Club had 10 teams of 15 players each with 20 players on each roster. Compare this with senior hurling clubs in other cities that have Irish immigrant populations on which to draw, like Boston in the Northeast GAA organization, that can only boast 5 senior hurling clubs. New York [new Junior clubs did start in 2011) Chicago and San Francisco (as of writing) all have just three each.

Indeed, many of the newer all-American or mostly American player-run hurling clubs have looked to Milwaukee for inspiration and leadership. Clubs in Atlanta and St. Louis are running operations similar to MHC but Olson stresses that one size fits-all shouldn't be the approach to adopt. "The

Milwaukee model is Milwaukee. Everybody, every city out there is different. What we do when advising clubs is 'use whatever you can from our model'."

One thing that the MHC has discovered is that you need numbers for a hurling club to have any sort of a chance of growth and to have any hope of making an impact in a competitive and packed American sports landscape. Milwaukee hurling is also finding that when building a club, the community element has to be considered:

> "The biggest thing that everybody is learning is that it's like a community. I mean the games were started in the early days [when] games took place between villages and it wasn't about national championships hundreds of years ago."

MHC also picks a team they call the 'Traveling Team' to compete in the North American National Championships each season and over the years has had considerable success when winning back to back Junior B Adult Hurling Championships in 2007 and 2008. At this grade, MHC's American squad, would have had to compete against teams with several Irish natives involved and so on a national level the Milwaukee Hurling Club has been making steady progress becoming more and more competitive.

However, MHC doesn't look at success at Nationals as a barometer as to how the sport of hurling is developing and growing in the Milwaukee region. It is more concerned with continuing to grow numbers and build community and a culture of a new sport in a city that at one time had never heard of hurling:

> "Club-wise it's just the integration, the youth league is going but the amount of adults that we are getting to play is phenomenal. The unity of all the players and I mean the amount of marriages within the club that has taken place is one of the highlights for me ... that for us is success."

Milwaukee feel they need two referees on the field at all times because of the speed of the game and the regularity of how play, with one bat of a ball, can change down-field in an instant, hence the need for a second referee.

Practice for the MHC is also something unique to the world of a Gaelic sports club anywhere be it in America, Ireland or anywhere else. Actually from any sporting perspective it's unique. Adult practice takes place at the exact same time as youth practice. This means that when Mom is practicing alongside hubby, junior might also be knocking the ball about.

The folks in Milwaukee came up with the novel idea of having the entire club practice at the same time. Moms, Dads and the kids all out there swinging. The club has found that not only is this beneficial to everyone's schedule, it also has the added bonus of acting as a valuable promotion tool.

Picture it this way, over 220 adults and 70-80 kids all out on a green space at the same time playing a game that a passerby has never witnessed before ... it's only natural that people stop and ask, 'what the heck is going on'? People have been known to join the ranks on seeing the whole club in action.

This type of approach is unknown within the more traditional Irish-run clubs in America as most of the senior clubs do not have a youth program or set-up for women players in men's teams.

Traditionally, when women play the game of hurling it's called Camogie – a few slight changes in the rules but basically the same sport – and there are relatively few Camogie clubs in America even though of late new interest in starting camogie clubs has begun in the Denver, Seattle, Minnesota and Washington DC areas.

The youth hurling program within the Milwaukee Club has been growing year on year with little if any Irish American heritage on show. It's American kids playing a new sport and apparently loving it.

It is not an overstatement to say that when you compare their youth hurling league with other youth Gaelic Sports Leagues which have been off and on in operation since the mid 1970s (New York and Boston), that MHC is ahead of the curve in regards to hurling. Other youth leagues have tended to focus on the development of Gaelic football primarily, a trend that is slowly changing.

Illustration 10: Milwaukee Hurling Club photo (Photo Andy McKee, Milwaukee Hurling Club)

Milwaukee is also unique in how they celebrate the start of a new season. Milwaukee Hurling Club's 'Opening Day' has become legendary in the area.

Following in the practice vein, the whole club gathers on the day to have a 'Walk Out' with each player in full gear accompanied by music. This is capped off with a huge team photo of all the club together, adult and young players alike. The display points to the essence of inclusiveness and togetherness as a club. Nowhere else is this duplicated.

In places like Boston and New York, season openers will start with scheduled games but the whole league will not be present and geared-up.

In 2010 MHC celebrated their 15th anniversary and for their Opening Day a call out of the oldest playing members of the club to the newest took place. Says former club administrator, Karen Fink, "Opening Day ceremonies are always a big deal for us but with the 15th anniversary of the club we wanted to have much more pageantry than usual."

"As the players from the different years were called out and the circle got larger and larger until the year when we called 2010 and then everybody put there sticks up in the air and yelled 'Up the MHC' and that was pretty cool to see how the circle grew," she said in an email interview.

The 'Up' cry is a throw-back to traditional cries, when on game day in Ireland, supporters will shout on a team by calling 'Up Cork' or 'Up Kerry'; however, when you add in the MHC 'Opening Day' ceremony a more American flavor is added to the pot.

The impact of the MHC is not to be underestimated as a new aspect to the GAA story in America. MHC co-founder Olson, because of his work in promoting hurling in the Milwaukee region, caught the attention of the governing body for Gaelic Sports in Ireland, the Gaelic Athletic Association (GAA). In 2006 he became the first non-native of Ireland to be honored with the GAA President's Award for his efforts in bringing hurling to America. Olson would go on to serve as the North American Hurling Development Officer (non paying role) over the next few years with many young all-American hurling clubs looking to him for guidance on how to start and grow a club.

The Milwaukee Hurling Club has also differed from the more traditional Irish hurling clubs in America in its approach to marketing and in particular how it reaches out to local media.

The Irish clubs have always maintained a relationship with Irish American local newspapers like, 'The Pilot' and 'The Gaelic American' of yesteryear, and today with the 'Irish Voice' and 'Irish Echo' weeklies in New York as well as the 'Irish Emigrant' (now Irish Central) in Boston. But clubs never formed any relationship with local TV networks. There has never been a culture of reaching out to TV outlets in an effort to promote hurling and other Gaelic sports. In the modern era between the 1980s and present day America, there are many Irish clubs in the states that would have undocumented immigrants among their ranks and so placing a spotlight on the club would not necessarily be in anyone's interests. But over time this would change as more people became documented.

Overall, Irish clubs have been very poor at promoting the likes of hurling to local Americans. Because of this Americans have had no idea that hurling is played in most major urban centers each weekend from May to Labor Day. Not so in Milwaukee.

From the very start the MHC reached out to local TV outlets in an effort to promote their new sport and club and it has paid off with, on average, 25% new members each year.

An examination of American hurling stories on You Tube sees MHC in the front row when it comes to reaching out to local TV stations.

Milwaukee WISN 12 TV News reported in 2008:

> "the game's been around since the 14th century [as noted it goes further back than that] but it doesn't get publicity. That's hurling with an 'H'. It's always been huge in Ireland and it's growing in numbers and interest here in Milwaukee ... and local players just can't get enough." The name of the TV news feature was 'Hooked on Hurling'.

In the WISN report, American player Gwen Barker tells of how:

> "There's a lot of finesse involved but it's a good mixture of both [physicality]. Good players can do both. You can't be too physical, you got to be able to finesse it as well. You can't be afraid of the ball or getting hurt."

Reporter Bob Brainerd tells how other clubs "are using Milwaukee as a model." The report ends with information on the club and its season. This kind of TV promotion to local American audiences is unheard of within the realm of the more traditional Irish hurling club in the U.S.

Reaching out and recruiting new players is something MHC has been doing year on year with the club themselves producing their own short promotion reels for You Tube and their website – hurling.net. An example of this can be seen in a 2011 video showing their MHC Championship game and a noteworthy aspect to this is the good sized crowd in attendance and that audience 99% American.

The role of the Internet, particularly You Tube, has been paramount in helping promote the sport of hurling in recent times. An examination of American oriented hurling stories on You Tube again highlights how new American clubs are following Milwaukee's lead and reaching out to local TV stations.

Over the past decade at least 8 local TV stations have presented News pieces on American hurling clubs. This is unheard of in the history of Gaelic sports in America. News clips are republished on You tube and give an insight into how America's 'new sport' is spreading across the country.

In Washington DC, TV outlet 'myFox DC' did a piece on the Washington DC Gaels, a mostly all American player and recently founded club.

In the state of Missouri, another area not known for modern-day Irish immigrant populations, the St. Louis Hurling Club was featured by the public TV station, KETC Channel.

In Minnesota, the local public radio station did a piece on the Twin Cities Robert Emmets Hurling Club from St. Paul, Minnesota in the summer of 2008. A couple of years prior to that in 2006, local Denver TV outlet WB2 News produced over a nine minute segment on the sport entitled, 'Irish Hurling'.

Even word of hurling's growing popularity caught the attention of one of the major TV network's, NBC. The network featured hurling in a three minute segment showing hurling drills in Ireland in 2009.

The following year we see two more local TV channels highlighting the sport. In July of 2010, News 12 Sports from Augusta did a story of the arrival of hurling in their city when profiling the Augusta Hurling Club.

Then back in Wisconsin, in the state capitol of Madison, NBC 15 did a story about the Hurling Club of Madison. This club was founded in 2006 and was influenced by goings on in Milwaukee as several players who traveled down to play with the MHC decided to start their own club closer to home in Madison.

Across to the Northeast, a local TV story featured Maine's Portland Mauraders. The Mauraders, a new mostly all American team, have been making steady progress growing the game locally. The local TV channel, WCSH Portland, did a news piece on the hurling team where club player Matt Ryle pretty much sums up the general feeling of what is happening on the ground in that once you try the sport ... you're in for life. "'Come out, we usually have spare hurleys, spare sliotars, spare helmets, and just come out and try it," says Ryle. "'You'll be hooked.'"

THE MARAUDERS

The Portland Hurling Club began life in Maine in the summer of 2007 but it wasn't actually there that it got its start.

Illustration 11: Portland Mauraders Crest (Courtesy of Portland HC)

Like many of the new hurling clubs spreading across the country, hurling came to Portland via an American who had started off playing the sport elsewhere.

Back in the late 1980s, Pete Marietta, research scientist and Portland HC founder, was big into rugby.

He started rugby in college then played for the Saranac Lake Mountaineers in New York state for four years before switching over to Rugby League and was good enough to make the U.S. team. Moving to Colorado, he played major rugby games in Denver, and it was here that he first came across hurling.

He liked hurling's fast pace and physical nature and when moving back to the east coast he thought of trying something new and hurling seemed a good fit. He came across the U.S. soldiers and hurlers, the Barley House Wolves – who we meet in the next chapter – and began to play with them in Concord, New Hampshire.

When he got trained up and some skills in, the Wolves suggested he start a club in Portland as a means of growing some local competition and what with a one and half hour trip for practice twice a week it was an easy decision for Marietta.

Back in Portland, Pete Marietta just like Michael Cusack, the founder of the GAA in Ireland had done, rounded up a half a dozen interested folk and began playing scrimmages – this time on a softball field.

Marietta could draw on his soccer coaching experience at Paul Smith's College while in Saranac Lake, and he had also coached woman's rugby while living in Colorado and along with his masters degree in exercise physiology, 'and a whistle,' he was the perfect candidate to get a sports club going.

He got more equipment and from there things took off:

> "I bought 15 hurleys and 10 sliotars with my own coin and the rest was easy. Well, the first 'practice' ended early because of stitches to the eye. Actually, the first three or four practices had blood ... but they kept coming back!" explained Marietta in an email questionnaire.

The numbers began to grow and the young club saw their first competitive action the following year. Portland club's website looks back on that fateful day:

> "The first game was played on May 18th, 2008 in Concord, New Hampshire against our brother club: The Barley House Wolves. They put on a great show with bagpipers and a nice showing all around. It was not about winning or losing ... we won!"

Brotherhood is important but Americans also like to win.

Then something that has happened in other places saw local Irish natives get involved and take on coaching roles. Five years down the road in 2011, the Mauraders have 45 players that includes a traveling team that competes in the Northeast GAA's new competition for Junior C Adult clubs and at local tournaments in the region and also in Canada.

The club has also been able to expand to form their own league of four teams. There is a good mix of players with young and not so young ranging in age from 19-56 all enjoying the sport. The Portland club also started a youth hurling program in early 2011 with the help of the Northeast Games Development Officer, Mike Moynihan, who supplied equipment, and this new initiative has been very successful with some 25 kids regularly at practice. The kids, who play all other American sports, are getting into the game.

James Tierney, who had remembered hurling on early ESPN, is heavily involved with the youth program and says feedback is positive:

> "Hurling does offer an element of many of the major U.S. sports, so it wasn't terribly hard to sell. And, once kids got into it, you know we said the same thing as we do to the adults, 'once you play once, it's very difficult to not play'."

Several of these new clubs name their organization after localities and cities where as the more traditional Irish club in America name their club after an Irish county, GAA founder member as in 'Michael Cusack', or after a national and mythical hero. There is also placement of some Irish cultural reference as in putting 'Gaels' after the locality.

The majority of Irish traditional clubs in New York, Boston, Chicago, Philadelphia, Chicago and San Francisco name their clubs after 'Counties' back in Ireland as has been the practice for the past century. Many clubs sprang from county societies or networks in places like New York and Boston, and hence the continuation of the tradition, even though the concept has no real bearing in relation to player makeup, as both home based and summer players hail from all over Ireland. The naming of a club in America after a county in Ireland for whatever traditional reason is contrary to the notion of inclusiveness and local community. It has zero cultural meaning for Americans today.

Looking at the American clubs mentioned such as Madison, Milwaukee, Portland, St. Louis, and Augusta, they all name their organizations after the place. This aspect alone is another step in how the landscape of hurling and Gaelic sports is shifting across America. With more and more Americans taking up the game, there will be less and less Irish cultural attachments as the sport itself, will in essence, be allowed to speak for itself.

Hurling's soul will always be in Ireland but the time is fast approaching when its heart roams free.

HURLING CLUB OF MADISON WI

We prolong our focus on the state of Wisconsin by highlighting the Hurling Club of Madison.

Illustration 12: Hurling Club of Madison Team (Photo courtesy of Hurling Club of Madison)

The General Manager of the Hurling Club of Madison, American Michael Stapleton, in his summation of the club's activity for the 2011 season gives a bird's-eye view into how new American clubs are shaping the sport from grassroots level up.

In his summary he talks about the club's new pre-season league initiatives, finding a suitable place to play, forming working partnerships with other sports – an important issue – sponsorships, and commentating on local and inter-club tournament performances.

It is necessary here to reproduce in full his one page summary of a young American club's year in review and on how the sport may develop in the future:

"Hurling Club of Madison – 2011

I'd like to thank you all again for supporting the Hurling Club of Madison again in 2011, we really appreciate everyone who comes out to our matches and spreads the word about our ancient Irish game in the Madison area.

I wanted to give you all a year end overview of the club activities.

This year we were able to get the hurling season started earlier than normal when we held our first ever indoor hurling league. We were able to shake off some of the cabin fever a couple of months earlier than usual with the three team (consisting of green, orange, and white) league. It was great to get some extremely competitive matches going right from the get-go. It also provided an opportunity for some brand new players to get exposure to the game right away. When all was said and done, the green and white teams played in an extremely competitive final with white just barely edging out the green team for the championship.

With the season getting underway, we really wanted to do something for the club that would not only help grow our sport, but also the culture of the club. One of the ways we've been trying to do that is to find a "home pitch." A field where we can play our game and call it our home when playing our summer league games and holding our year-end tournament. In 2011, we were able to do that through an agreement with the Wisconsin Rugby Club.

Over the past few years, the Wisconsin Rugby Club has been developing a field/sports complex in Cottage Grove, WI for their players. We were able to reach a mutual agreement that allowed our club to call their complex our home. Through the agreement and small financial arrangement (which we were able to meet thanks to our sponsors' generous support), we were able to hold half of our training sessions, all of our league games, and the year end tournament at the complex. The pitch was well taken care of and we were able to adjust its dimensions to meet our needs easily.

We held our third annual city league this year, again comprised of two teams (the PBR/The Coopers Tavern-Blue and PBR/Brocach Irish Pub-Red teams). Our membership was just under the amount of people needed to get a third team together for the league. The league was extremely competitive this year, despite the PBR/The Coopers Tavern-Blue team taking the championship. It was an all around excellent time for player and spectator alike. After our matches (among other times), our members would frequent either Brocach Irish Pub or the Coopers Tavern (or both) and have a pint or two of our favorite beers (especially Pabst Blue Ribbon).

On the inter-club match front, we had somewhat of a challenging year. We traveled to Minneapolis in June and Chicago in August to play their respective clubs. Additionally, Minneapolis, Milwaukee, and Chicago traveled to Cottage Grove, WI for our end of the year tournament. This year, we certainly realized there is a lot in the way of development.

Quite a few of our matches were competitive this year, but each time it seemed like the other clubs had an extra player in their squad known as the clock. We seemed to be making a run, but then time would run out. We're looking forward to making our play much more consistent and competitive next year as we have been in the past. The tournament was a success this year. We changed the format up a bit, so there was plenty of action for everyone. There were probably between 150-200 (including players) on hand to watch the event, which isn't too bad for a little known sport.

We truly appreciate what our sponsors, Pabst Blue Ribbon, Brocach Irish Pub, and The Coopers Tavern have done for us this season and we worked hard to ensure we're getting the word out there regarding our favorite beer. We encourage everyone who supports us to support these fine organizations.

I have several photos of our matches that I'd be happy to send you all (due to their large file size even after cropping, I didn't want to send them initially unless you'd like to see them). You can also see video of some of our indoor games here: http://madisonhurling.com/abouttheclub/clubmediagallery.

Finally, I wanted to let you know that I've included our new public relations officer, Ted Bach, on this e-mail. Our club would love to continue our relationship with all of you in 2012. If you have any questions, concerns, or comments about what we can do to continue the sponsorship, Ted would be the person you want to talk to. He is excited to continue the conversation and keep everyone in the loop on our club happenings for the next season.

Thanks again for your continued support for the Hurling Club of Madison.

Michael Stapleton

General Manager, Hurling Club of Madison."

In his address, Stapleton points to new beginnings in a first 'Indoor League' comprising of three teams.

This is something that many American hurling clubs are starting to do as with the St. Louis Gaelic Athletic Club, Indy Hurling out of Indianapolis, Denver, and in Ohio with the Akron Hurling Club, to name a few. Playing indoor in the off-season appears to be paying off as St. Louis, who started their indoor hurling league in 2010, came out the following year and won the Nationals Junior C Adult Hurling Championship (outdoor).

With fewer players on an indoor team, new players get a chance to get more touch in and game time and this is also the case for the folks in the Indy Hurling Club. Indy run a 16 weeks Indoor League and in 2010 out of the 63 players, a whopping 34 of them were new to the game.

In December 2011, the Akron HC held their very first indoor hurling session with the club running drills and a scrimmage and according to the club's website this attracted "very curious crowd of onlookers" at a local indoor soccer complex.

This brings us to the topic of sports grounds and partnering up with other than Gaelic sports organizations which Stapleton alludes to in the case of Madison. One of the biggest problems historically and to this day that any new outdoor sporting organization will encounter is where to play their sport.

Applying to local County Parks across America for green field space is always going to be a hit and miss scenario as some localities will have adequate space and free schedule time while others will not have enough space and any that is available may already be booked.

Madison with little or no resources have no option but to join forces with other sporting bodies in order to have a place to call their own as it were. The Denver Gaels (Irish and American mixed player club) in 2011 have done something similar in that they have hooked up with the Denver Raptors Rugby Club who play out of Infinity Park Stadium, Denver.

In Ireland, the governing body of Gaelic Sports, the GAA do not share their grounds with other sports. As stated, there are circumstances where they have and may do so in the future in relation to their main stadium, Croke Park in Dublin, but not outside that venue.

This notion is cemented within the rules of the GAA and stems from an introverted approach to preserving 'our games' from a cultural and political stance when the whole of Ireland was formerly under British colonial rule. The idea being that sharing of venues with the likes of rugby and soccer would dilute and weaken the Gaelic sports tradition. Yet today across Europe, Asia and America, Gaelic sports clubs see nothing but positives and opportunity in reaching out to other sporting organizations.

The more traditional Irish clubs in areas of large immigrant populations have over the past 100 years been successful in being able to lease and acquire land to furnish small stadia in Gaelic Park in New York, Canton outside Boston, Chicago Gaelic Park, Treasure Island in San Francisco, and new facility, Rockland north of New York. Another small stadium is being developed in Philadelphia. The GAA in Ireland has supported such developments with capital investment and are set to continue this practice into the future.

Apart from the huge price tags associated with buying a parcel of property zoned land or a long-term lease arrangement, the costs alone associated with running and maintaining venues is also considerable.

Illustration 13: Canton Gaelic Park (Photo by Denis O'Brien)

A look at some of the expenses associated with maintaining the Canton GAA venue, which hosts the Northeast Division League, sees costs for the year 2000 almost $225,000.

Seat scaffolding and stands comprised most of the expense running to $130,000 with a sod for a new pitch at the time costing over $50,000 while a new sprinkler system alone cost $6,000. It's not every year that a venue would need such major infrastructure investment but with 3-6 games being played at Canton between May and Labor Day each weekend, and sometimes more, monthly field maintenance can amount to almost $1,500 per month (at 2000 prices).

Returning to Madison we notice the club is also running its own local tournament and participates with others in inter-city games. These two competition formats have been a relatively new phenomenon over the past decade.

The local tournament amounts to mini leagues whereby three to six teams (in Milwaukee's case 10 and counting) are made up from within the one club. In the North American GAA organization, the NACB, (exclude NY) teams are made up of 13 players a squad but in order to get a mini league going a club might choose to start 7-11 aside style games, or what best suits their needs. Then there are formats where a club might play a mini league but this time feature clubs from different states as in the New England region where the likes of all American clubs, the Barley House Wolves (NH), Portland, and Allentown HC, PA have played each other in a home and away format. The former two recently hooked up with new all American club, Worcester HC, MA, to form the new Northeast Division Junior C Adult Championship in 2011.

This is the first time in the history of the sport of hurling in America that a league comprised almost entirely of Americans has been set up in the Northeast and is another example of the growth of the sport in recent times. Directly across the country in the Northwest, another new league sprouted up recently which sees new all-American clubs also taking to the field. Once more they are coming from places with very little Irish immigrant populations and certainly no history of the sport of hurling played competitively in the region.

Six clubs have taken root in the Northwest with all but one forming in the last couple of years. They are Benton Brigade and Eugene Trappers from Corvalis and Eugene in Oregon, Seattle Gaels and Columbia Red Branch from Vancouver Washington State, with two newer clubs formed recently, Williamette Hurling from Corvalis and Pocatello Hurling out of Idaho.

In 2010 the clubs hooked up with Vancouver GAA across the border in British Columbia, Canada – players largely of Irish origin – to play in the new Northwest Hurling League. Consider that as of 2011 there are only five senior hurling teams in the Boston area, and the city with a huge Irish demographic, one immediately sees that something different is taking place.

That there is a hurling club, and an all American one at that, in the state of Idaho speaks volumes as to the sport's spread into what one could deem uncharted territory for hurling. The folk in Idaho when practicing in a rural location have to watch out for the local wildlife: Cougars.

Meantime, the Benton Brigade who formed in 2008 under the stewardship of American Dustin Herron - similar to Madison - have gone about things in a very different way to the more traditional Irish clubs.

In modern times sporting organizations have had to keep up with how information is distributed and consumed, and this usually means having some sort of Internet presence. Setting up a club website and more recently a Facebook page has been the norm as to how any sporting club is organized in the modern day.

Benton Brigade have a website and Facebook presence but the kind of site and content it distributes to members and indeed to the world is more local promotion orientated than the hurling clubs in Boston.

There are five hurling clubs in Boston: Fr. Tom Burkes, Galway HC, Tipperary HC, Wexford HC and Cork HC. According to the Northeast GAA Division website (and at the time of writing) not one of these clubs has a website presence. Galway HC does have a domain name but not a functional website.

Meanwhile New York, a city that once boasted 22 hurling clubs back in 1967, is left (until 2011) with three senior hurling clubs. When a club is dependent on the immigration model alone this type of scenario arises.

It appears that all three clubs: Galway, Offaly and Tipperary do not have a website presence either (at time of writing).

Their dependency on the Irish market places their existence on a precarious footing year on year, as in the case of Boston, in recent years several clubs have had to fold for a season or two due to lack of numbers. This is in stark contrast to what is taking place with new hurling clubs in the Northwest, Northeast and in places like Milwaukee who train rookies to play and enjoy the sport.

In the Northeast in 2011, the first competition of this sort at a rookie Junior C Adult League level was introduced, principally driven by the New Hampshire and Maine contingents, who reached the final, and it turned out to be a great success.

At Junior C Adult Hurling only Americans and resident Irish-born players (3) are eligible to play. No Irish summer sanctioned players are allowed at this grade.

Northeast GAA PRO, Rory O'Donnell, commenting on the final and the new competition to the podcast, GaelicSportsCast in 2011, felt that it is a step in the right direction:

> "It was a very exciting game with lots of good hurling. A great final for the Junior C competition. It's great to see hurling at that level and

being played in the Northeast and we look forward to it becoming more competitive as time goes on."

These three new clubs actively recruit local players each year and have a much better chance of sustaining their club over the long-term in contrast to the more traditional Irish club that rely on the vagaries of immigration to fuel their existence.

The fallout of non-local promotion is that in essence, as far as sports athletes in Boston are concerned, there is no such thing as the sport of hurling as they are not invited to become part of a sporting club and learn a new game. The core thoughts of the traditional Irish club, and this goes for the majority of such clubs in the big American cities, is that fielding a team of home based immigrants and Irish summer players to win the local championship is the sole priority. Not all have this aim, but most do.

North American GAA Divisions that run stadia in the larger cities with high Irish immigration, have a vested interested in seeing competitive games that attract crowds. The senior grade in hurling and Gaelic football, which comprise largely of Irish resident and short-term summer Irish, are revenue earners for big city divisions but with the constant ebb and flow of immigration/migration, depending on such a system for revenue sustainability is precarious.

There are a lot of people involved with the Irish traditional clubs and big city divisions who have put an enormous amount of work into running their organizations over the years, but if the growth of the club and division is not key then such entities will always be threatened with extinction.

For many Irish immigrants living in the bigger cities, playing and attending hurling and Gaelic Sports competitions is a means of integrating with their fellow countryman and culture. Gaelic sports events are used as a networking and job seeking opportunity.

Often people will go the games at Canton in Massachusetts, or Gaelic Park in the Bronx, for the social aspect of being with your own and getting a taste of Ireland if only for a day. This social and cultural aspect has always been a part of Gaelic sports in America and indeed wherever Irish emigrants find themselves down through the years.

Playing the games on a Sunday in Boston or New York has acted as a central part of the lives of immigrants but all too often this important aspect has been left out of the historical cannon in America. The games have also been left out of TV features on Irish immigration. You'll get the series about the Irish Potato Famine, Irish immigration, the Kennedy's, Irish organized crime in America, but you'll get nothing about the likes of hurling and Gaelic football and their significance.

While American public TV has done some great series such as, 'Out of Ireland' and 'The Irish in America', it has failed dramatically to show how the likes of hurling has played a crucial part of Irish immigrant life in the U.S.

Meanwhile academics in America, for generations, mostly explored only the socio-political Irish immigrant landscape. It is only people like sports scholar Paul Darby who has recently addressed from a historical and cultural perspective the importance of the games to the Irish in America. The Irish Gaelic sports community can feel rightly grieved that the games haven't been given more exposure, at least from a historical perspective, but they haven't always helped themselves.

This author lived in New York City for eight years in the 1980s but did not make any contact with the local Gaelic sports community at the time. When later moving to Boston (1997-2007) things changed as the last 5 years of living in 'Beantown', saw regular attendances at Canton, MA, when reporting on games every Sunday.

There is no doubt that one looks forward to meeting friends and being able to see games like hurling or Gaelic football played each summer weekend. There is no doubt the entertainment is good with high level of competition due to players – mostly third level students on J1 short term visas - coming over from Ireland for the summer. But it is all too easy to get wrapped up in the Irish summer player culture and keeping things going in this fashion in Boston, Chicago, New York, and San Francisco.

A sport like hurling itself is sacrificed to entertainment value and club championship pride. It deserves better.

Rules are brought in each year that only allow a certain number of summer or sanction players on the field at all times but this model is only a short term fix in its current format and does nothing for growing the sport locally.

Some will tell you that this model has kept the flame alight and the game going in America. To a certain extant this is correct, however the model of dependency on Irish immigrants and summer players, hinders the good work in setting up a local sporting club in the first place. Most of all it hinders the development of a sport to and for the local community.

The game continues within the Irish immigrant enclave where hurler-imports fly in like geese for the Summer and leave by Fall. The traditional Irish clubs are boosted with an influx of resident Irish immigrants and summer players, but by the end of the year things may be completely different with just the long-term resident player left to backbone a club.

The summer player model is destroying the sport's development and many clubs are beginning to move away from this dead-end street. The newer Junior C Adult clubs are growing the sport locally. They are reaching out with marketing campaigns in the form of videos on You Tube, Facebook and on their websites. As well as this very creative local tournament and recruiting posters are also helping spread the word about hurling.

FOX RIVER HURLING CLUB

Illustration 14: Fox River Hurling Club logo

Hurling's spread through the state of Wisconsin gained further momentum in 2011 when another new club arrived on the scene. Like others before it, the Fox River Hurling Club (FRHC) was set in motion when several people gathered around a few beers and started to talk.

The setting was the McGuinness Irish Pub in Appleton WI in late 2010, and around the table, a bunch of Americans. One was the soon-to-be founder of the new club, Brandon Salfai and his friends, Clodagh McGuinness (daughter of the proprietor who is now club sponsor) and Brian Christ. The conversation soon spread to hurling as both Brian (who lives in Milwaukee) and Clodagh had taken up hurling with the Milwaukee Hurling Club, and like what Dave Olson had heard years before, Salfai's friends started talking up hurling.

The Fox River founder recalls the moment in a recent email interview.

> "He [Brian] couldn't stop talking about how much fun hurling was, and the club and camaraderie down in Milwaukee. Brian had helped

build the pub into what it is today, and he figured that Milwaukee had a great pub league, why shouldn't Appleton?

I didn't have an good answer for that, but I didn't know enough about hurling to be enthused about it yet. We went into the back yard where he handed me a hurley and ran about 20 yards away with his. I took a swing at the sliotar and got hooked."

From that moment, no matter what happened, the idea was to keep the "spirit of fun and friendship" at the center of any new organization. Soon after, Salfai, with MHC member and friend Tracy Sherman, found himself attending Milwaukee Hurling Club's events, like their Christmas party, or their "Pales, Ales, Sticks ,and Stouts" party night. Tracy was in the process of moving to Green Bay, just up the road from Appleton, and so now there were two hurlers in the area eager to start a club.

Salfai acquired a sliotar (ball) and hurley and started Hurling 101 at home.

"I enjoyed hitting around and practicing soloing and other stuff in my yard. I had bought a pitching re-bounder, like the ones baseball players will throw balls into. It springs the ball back at you pretty fast, so it was perfect for playing a form of wall-ball (bating ball against a wall) I would get a lot of repetition, but it still wasn't hurling."

The idea of heading down to Milwaukee to play each weekend didn't appeal with the long commute, so starting a club locally was the preferred solution.

"So there I was, wanting to hurl, but not wanting to drive 218 miles each weekend to do it. We had just gone through our census and I remember seeing a statistic that said that there were a million people in the Fox River Watershed including Lake Winnebago. That area covers most of the cities in a 35 mile radius of Appleton. Well, a million people isn't anything to sneeze at! I thought certainly this is enough to support a pub league."

But Salfai's next step was novel. Instead of waiting for folks to come to him, he went to them. He followed the notion that if you build something for people they will come.

"So I thought that in order to get folks to want to join, I needed to develop some marketing presence. So I went out and built our webpage, and a Facebook presence. The idea was that if I told someone about the game, and got them enthused, if there wasn't a place for them to "go", they'd quickly lose interest."

It worked. McGuinness Irish Pub soon gave support in the way of sponsorship and he got equipment from the only supplier of hurleys, balls and gear in the U.S. the American Hurling Company out of Greenville, South Carolina. This family run company was set up by Irish immigrants, Joseph and Stephen Quigley. The family have been long-time supporters of hurling in America and this new hurley making tradition springing up in America is another indication of the changing landscape for hurling across the states.

Soon the number of players joining the Fox River club started to grow and in an effort to retain players and interest Salfai immediately set about starting off practices, leading to a league, and hopefully a community.

> "I then wanted to be sure to retain as many members as possible, so I went out and got some pub league jerseys. Once you get a guy in a jersey, he's got a new family, so to speak. There's an identity to it. There's a face to the club, and it inspires folks to bring their friends next time ... that and the coolers full of cold beer for after practice didn't hurt either," Salfai added.

Each practice brought new faces and by the time of the big Irish cultural festival in the region, the Oshkosh Irish Fest in early June, the fledgling FRHC boasted 13 members. Promotion efforts at the festival proved hugely important.

"Naturally, everyone wanted to go down to the festival," recalled Salfai.

> "So we all carted down individually and wore our pub league jerseys. I was able to get a last minute table in the cultural tent on Sunday because Milwaukee Hurling Club (MHC) had to go down for their pub league the same day. They let me occupy their spot at the table, and left me with their marketing gear. I added some of the FRHC marketing merchandise and sort of drew an imaginary line through Fond Du Lac, WI. I wanted to respect MHC's area, as they too wanted to grow their club. Anything in Fond Du Lac or south, I'd talk about MHC. Anything north of there, I'd pitch FRHC. That really drove up membership! I remember thinking that we've got enough to make a full squad now!"

Soon neighbors to the south, Hurling Club of Madison, heard about the new club and came to play a friendly match. This progressed the club further, especially with club 'fence sitters' and the commitment level within the new sporting organization "increased dramatically". Interest was stimulated by a 'Poc Fada' (Gaelic for long puck) style event in October of 2011 with a turnout of 30 contestants. The 'Poc Fada' competition is a longest bat of a ball event and takes its name from the legendary all day 'Poc Fada in the

Cooley Mountains in County Louth on the east coast of Ireland. The event takes place over a three mile circuit through mountainous terrain and is inspired by the legend of Cuchulainn, as a boy, hitting the ball in front of him as he went along.

The Fox River Club recently started an indoor winter league and are now up to 40 playing members with two rosters for their league. They have also initiated a youth league. The new club draws on athletes who live in eastern Wisconsin and boasts players from three different cities Oshkosh, Appleton and Green Bay. The club drawing inspiration from the region's geographical center piece, the Fox River, had christened the club after the waterway.

The club core values as laid down in their documentation reads:

> "We are hurlers, men and women of all races and nationalities, advancing this ancient game by playing for enjoyment, friendly competition and a mutual respect derived through team and club camaraderie."

The mission statement is reflective of what is happening on the ground at other new American clubs where reaching out to the local communty and playing hurling within a friendly and enjoyable enviroment is paramount.

Salfai hopes that, like Milwaukee and Madison, the fledgling club can put down solid roots in the area.

> "It's our vision to popularize hurling in these three cities, and ultimately have three or more teams in each city, that can play intra- and inter-county games culminating in a regional championship series."

Just before publication, news arrived of yet another new hurling club starting in the region. The latest arrival is located in the state of Minnesota at the north western border of Wisconisn in the city of Duluth. A few hurlers from the Twin Cities club moved to Duluth and are now spreading the game in that region. The Twin Cities Hurling Club is another progressive organization that reaches out to the local community. The club is also looking to promote and develop the sport in the city, region and throughout the state of Minnesota.

Looking south to Colorado, the well established Denver Gaels Club have also made huge progress over the past number of years where 2011 saw them initiate an exciting and trend setting project.

DENVER GAELS

In the mid 1990s Denver was abuzz from sport's mania. The Broncos were building a football legacy, the Colorado Avalanche in just their first year in the state won ice hockey's Stanley Cup, the Rapids soccer team was in the mix in that game's new competition, Major League Soccer (MLS), and some Irish men inspired by it all decided to start off a Gaelic sports club. In 1996, Dubliner Shay Dunne called the first meeting and so was born the Denver Gaels, the first official Gaelic Athletic Association (GAA) club in the Rockies in the modern era.

In the beginning, the club was comprised of Irish immigrants who played Gaelic football and in 2000 they won the Junior Adult B Championship at the Nationals.

With a small Irish community to draw upon the club soon realized that recruiting local players was the only way forward in order to sustain the young organization. "We began recruiting and training young Americans to adopt and play the sports of Ireland. To our delight they learned quickly and have proven to be very capable Gaelic players," the Denver Gaels inform on their website.

The club continued to attract local players and the organization received a big boost when the Mile High City was chosen to host the 2004 North American GAA Nationals. Club Chairman, Irish native Eamonn Ryan, told of the significance of the event when speaking with GaelicSportsCast in May 2011:

> "[When] the Denver Gaels hosted the North American finals, we had a couple of thousand people come in and it really raised the profile of Colorado and the club here [from Gaelic sports perspective] and at that point a few of the lads here decided we might as well launch a hurling side of the club. So in 2004 hurling started and hurling has been going from strength to strength ever since."

The hurling tradition grew rapidly and with two Junior Adult sides (grades B and C) has overtaken Gaelic football with almost 90% American player participation. The hurling team tasted their first success in 2008 when they won the Junior C Adult National Championship in Chicago.

Today the club has some 120 members and such has been its success that it has added Camogie (ladies hurling) and Ladies Football teams as well as a Youth Development program. The growing numbers have allowed also for annual Hurling and Football leagues, Fall Scrimmages and popular Indoor Winter Hurling.

The Denver Gaels is an example of a progressive club with a mix of Irish and Americans, who work together for the betterment and development of Gaelic sports in the region.

Ryan said that one of the strengths of the hurling program was its competitiveness:

> "One of the ways we achieved that [growing local numbers] was to make sure that we had competitive games every weekend for new players joining and actually get involved as opposed to just focusing on the North American Championships. When everyone joins the club now they are guaranteed a game every single weekend."

The club welcomes all players but at the same time thinks that looking to Irish summer players to keep things going is unworkable:

> "We welcome all players coming out but we don't focus on that. We don't believe in sponsoring players to come out who just come for one summer. We prefer to have fellows that are living here or local people – it helps to grow the club a lot better ... our focus is to grow from the ground up, locally," he told GaelicSportsCast.

Helping to get rookies into the swing of things in their new sport, New Player Clinics are held each Spring. The Hurling League comes to a conclusion in mid summer and towards the end of this competition, the club hosts a major inter-state tournament.

Every year the Gaels make the most of the local three-day Colorado Irish Festival as they organize a Gaelic Sports Tournament on festival weekend in the summer. This is one of the biggest tournaments in America with teams from all over the country traveling from Oregon, Washington, Illinois, California, Texas, Kansas and even New Mexico.

Games of hurling, mens and ladies Gaelic football, and camogie take place over Saturday and Sunday and to facilitate the some 50,000 people in attendance over the weekend, the Denver Gaels organize an information booth at the festival. The club over the weekend also organize a Kids Clinic in hurling and Gaelic sports for boys and girls of all ages.

In the Spring of 2011 the Gael's embarked on an exciting experiment that could yet reap rich rewards for the club and offer other clubs a valuable promotional tool.

Looking to boost the Gaelic football side of things, the Gaels played a half time exhibition game during a U.S. college rugby match at Infinity Park stadium, the brand new Municipal Rugby ground in Glendale Denver,

Colorado. This stadium is one of the premier rugby venues in America and regularly hosts national championship games.

The Denver Gaels, along with the stadium and Diageo (Guinness) – the sponsors of the Gaels and the Glendale Raptors – wanted to promote the stadium as well as football and hurling in the area. An arrangement was made and U.S. rugby followers got exposed to Gaelic sports exhibitions during a game.

The first exhibition was played in April 2011 and centered around football as a means of kick-starting interest locally. The games took place on a regular basis throughout the summer at Infinity Park. The facility is located just outside Denver in Glendale, and is one of the few city owned rugby stadiums in America.

Eamonn Ryan explained how the Gaels got the invite to play in the stadium:

> "It's the home of the Glendale Raptor Rugby team and they happen to be sponsored by Diageo Guinness, and we're also sponsored by them. So one of the things we talked about at the start of this year [2011] was well (1) raise the profile of hurling and Gaelic football in Colorado and (2) raise the profile of Infinity Park itself. We talked to Guinness about this ourselves and so we basically team up with the stadium."

After the first football exhibition, which took place between two college rugby sides, Ryan said the reaction was very positive:

> "We had our logo up on the big screens and they announced the club and the fact that we have a league starting. So we had a lot of inquiries from it and it was good to play in front of a crowd and people were curious after-wards as well."

Denver Gaels PRO, Brian McCarthy commenting on the initiative to Denver media outlet, The Onion a month later said that it was great to play at the state-of-the art facility. "Infinity Park is a fantastic facility for us. The new pitches are top quality, and the rugby goalposts are similar dimension to Gaelic goalposts, so it works really well."

Infinity Park is just about rugby regulation size but is too small and restrictive for a full-on game of hurling.

In 2011, the Denver Gaels recruited 13 rookie adult hurlers (also recruited Gaelic footballers). The club has recently begun its 2012 four team hurling league, consisting of 20 players per roster, and it looks like it will be another good year for the club as it has already recruited a further 15 players for the season.

The Denver Gaels website is one of the most informative and interactive of any Gaelic sports club across America today. The club chairman says that the organization has put a lot of effort into the site and told GaelicSportsCast of its importance:

> "We have actually put an awful lot of work into the website this year [2011]. We have a great committee this year and a few of the guys and girls took it upon themselves to really just revamp the website with a discussion forum and up-to-date events calendar.
>
> We've found that without that it's very difficult to grow. People new to the club need to go somewhere and try and understand what the game[s] are all about and understand when is the next training session. We've such a spread of people here in such a vast area that having everything up to date on the website is very important."

It seems Fox River in Wisconisn and Denver are on the same page and working towards similar goals.

People come from all over Colorado to training sessions with some traveling an hour each way. The Gaels put a lot of effort into recruiting through their local Irish media outlets, sponsors, and especially promote the club during and after the annual St. Patrick's Day Parade.

ROGUE CAMOGS

While this book focuses primarily on the sport of hurling, the ladies version of hurling, Camogie, is also beginning to stir American imagination. This is seen very clearly in one particular team who go by the name of the Rogue Camogs.

As the name suggests The Rogues are a little bit different and not exactly like any other Gaelic sports club in America. In 2010, the Rogue Camogs were founded more out of necessity and practicality than anything else. Made up of three different camogie teams from Denver, Seattle and Twin Cities, MN, the idea was that each had numbers problems and especially when it came to traveling to Nationals each year.

Camogie started in Denver back in 2006 with current team manager American Kyle Shane the driving force behind the initiative. Kyle's introduction to camogie is a carbon copy of other Americans' stories of picking up hurling while in Ireland.

Kyle went to Ireland in 2001 for a study abroad program, and it was there she discovered the sport, she also told GaelicSportsCast in a 2011 interview:

> "I was studying at the University of Limerick and I was actually playing rugby and I saw some of my roommates playing hurling. At the time I was stuck into rugby pretty good but I got injured, and when I moved back to the states and came to Denver, I saw that the Denver Gaels had hurling.
>
> There was only one girl playing [with the men's hurling team] at the time, and I had to get in on that. So I started playing hurling and convincing other women that it's a good idea too so we kind of got camogie started."

Hurling and camogie speaks to the athlete and another rugby player gets hooked. Shane has taken a shine to her new sport. "I adore camogie. I absolutely love it."

Twin Cities Camogie Manager, American Sarah McFarland, in her discovery of the sport in the same interview, highlights the importance of an Irish festival as a promotional tool for hurling and Gaelic sports:

> "In 2008, my husband and I saw an exhibition of a hurling match at our local Irish Fair and that was the spark. At the time there was only one girl playing as well, similar story to Kyle's, who was also the wife of a male player. So when I began next spring 2009, I was the second player on the team."

Meanwhile, Seattle Camogie Manager, American Kim Beckett had known about hurling and camogie as she already was a Gaelic Football player with Seattle Gaels:

> "I saw camogie for the first time at the Nationals before last (2009) when I played Gaelic Football ... but I had seen hurling before. We had a player that helped start our camogie team in Seattle that had been playing with the guys, playing hurling, and so we were just like 'let's do it'.
>
> You know it's newer in the states in general and there's a lot of new teams so we thought that we would start a team, be competitive and have some fun," she also told the podcast, GaelicSportsCast.

It took many emails and phone calls to get things organized but nevertheless the Rogue Camogs made their debut as a tri-state hybrid Junior Adult B club at the National Championships in Chicago in 2010.

At Camogie Senior grade, there have been mostly only three teams, Chicago St. Mary's, Boston Eire Og and San Francisco Shamrocks and primarily of Irish born players in competition at the National Championships. At Junior Adult level the number of teams competing over the last few years at Nationals is greater with teams of mostly American players from Milwaukee, Washington DC Gaels, St. Louis, and Indianapolis.

Playing at the North American GAA Nationals is especially a great source of pride for American players and has resulted in boosting playing numbers. Playing as a combined team helped grow camogie in each individual area of Denver, Seattle and the Twin Cities.

At the 2011 Nationals in San Francisco, the trio had become a duo as Seattle Camogie team had enough traveling players to compete on its own with the Rogue Camogs represented by Denver/Twin Cities.

In the first round of the Junior Adult Championship, the sister teams unfortunately met with the Denver/Twin Cities combo coming out best. The Rogue Camog combo had a great tournament as they went on to win the Championship, nipping DC Gaels in the final by [5] 1-2 to [4] 1-1. Seattle also had an excellent nationals when finishing runners-up in the Camogie Junior Shield Final.

Twin Cities Sarah McFarland lauds the idea of the North American GAA Nationals as an inspiring and motivational American sporting championship:

> "The experience of going is so energizing and so positive and so amazing that you come back with a whole wealth of knowledge.
>
> You see teams play. You get to form relationships and you bring that back and the energy carries over into everything we do once we get back home.
>
> I think that shows up in our practices, it shows up in our recruiting. For adult females, the ones who are in college or out of college, the competitive piece is something that they are used to seeing especially if they played college sports. So the traveling and those kinds of things really help in promoting the sport and encouraging adult women to play."

In 2011, the Denver Gaels Camogie team added seven local new players and this allowed them to host their very first camogie competition during the summertime. The Rogue Camogs combo idea has been a positive development for growing the sport regionally but on a national level American players like McFarland feels the sport needs to get on TV:

"I think really it is just being able to show the sport on a wider spectrum. You know, getting it air-time on TV - one of the camogie finals (from Ireland)... Or, showing up at a sporting event and doing a half-time exhibition match. Because the sport itself is exciting, it's amazing on so many levels and so appealing to many women out there who play soccer, lacrosse, rugby that it's really just getting the word out."

Denver's Kyle Shane thinks along similar lines:

"I couldn't agree more. It's really just exposure. Once people start to play in the U.S. most people either love it and become addicted to it within the first couple of times playing in it and we just need more exposure. We've had women who play [ice] hockey and field hockey; the skills transfer over so well, we just need to get it more visible."

Kim Beckett in Seattle thinks the coaching clinics are an important factor for promotion, saying:

"that's really good and to keep that going." She also feels that a recent visit by Ireland's Camogie Association at National's in 2010 and "working with us was really exciting and I think that everyone was really excited to have some talented Irish camogie players teaching us some skills. I think that's great and I think we are heading in the right direction as regards evolving the sport."

An important part of Denver Camogie teams growth and the Gaels as a whole has been the work of club photographer, American Amanda Reiker. The professional photographs Reiker has shot allow for better branding for the likes of hurling. In the Year in Review for 2011, the club website said:

"In the past few years she has snapped countless photos and made us look better and more skillful. She has emerged as a tremendous asset to our club, and one of the premier Gaelic Photographers in the Country. We are incredibly lucky to count her as one of our own."

Recently, her Gaelic sports photography work at tournaments in the Denver region and at past Nationals, caught the attention of the NACB who now use her professional images.

Denver Gaels are growing from strength to strength but there is still another hurling club that recently caught the eye and in a very big way.

INDY HURLING

The Indy Hurling club out of Indianapolis, IN, have been marketing the sport locally for a number of years and in January 2012 they hit the jackpot. Actually, the 'Super' Jackpot.

A little over a week prior to the Super Bowl XLVI in Indianapolis, the local Super Bowl Village Committee invited sports in the area to come and feature their club to the thousands of visiting football fans in Downtown Indianapolis – Indy Hurling was one of those chosen to exhibit.

"We have a very unique and rare opportunity to showcase our sport on a national level. We encourage EVERYONE to come out and help show the world what the Indy GAA is all about," said Indy Hurling PRO Kyle Keesling on the invite, in the club website, prior to the event on Jan. 31, 2012.

Indianapolis was also the venue recently for the first ever Midwest College Hurling match on April 4, 2009. Back then spectators lined the field at Lake Sullivan Park to see the two all American college hurling clubs from Purdue University and Indiana University meet for the first time.

Hurling has started to spring up on Midwest colleges in the past two years and when a sport gets to be played at this level – though fledgling at present – it does get noticed by the local community. When you get noticed good things happen as per the Super Bowl gig.

"We were approached by the Super Bowl Committee to help participate in their sports club night. A few of the members had seen/heard about the club from prior events," Indy Hurling said in a Press Release on their website and Facebook. This speaks to the importance of reaching out to local community and city, and as a result, a club reaps rich reward.

So on that night Tuesday, January 31, 2012, a bit of hurling history was made in America. For a period of four hours, Indianapolis Hurling Club showcased the sport to thousands of Super Bowl fans at the Super Bowl Village.

Illustration 15: Indy HC - Solo Run Drill at 2012 Super Bowl Village, Indianapolis (Photo by Kyle Keesling)

The event took place on Capitol Street in the midst of the NFL Experience activities.

As part of the various events a large section of the street had been turned into a carpet-like playing surface. Crowds swarmed around the whole Super Bowl Village and there smack bang in the middle of everything was Hurling.

The local club pulled out all the stops with an American club player hooked up to the PA system doing MC. Throughout the evening, he told of the sport's history and about the local club. He also explained the rules with interactive demonstrations and invited the football hordes to try out various hurling drills and skills with club instructors. A hitting cage was also on hand for some of the younger members of the audience.

Little scrimmages showcased how the game would look when played and various plays were showcased and broken down. Over the course of the night, Americans lined the artificial playing area and many took part in trying their hand at Hurling 101.

The event turned out to be a great moment for both the local club and hurling. Indy HC PRO, Kyle Keesling, live at the event, told the podcast GaelicSportsCast that night of it being a fantastic event. "It's been pretty crazy but it's been great. They've hooked us up with the PA system ... and they've really set it up for us to showcase hurling on a national level ... It's been great!"

Feedback from participants on the night was very positive, he said. "We've had a lot of crowd interaction and everyone seems really into it and wanting to get involved."

Illustration 16. Indy HC – Showcasing the hurley grip at 2012 Super Bowl Village, Indianapolis (Photo by Kyle Keesling)

Indy HC, like many of the newer American player clubs, had been playing an active part in promoting the sport to local audiences.

The prevalence of Irish festivals throughout America is prolific with over 70 events and the Indy club, like others, took full advantage to market hurling when setting up well stocked information booths at their annual local Indy Fest. This three day festival attracts over 50,000 annually and Indy HC is a willing partner in attracting new recruits at their booth.

Illustration 17: Indy exhibit at Irish Fest (Courtesy of Indy HC).

The club packed their booth with hurling memorabilia and also featured a multimedia hurling video, while on the field of play, they showcased the sport. Afterwards the club issued a report on their efforts:

> "Indy entertained scores of onlookers with a two-round tournament held over Friday and Saturday ...The field immediately adjacent to the festival's entrance was available for our games ... Our booth attracted sports-fans of all ages [and] this year we added a hitting cage to our display where folks could try their luck at the hurl.
>
> It was our pleasure to introduce our club to many people from the area, as well as a handful of Irish-born Hoosiers. We look forward to working with Irish Fest next year for more of the same, only better."

Prior to the festival the club had this to say, "We will be introducing hurling to the masses with our booth, and actively recruiting at the same time. This is a great opportunity for the club to reach out to showcase our sport!"

Reaching out has paid dividends as their club continues to grow in number. Their annual inter-club/state competition, the Hibernian Invitational – started in 2008 – regularly hosts up to six clubs from the Midwest and is growing in popularity each year.

Indy hurling says that it is proud to host a local tournament and highlights the sport's growth in America:

> "Hurling, one of the national sports of Ireland, has been gaining a dedicated following of both players and enthusiasts in the U.S. The Indianapolis Hurling Club is proud to host an exciting day of competition between some of the Midwest's strongest clubs. This six team tournament will feature competition from around the region, giving Hoosiers a real taste of the excitement around Irish hurling."

The club set out goals for themselves each year and 2008 was a particularly good year on and off the field:

> "In 2008, our coach and executive board led the club to accomplish every goal they set forth 1 year ago. These included community involvement, expansion of our membership, and a national championship win in Boston – a feat accomplished only two years after Indy Hurling joined the North American Gaelic Athletic Association."

While winning championships is important, the emphasis is on club and sport growth as mentioned in a website news update. "The new year (2009) promises to bring more excitement as we renew our goals, improve our game-play, and introduce more Hoosiers to the sport of Hurling."

The club was initially formed after a wedding back in 2002 when an impromptu game took place and later reformed in 2005 by two Irish immigrants, Neal Mulrooney and Shane Powell. They had a great love for the sport and brought "leadership for the club's future," the club website reports.

Things got really motoring when the club marched in the local St. Patrick's Day Parade, then further growth, sponsors and soon a co-ed league got off the ground. Indy hurling is mostly an American player club but Irish immigrants who became chairpersons and coaches have also played a crucial role in introducing the sport to the local community.

In the newer American-player clubs, there are many Irish immigrants who have played huge roles in getting things off the ground. These immigrants are a new breed with a new vision for a sport like hurling. They are keen to grow the sport locally and not be dependent on Irish summer players.

By their very nature sports clubs have to grow from out of the local community – Michael Cusack understood this. Without local growth at the heart of a sports club there is no club, and clubs who have to depend on importing players, are in essence clubs by proxy. They don't fully exist and little wonder then that Americans have never come across the sport of hurling.

BENTON BRIGADE, CORVALLIS, OR

Benton Brigade Hurling Club in Oregon also tries to reach out to the local community. They even borrow from a corporate approach to organization in that they have a Mission Statement on their website that sets out to say exactly who and what they want to do:

> "The Benton Brigade Hurling Club is hereby formally established to provide members of the community a means of participation in the sport of Hurling.
>
> The club, led by its officers, will strive to promote and support the sport both in and outside of Benton County. The club will make reasonable efforts to support and help grow neighboring county/city teams.
>
> It will aim to create a fun atmosphere composed of dedicated individuals as well as casual members. Goals for the development and growth of the organization will be submitted and pursued to achievement as needed. The club will be managed by volunteer officers and will work to build a professional and organized image in the community."

This Mission Statement is similar in its outlook and aims to other new American clubs in that it wants to recruit from within the locality. The Benton Brigade club also wants to forge relationships with other hurling clubs in the region in an effort to promote on a united front as opposed to seeing other clubs as purely there for competition – although it would be a mistake to think that American clubs don't want to win. They do, but they place an equal importance on forming partnerships off the field.

Further, the club wants to build an atmosphere of fun around the games and not only grow player count but build a community following. This formula seems to be working evidenced by growing numbers in March of 2011, where player membership increased. A News item on their website read, "Membership is up!!! The Brigade has 23 registered members and is continuing to grow! Keep working on recruiting, we may be able to field two teams!"

Benton Brigade was founded by American Dustin Herron in the summer of 2008. With sponsor restaurant and brewery Block 15 on board, Herron was able to get equipment and next started recruiting locally. Over that winter hurling clinics got organized with members from other regional clubs, Columbia Red Branch and Trinity Willamette.

The Brigade's first match was held at the Eugene Irish Festival with the Brigade and Trinity members playing the Columbia Red Branch of Vancouver, Washington. From there a solid core of players began to develop.

Growing club numbers over the years is not only a clear sign of positive health but that their local recruitment of rookie American players has worked. This is very similar to how Milwaukee, Madison, and Portland Mauraders go about things.

When looking back at how the man who started hurling's revival in Ireland, Michael Cusack, we saw that he also began with a few others hitting a ball around in a local park. This would eventually lead to more and more communities in Dublin and beyond starting off clubs in similar fashion and this local start-up model is a proven winner.

The importance of growing the sport through local competition and at a very basic skill level in a culture of camaraderie and cooperation is typical of one day inter-club blitz type competitions.

Another example of such tournaments is the Annual Hibernian Hurling Invitational held in early August in Westfield, Indiana. Teams from across the Midwest participate like Chicago's Michael Cusack HC, Akron Celtic Guards, the St. Louis Gaelic Athletic Club, and the Bloomington Gaelic Athletic Association.

A typical blitz commences at 12 noon and will run till late afternoon with each club getting in 2-3 games. The competition will be very keen but a sense of camaraderie and bonding takes place that can only auger well for a new sport developing in America. This spirit created around playing the sport on a blitz type inter-club tournament format is something beyond what you would get in a typical Irish immigrant league.

There is plenty of spirit and team bonding there also but for the most part it's summer players from Ireland who are in the thick of the action and whatever it means to them in the short-term, it doesn't have the same feel about it when you see home grown Americans playing and loving a new sport. Too often the Irish leagues are all about winning where clubs will outdo each other year after year to bring over a top summer recruit to bolster their chances of winning their local city championship.

You get the feeling when you talk to American players after an all day Inter-City club tournament that it's not just about winning but about having fun playing a new sport. One gets the feeling that it is this type of approach that will grow a new sport in a new country. And, in many respects, hurling *is* a new sport in America.

The folks in the Portland club call themselves the Portland Mauraders but they look upon their fellow competitor in New Hampshire's Barley House Wolves as their 'brother club'. This is something that the more traditional Irish clubs and leagues struggle to achieve.

Attracting sponsorship for local clubs and regional leagues is an essential element in sustaining and growing any sport and hurling clubs are by no means exempt from this formula.

The traditional method of seeking sponsorship is to get the local watering-hole to support the club and this continues to be a club's only real revenue source. The Hurling Club of Madison, however is one of the first clubs to garner the interest of a large American company, Pabst Blue Ribbon beer.

Perhaps with the growth of more and more Americans playing hurling, larger companies will take notice and when this happens usually the chances of the sport being highlighted by local and national media get increased.

ST. LOUIS

Hurling fever has also spread to the state of Missouri and to the city of St. Louis. Though hurling did have a prior history in this urban center during the late 19th century, born out of the arrival of Famine Irish immigrants in the 1840s, it's modern-day arrival in the city has turned heads and is slowly weaving its way into the sporting fabric of the region.

Milwaukee Hurling Club's (MHC) influence is felt here also as former MHC players, Paul C. Rohde, Dan Lapke, and Patrick O'Connor founded the club in the summer of 2002.

They started back then with small scrimmages in a local park and were proud to affiliate with the North American GAA organization at an early stage. "The St. Louis Hurling Club is the first association of American-born hurlers ever invited to join NACB in a club's first year of organization; its membership is primarily American-born."

This sense of pride is expressed in the club's website history page where they talk about their intentions of "introducing the sport of hurling to the metro St. Louis area, creating opportunities to play the sport, developing better hurlers, and developing strong St. Louis representation in nationwide competition."

The club laid this vision out in a very work-man like and no nonsense fashion with objectives:

> "(a) recruit at least 30 active members (exceeded), enabling a minimum two-team league, (exceeded, with a three-team league) (b) increase awareness of the sport and the club in the metropolitan area through aggressive marketing, (achieved) (c) establish a strong national reputation of St. Louis hurling through victories in nationwide competition, (achieved) (d) improve quality of play to a level adequate for consideration into the North American County Board in 2004 (achieved one year ahead of schedule)."

In March of 2003, history was made in St. Louis as the club marched in the St. Patrick's Day Parade showcasing the sport of hurling for the first time in the city's history. Later in September more city heads were turned as "aggressive marketing" bore fruit with "television, radio, newspaper and magazine exposure increased the number of interested Hurlers."

That month the first ever St. Louis Hurling Club season saw an 8-week league featuring three teams: Brown & Brown Financial, Black Thorn Sons of Liberty, and McGurks Black Shamrocks. McGurks would go on to defeat Brown & Brown, to win the first ever Gateway Cup on November 22, 2003 in the state of Missouri.

Still in September and more publicity in the form of a Proclamation from the Irish Consulate Office, "'commending the Club on its league and advancing the sport of hurling'".

Illustration 18: St. Louis Club logo

The following year in April the club started a Spring League, added a new team and further kudos arrived with the Missouri House of Representatives through 'a state resolution commending the Club for its success.'

Fall of 2004 would bring further accolades, this time on the field, as St. Louis Hurling Club at Bolder, CO, won the inaugural Junior C Adult Championship 2004 for mostly American born players.

The club was again rewarded for their efforts when this time:

> "a Proclamation from the City of St. Louis, congratulating the Club on its National Championship and commemorating the first anniversary of the inaugural league, where Hurling was played among St. Louisianans for the first time."

Illustration 19. St Louis Junior C Adult Championship Team 2004. (Photo courtesy of St. Louis HC).

Mayor Francis Slay proclaimed September 25, 2004 – St. Louis Hurling Club Appreciation Day. That November, the United States Senate recognized the Club for its national championship in the Congressional Standard.

These types of commendations and publicity for a hurling club in any of the major cities is unheard of in both the modern era and throughout the history of Gaelic sports in the country.

The club's progress since its inception has been impressive. St. Louis continues to grow as its current status (2012) sees the club with 8 teams, with a women's Camogie (hurling for women) two-team-league, starting off for the very first time.

The club runs an annual 20 week league and continues to look to recruit new local players. "Anyone interested is welcome — our club is committed to teaching the game to new members as well as improving the skills of our returning players. See you on the pitch."

WASHINGTON DC GAELS

Another innovative club is DC Gaels from Washington. Though a major urban center, Washington doesn't have the same Irish immigration numbers of either New York or Boston.

During the 1980s, the number of Irish arriving to DC did increase and by the end of the decade saw the start of the first Gaelic sports club in the city in the modern era. Hurling had been played in the city during the 50s and 60s and it wasn't until 2004 that the sport got going again.

The DC Gaels play in the Mid Atlantic Division and play in all four Gaelic sports codes – hurling, Gaelic football, ladies football and camogie. The club has been very successful on the field as they have won national titles in each of the four codes. Americans comprise the majority of players and the club also put a lot of emphasis into recruiting locally.

Liverpool born, Nora Reilly is the WDC Gaels Chairperson and in an interview with the podcast GaelicSportsCast in early 2010 she talked of the club's commitment to local growth and how recruiting grew beyond the pub circuit:

> "We have to find home grown American born players and we have done a lot of recruiting in colleges, universities, and you know, we have found that you need athletes to play these athletic games so we don't find people in bars anymore."

The Gaels took the athletic and fitness aspect of recruiting a step further when they saw an opportunity for exposure in the city with the annual NBC 4 Health & Fitness Expo at the Washington Convention Center.

The two day Health Expo is considered one of the largest of its kind in the country with some 25,000 people in attendance availing of free health screenings, health and fitness services, and sporting activity offerings.

American Mary Beth Ginder, DC Gael's club Development Officer (2010), explained in the same podcast, how the organization got involved for the first time with the Expo in 2010:

> "We looked into it because it made sense. The DC Gaels saw a great option for people who are interested in playing very competitive very high levels sports that you know you are going to have to train and be fit and be healthy in order to compete. So we felt that getting this sort of exposure going to this event would get our name out there a bit more in the community."

Ginder added that to let people know that the sports exist you have to reach out:

> "I mean we do have an Irish American community here but many people don't know or have never heard of Gaelic football or hurling or camogie, they don't know what it is. So it's a big challenge here to put ourselves out there and get exposure for the sports."

At the NBC Health Expo the Gaels had an information booth informing people who they were as a sport's club in the area and engaged people with various drills for hurling and Gaelic football.

Illustration 20. DC Gael's Camogie & Gaelic footballers at the 2010 NBC Health Expo at the Washington Convention Center (Courtesy of Washington DC Gaels)

The efforts by the club at the Expo reaped rich rewards with some 50 new recruits signing up to attend the Gaels Spring field days and to get fit through Gaelic sports. On top of this and as a direct result of the Expo, the D.C. Gaels went on to collaborate with Gonzaga High School, the Miss D.C. International pageant, and a local YMCA branch to spread Gaelic sports in the community.

In 2009, the Gaels all American camogie (ladies hurling) team went to the National Finals in Chicago and came away with the C level Camogie championship. Ginder is another American who has fallen in love with the sport:

> "I like camogie a lot. I think it's a very intense sport. It's fun. It's fast paced...I think most people are very impressed when they see it for the first time. There's one or two reactions either very impressed or a little scared with the sticks and all.
>
> But to recruit Americans and my friends especially, a lot of them have experience playing field hockey, or lacrosse or ice hockey. So you just say 'look you just take your skills that you already know from field hockey and we'll teach you how to hit the ball in the air. You know how to field the ball with a lacrosse stick we'll teach you how to hit it on the ground and pick it up then it's not quite as intimidating.'"

After the Expo, the club partnered with a local Irish arts group, Solas Nua, for a little 'street theater' and 'Guerrilla Hurling' in Farragut Square a block away from the White House. It took everyone by surprise and Washington folk are still talking about it.

People are also talking about another all American hurling club. An unlikely, yet extraordinary decision one fateful day describes the American spirit at its very best.

Chapter 6

The Barley House Wolves – Warrior Hurlers

It was exactly eight years ago to the time of writing that a special group of Americans set out on a life changing journey.

Early on the morning of St. Patrick's Day 2004, U.S. soldiers from Charlie Company, 3rd Battalion of the 172nd Mountain Infantry of the New Hampshire National Guard, arrived at Shannon Airport, Ireland.

A fuel stop-over saw just enough time for soldiers to call their loved ones and even get a taste of Ireland in one last pint before heading for a one year tour of duty in Iraq. The airport represented a poignant setting for many as it was their last glimpse of every day life in the west before the Middle East and war.

Over the course of that 12 month period Charlie Company engaged in many challenging duties – keeping convoy and supply routes clear, Improvised Explosive Devices (IED) clearance and sniper missions. "We faced direct combat on a daily basis," reflected the company commander then Captain Ray Valas (time of interview, Major and currently, Lieutenant Colonel) in a podcast with GaelicSportsCast in early 2010.

In their time in Iraq, the unit was honored as the best in the eight-company battalion which included active duty and guard reserve. Charlie Company received 12 Purple Hearts but everyone made it home alive. Early one morning a year later they arrived back into Shannon for refuelling:

> "When we left we had 14 of our men wounded but everyone made it back alive and in one piece. So we felt pretty blessed at that and it ended up that we were going back out through Shannon on our way back home," Valas recalled.

Coming back into Ireland had special significance for the unit as it was the last place they had seen 12 months prior to war and the first on their journey home to America:

> "There was some strong memories there from the beginning of the tour and it was kind of a moment for reflection because you think about how much you've changed and how much you faced over the course of that year so it was a pretty special point of departure for us," Major Valas stated.

This writer over the course of his 18 years in America returned regularly to Ireland to visit family and often witnessed U.S. military personnel in their sandy colored khaki uniforms in the large departure lounge at Shannon.

You saw them in line for that last pint. You saw them at a bank of pay phones talking to loved ones far across the ocean and you saw them sitting in groups perhaps contemplating what lay ahead, or was left behind.

On their homeward stopover, a bunch of soldiers from 'Charlie Company gladly sipped some cold ones at the bar.

They talked about their return to the states, when many in the unit who had experienced a lot together, would spread to the four winds. They thought of maybe a solid activity that could keep them together as a unit:

> "A few of us were talking that we wanted something that would be a rallying point that would keep guys together and keep in touch but we didn't want it to be something like going to a bar or just a social club, we wanted an activity or a healthy outlet to rally around," Valas explained.

It was then they happened to see a TV screen that was showing a weird game. They became captivated and wondered what the heck was this weird looking hockey game they had never seen before. They were looking at the sport of hurling.

True to their American and warrior spirit, their next thought placed them in uncharted territory and they asked ...'what if'...?

Major Valas and colleague, Ken Kinsella began to wonder aloud:

> "We thought wouldn't that be something if we actually started a hurling team.
>
> Some of the guys thought we were kidding, it seemed kind of outlandish but hey, why not give it a shot. It's unique enough to get people's interest and for us it was also important that if you picked a sport that a lot of people had played since they were little and some hadn't played before, everyone would be at a different level, but with hurling we were absolutely all beginners. So it put us all on a common point that everyone could enjoy it that way," said Valas.

When Sgt. 1st Class Eddie Clements saw hurling for the first time, his reaction probably summed up the view of his fellow National Guard comrades:

Illustration 21: Sgt. 1st Class Eddie Clements at a rest break while moving the Korean Army into Northern Iraq 2004 (Photo SPC Eric Madson)

> "It was definitely interesting. Of course the first thing we thought when we were looking at it is 'that's a really weird way to play field hockey,'" he remarked in the same interview.

The sport would go on to become something very special for the soldiers.

Charlie Company returned home to America but the idea of starting a hurling club stayed with them.

It took time for the soldiers to adjust to something approaching a normal life – though some in Charlie Company would see redeployment again – many made that adjustment in various ways.

Lieutenant Colonel Valas would later explain the process to a Boston Herald reporter:

> "When you come back, it takes time to readjust and get back to whatever normal was before you spent a year in a combat zone.
>
> The path that gets you there are different for everyone. Some of my soldiers turned to art, some turned to writing, some to the gym. There are good directions you can turn and not-so-good directions. The more options we can offer, the better we will be as a unit," he

told the Herald's Tenley Woodman in a January 2011 article entitled 'Caution: Hurling zone. N.H. Guardsmen promote ancient Irish sport in the Middle East.'

The latter refers to another redevelopment that took on historic elements.

So in late 2005 at another bar, this time stateside at the Barley House Restaurant & Tavern in Downtown Concord, New Hampshire, comrades from Charlie Company assembled. They had downloaded a few hurling clip videos off the Internet and acquired a projector:

> "We said 'here's what the sport looks like' so everyone knew what it looked like and we said 'if you thought we were kidding before, we're not – we're actually going to do this. We are going to give this a shot," Valas told GaelicSportsCast.

The unthinkable was beginning to happen ... the 'what if' ... was taking shape. The owner of the bar got behind the idea and became their sponsor. They took the Barley House for a name, but not forgetting their unit and what they had been through together, they added something from their year away. In Iraq the 'Wolf' represented 'Charlie Company's' call sign, and so the Barley House Wolves hurling club was born.

Illustration 22: Barley House Wolves Crest

"Wolf" was the company designation, followed by numbers indicating a duty position. The nine stars represent New Hampshire, the ninth state to join the union, as represented on the state flag by the nine stars around the wreath. The broken collar, below the wolf's neck, and broken crown, represents the Irish saying; "Bona Na Croin" or "No Collar No Crown", which was taken from New Hampshire's military roots in the American Revolution, representing men who would stand to be neither slaves nor subjects.

They had first practice January of 2006 and spent most of the year educating themselves about the game and sourcing equipment.

Getting that equipment was an issue but that was overcome in the short term when Valas bought a hurley online and gave it to a carpenter and told him: "Make me 20 like it!"

He bought 12 hurling balls as well and they still have some of the original ones to this day. They soon realized that hurley making required a bit more finesse and knew they had to get "real" hurleys.

Despite equipment setbacks something 'real' was starting to happen once the soldiers took to the field. The sport was beginning to speak directly to them, recalled LTC Valas:

> "Guys were hooked right away. All we had to do was put a hurl and a sliotar (ball) in someone's hands and they were hooked. Once you play that sport ... it's a great sport. That's all we have to do to get guys to join the team.
>
> We say 'come out one time and if you don't like it don't worry about it you never have to come back' and they always come back."

Sgt. 1st Class Clements grew up playing ice hockey around Manchester, New Hampshire. He also played a little soccer, and like Valas, who had also played ice hockey and lacrosse, eye hand coordination skills were present:

> "I grew up on a lake playing hockey so the stick skills were there for me when we started up. A lot of that transferred over for me and it worked real well," Clements told in that same podcast. But little did he realize then how the game would take hold of him.
>
> "I've been playing for four years now and it's honestly the greatest game that I have ever played. When I first came to the team I said I'd play as I thought it was going to be a drinking or social club, and I entertained the idea. Then, when I went out for the first practice, that was it for me. I was hooked right in."

Soon a story about the soldiers and their new sporting passion appeared on a local New Hampshire paper and a resident Irish native read the article and was impressed.

In the GaelicSportsCast interview, Daragh Madden, who had immigrated from Athenry in County Galway in the West of Ireland, explained that the story caught his imagination and he wanted to join up. "I read it on the local paper and I emailed Ray and said, hey, I'd love to play too!"

Valas was delighted to have an Irish man on board who could help the fledgling hurling team develop. He told Madden to come along and the Galway man arrived for the game clad in gear connecting him to that land across the water:

> "He came down suited up in his Galway outfit, and I said 'here you go, here's the blue jersey for you. You are on our team'. I said 'you are starting midfield and you're the best player on the team right now whether you know it or not!'"

Daragh had not played hurling since Elementary School but over time he began to teach the soldiers the basics of hurling. Their new coach was immediately impressed by the Wolves approach to learning the game:

> "To just watch the guys out on the field; [their] determination to learn the sport. As military guys they can take orders so well, you tell them once and they have it," said Daragh when recounting drill sessions.

During that summer the Wolves traveled down to Canton MA outside Boston to see how the game actually looked in reality.

Illustration 23. Canton Gaelic Park, MA (Photo by Denis O'Brien)

Valas, who is a Canton native, told of how the trip was well worth it as they got a lot of help from those playing at senior grade in the Northeast GAA Division:

> "Going down to Canton, Massachusetts, where our GAA division was incredibly helpful; just watching games there in the Boston area. Looking at the senior teams play gave us a better feel for the tempo. They were incredibly helpful down there as they helped us with some drills, training advice and it was great to get us going."

This alone shows the potential of the traditional Irish clubs that when they decide to turn their focus away from purely winning local championships and using the summer player model, they can be a very positive force in helping clubs like the Wolves or a college team like Stanford get started. If they can help the likes of the BHW get going then they can surely help themselves if the summer player model was to be phased out in the future.

Slowly the new club started to grow to about 20 National Guard members by 2008 with just the sole Irish man in the team ranks.

By setting up the club, the Wolves had created history in New Hampshire as the only hurling team in the state. Another milestone followed in September 2008 as the club participated in their first major competition, the North American GAA Nationals on Labor Day in Boston.

Naturally it was a baptism of fire for the rookie hurling team but the players learned a lot from the experience. The Wolves were drawn against the Milwaukee Hurling Club's second team in the Championship and though humbling it provided the soldiers with something to build upon. Milwaukee, though an all American club and league, had been playing hurling for well over a decade at the time and so there could only be one outcome in that contest. "They have a pretty strong pool from which to draw from and that was a very informative experience and incredibly humbling," Valas recalled in the GaelicSportsCast interview.

But always looking to take positives from the experience the soldier hurlers broke down the game into components in order to get some perspective going forward:

> "It came down to we would consider it a success if we could move the ball past the midfield line. They were a lot more experienced than us and had a lot more highly developed skills. You know we learned from that and we took it back and said we are going to do better next year."

Though defeated they used their time in Boston well as they watched a lot of games and talked to a lot of people about their new sport. They also set up informal drills and scrimmages with other first round casualties.

The Wolves thought that the best way to learn the sport was to play more local games and that meant helping to grow and promote hurling in the New England region. The club was influential in getting Portland's team off the ground and later helped the Worcester, MA club get going. Valas is a firm believer in that when you help another club you help yourself. "If we don't grow our competition it's going to be hard to make it happen and so growing other teams helps us to grow our own club."

The Wolves have also built connections next door to New Hampshire in Canada. The U.S. Army National Guard does a lot of training with the Canadian Army and a group of Nova Scotians in Halifax expressed interest in starting up a club. The Barley House Wolves have since been supporting those efforts.

The Wolves have also been trying to grow interest among other national guard units and apart from reactions of "bewilderment" the biggest issue they face is that war inevitably gets in the way.

The soldiers love the sport and want to spread hurling far and wide but for them 'mission comes first'.

In 2009 the Wolves grew to some 37 members, however scheduling was a challenge as people continually got redeployed to Iraq and then more to Afghanistan.

The following year the team went again to the Nationals and though falling victim to a first round defeat to Allentown Hibernians from Pennsylvania the team showed considerable improvement on their first outing.

Illustration 24. Barley House Wolves 2009 Team (Photo by Sean T. Noonan)

As word spread about the team in Concord and around the state, interest grew and soon civilians looked to try out the sport and get involved with the club. One of the recruits was a police officer from Belmont and soon four other officers joined ranks. Along with several fire-fighters also from Belmont, the rookie recruits got their first taste of Ireland's national game in early 2010.

That year was another momentous occasion as the Wolves planned, as a club, a return trip to Ireland for a four day hurling appreciation tour, while later that Fall a large contingent got ready for redeployment to Iraq and Kuwait. On account of the deployment they were unable to participate in the Nationals in Chicago that year.

HURLING APPRECIATION TOUR TO IRELAND

The Wolves trip to Ireland was memorable.

This author got to meet and hang out with the soldiers over the course of several days and let it be said that every single one is a gentleman.

The 2010 tour was made up of 11 players and three civilian members associated with the club. Of the 11 players, eight were soldiers with six of those scheduled for redeployment later that September.

The tour was led by then Major Ray Valas (now LTC) and also, Sgt. 1st Class Eddie Clements, Lieutenant Dave Devoy, Captain Jim Pappaioanou, Captain Adam Burritt, 1st Sergeant Lore Ford, Staff Sergeant Luke Koladish, Corporal Mike Gregoire, and civilians, Dennis Trainor, Ben Hyman, and Daragh Madden.

The non players were club fund-raising chairperson, Karen McNeil, pitch setup manager Ed Hahn, and fund-raising assistant, club friend and professional sports photographer, Sean Noonan.

The tour wasn't without early hiccups but in typical American spirit these were readily overcome. Bookings had been made long in advance of April departure, but owing to the ash-cloud from the Iceland volcano disrupting air travel in the lead up, the club had to make speedy rearrangements. Determined to make it to Ireland they made things work and re-booked flights and accommodation for a new May departure back to Ireland.

The idea behind the tour was to immerse themselves in the sport's roots and culture as well as get a game or two in, and with a bit of luck try and attend a major match. Valas in an email communication before departure said, "We want to foster our appreciation of the sport and the tradition of it." They achieved all their aims and more.

Once again the Wolves arrived into Shannon Airport early of a Thursday morning, May 27, 2010. Five years prior they had left as U.S. soldiers coming home from war but now returned a hurling club from America.

Officials of the airport got wind of the story and organized a presentation and photo shoot. The touring party were met by members of their host club, St. Mary's of Athenry (Daragh Madden's club & former All Ireland winners) and escorted the group back to the stone walled fields of Athenry in County Galway.

Athenry, a cozy heritage town in the west, was their base for the four days and the club and town welcomed the soldier hurlers as long lost cousins.

One of the first duties was to source several hurley makers as getting equipment in New Hampshire was a challenge. In the afternoon, the group arrived at St. Mary's club house. They were decked out in sharp blue jackets.

The player number in U.S. military style font was on the front along with an NHNG Guard crest. On the back was an image of a hurley and in large letters the word, 'WOLVES'.

The jackets, military haircuts, and the calm yet focused look communicated U.S. soldiers proud to call themselves 'Wolves' and passionate about hurling.

The chairperson of the Galway County Board, Gerry Larkin, St. Mary's chairman, Leo Coffey, former GAA President and Overseas Chairman Joe McDonagh, club secretary Brendan Burke and Tom Carr then treasurer (acted as tour liaison) were all on hand to welcome the team.

Illustration 25: Athenry Club House presentation, Eddie Clements (left) Ray Valas, Overseas GAA Chairman Joe McDonagh and Galway GAA Chairman Gerry Larkin (right) (Photo Sean Noonan)

Gifts were exchanged with St. Mary's presenting Valas and Sgt. 1st Class Clements with a bronze statue of two hurlers battling for possession. Wolves leader Valas told the St. Mary's Club, "This is truly a humbling experience, and I only wish our hurling skills warranted such exceptional treatment."

Those skills would soon be put to the test as, only off the plane a few hours, the Wolves first match was about to take place later that evening. Their opponents would be St. Mary's Junior adult side and because there was 11 players in the tour, it was decided to allow some members of the host club to join the American team.

It was a beautiful sunny evening in the grounds of Kenny Park in Athenry – St. Mary's own facility was being renovated. The Galway GAA County officials, and the senior hurling squad in training for a major championship game that weekend, would have used the park but making other arrangements kindly allowed the use of the field for the guests.

Freshly cut grass, clean line markers and colorful sideline flags made Kenny Park a picture. It was a very welcoming venue for the American touring party.

The first order of business was a drill and workout session with a local coach. The Wolves followed each command as if there lives depended on it.

By the time of throw-in a nice sized crowd had gathered as news of such events – particularly if a bunch of American soldiers are playing hurling – travels fast in an Irish rural town.

The game was played at a steady pace if friendly rhythm but entertaining with the Wolves trailing at half time. The Americans on the mixed team had a heartfelt talk at the break and their 'hands in' and battle cry of 'WOLVES' rang out from the sideline as they re-engaged.

In the second half they fared better with the Irish locals on the side coming to the fore and went ahead approaching the finish. However a late burst of scores from St. Mary's saw them take the game.

The teams met in the center of the pitch with spectators joining and gifts were exchanged. A few minutes prior, and seemingly out of nowhere, two young boys marched in the park and one of them carried a large American flag. The timing could not have been better as when it came to a combined team photo, the American flag was placed in the middle.

Illustration 26. Barley House Wolves & Athenry Junior teams after game at Kenny Park, Athenry in County Galway May 2010. (Photo Sean T. Noonan)

Later that night at a bar in Athenry the touring party enjoyed local song and hospitality and a few well earned pints. The group seamlessly fitted in and enjoyed the occasion.

The following day they headed to visit Ireland's capitol, Dublin, and take in the headquarters of the GAA at Croke Park Stadium. They got a guided tour and even got to walk out onto the hallowed turf at 'Croker'. One of the highlights was seeing their club crest on the GAA Club Wall.

Tour member and Military Journalist Luke Koladish, writing about the trip later in the Fall 2010 edition of the New Hampshire National Guard Magazine, captured the feelings of the soldiers at Croke Park that day.

In the magazine Koladish told of one soldier's impressions of the venue, "'The sheer size and history of both the stadium and the sport was overwhelming. You could really feel the energy,'" Wolves fullback 1st Lt. David DeVoy III noted.

Valas also was impressed by the GAA ethos in having a new club's crest on the wall:

> "'It speaks to the inclusiveness of the GAA that they would have the crest of a newly formed hurling club from New Hampshire displayed in the same location as clubs over a century old. It's inspiring as a new team.'"

The next day, back in Galway, was another special moment as it had been arranged that they would play the Irish Army's 1st Infantry Battalion of the 4th Brigade hurling team, at their base, Renmore Barrack's in Galway city.

The Barrack's field venue was spectacular as it looked out over Galway Bay. The teams were again mixed with some of the Irish lads again joining in with the visitors. After the Wolves went ahead in the latter stages, a late goal turned the game and the match ended in a draw.

The 4th Brigade formed a guard of honor for the Americans as they headed for the lockers. It was an emotional time for the Wolves.

After food in the mess hall, the hosts arranged a guided tour of the Barrack's Military Museum where the visitors learned about the local brigade and Irish military history. The tour also relaxed with a few pints in the Barracks social lounge while watching County Galway winning their first round hurling championship match of the season on TV. Later members of the 4th Brigade introduced their American colleagues to the 'City of the Tribes', Galway.

The last day of the tour had been much anticipated as Sunday May 30, would see the Wolves witness their first live Inter-County hurling championship game. The occasion was the Munster Hurling Championship Quarter Final and it pitted age-old rivals Cork v Tipperary. Think Yankees v Red Sox.

Cork being the event venue, meant the tour had to take a trip down to the 'Rebel City' on the south coast. The group savored Cork hospitality in a quick pre-game-time pint before making their way to the match. In their blue jackets, emblazoned with the hurley and 'Wolves' imagery, they stood out as they made their way by the banks of the River Lee to a packed Páirc Uí Chaoimh stadium.

The party located themselves on the city end terrace packed between Cork supporters, bearing their red and white colors, and Tipp followers sporting the blue and gold in a crowd of over 30,000.

The game was fast paced and furious from start to finish with a great atmosphere. The Americans over the course of the game let out gasps of excitement and incredulity at certain plays. Cork came away with a surprise win. Later Ray Valas told in a U.S. TV production, that watching the sport live at its highest level was impressive. "Seeing the match was a big one for us. Just getting the appreciation for tempo and skills at the top level was a big deal ... It was an eye-opener!"

On their final night back in Athenry at a reception in a local pub, there was a far away look in some of the soldiers' eyes. The next time they would be abroad would bring them back to the reality of what they do in life.

In America that summer, the Wolves got help with coaching from resident Irish and Cork native, Ruari O'Mahony. Their skills began to improve and what they also found was that there was a marked difference in play between the players who went on the trip to Ireland and those who did not.

The Barley House Wolves while looking continually to grow numbers have also been looking at developing a youth program. They try and run one youth hurling clinic every month from June to September. The clinics usually run for about an hour before a Blue/White match. The club held the first youth clinic in 2009 during the National Guard Kids' Summer Camp.

Later in the Fall of 2010, 12 members of the Barley House Wolves headed off to the border areas of Iraq and Kuwait for another one year tour of duty. They passed through Shannon once more but this time the soldiers packed their 'warrior' hurls as well as their rifles.

While the club kept growing at home, a new beginning would take hold overseas with the Kuwait Chapter of the BHW determined to play the first ever hurling match on an American base overseas in Kuwait.

Illustration 27: BHW Kuwait Chapter Crest (Design by CPT Adam Burritt)

Sgt. 1st Class Eddie Clements was the point man for the Wolves in the desert. The Wolves were eager to get some practice in and this meant getting more gear and equipment to them but first they would have to get clearance from their commanders to be allowed practice on base when in-between duty. There wasn't much time for any sport with long days of patrols and missions but they hoped eventually to be allowed permission to drill and play a game.

Meanwhile, back home in the states things were heating up big time.

Before Christmas, Cork 2010 hurling captain, Kieran Murphy, who had played in the game against Tipperary, was over in Boston for a wedding. He was approached by friend and Wolves coach, O'Mahony to give the club a hurling coaching session in Concord, NH. The Cork hurling captain came up to Concord and conducted an intense indoor hurling session with the Wolves.

Illustration 28: Captain Robert Burnham (left), LTC. Ray Valas (right) and center former County Cork Captain, Kieran Murphy before the 'hurling' drill session in Concord NH 2010 (Photo by Ruairi O'Mahony).

Club leader Valas gave his reaction to the session in an email communication:

> "We just had an amazing training session last night with Kieran Murphy, from Cork. It was amazing because we actually watched him play when we went to that match v Tipp.
>
> It was a great workout. New drills, high intensity, and a lot of fun. I just couldn't get over how generous it was of him to spend his limited time with us while in the states for a short visit. He is a great guy, and clearly a leader. No surprise to me that he was Captain of the [Cork] County panel last season," the Lieutenant Colonel said.

Murphy was also impressed by the attitude of the Wolves.

"It was a great honor for me to coach the lads. Their skill level was actually surprising for lads that have only picked it [hurling] so late in only the last five years and they were very capable of doing technical drills," the former County Cork captain told the podcast, GaelicSportsCast in early 2011.

In considering the soldiers' unlikely discovery of hurling, Murphy feels that there is scope for the sport to really grow:

> "You know they saw the sport on TV and fell in love with it and it shows you the potential for hurling to be developed. When you see the passion the guys have for the sport and see what they're doing over there setting up underage structures is actually quite inspirational and very refreshing ... driving the game on and trying to encourage guys to join their club."

Earlier that summer, the Wolves had peaked the interest of the soldiers' commanders who felt their story was worth telling.

The Pentagon TV Channel (tPC), the U.S. Defense Department communications outlet, filmed the Wolves over the summer at practice and at games for a half hour feature special to be shown in early January.

This would mean significant promotion for the sport of hurling in America and within the military community as the channel is broadcast to U.S. units across the country, around the world, and picked up also by U.S. satellite and cable subscribers.

On January 3rd, 2011, the New Hampshire National Army Guard soldiers story came to light in the program called, 'Two Fields, One Team,' and it was broadcast to an estimated total audience of 30 million.

Illustration 29. TPC TV Channel promo poster for 'Two Fields, One Team' (Photos by Sean T Noonan, compiled by Judy Plavnik)

The story highlighted the unity of the soldiers on the field of battle and their bond when playing hurling. One helped the other and there were definite similarities with both.

The 'warrior sport' was a perfect fit for the soldiers in so many ways as it kept them fit, focused and united. The bond between them was growing all the time.

The BHW Kuwait Chapter meanwhile was busy with missions between Kuwait and Iraq.

The Pentagon special featured several times on base and some 25 soldiers expressed an interesting in giving hurling a try. The reaction to the program was very positive also in Ireland with many media outlets contacting LTC Valas for interviews. Hurling clubs across the U.S. were also delighted with the exposure and the North American County Board (NACB) website linked to the tPC Video Special.

About a month after the special the Boston Herald carried a story on the Wolves in Kuwait while later in the year, National Public Radio (NPR) did a news feature on the club.

In order to get permission to play on base in Kuwait, they had to brief the Commander on the player protection plan in relation to helmets, gloves, and shin guards with ankle protection.

It was a slow process getting protective gear shipped out from New Hampshire but eventually the equipment arrived and the Kuwait Chapter of the Wolves got permission to play. Organizations and clubs in Ireland who had seen the Pentagon special online also played their part in sending equipment to the U.S. for shipment to the desert.

The soldiers faced many perilous days and least of their difficulties was getting some hurling in, however they did, but first they had to skill-up the rookies. Later they got to play that very first game by active U.S. service men in Kuwait at Arifjan on July 17, 2011.

Sgt. 1st Class Clements took the time and effort to write up a report on the Wolves in Kuwait and on the game. He sent the following 'Unclassified' document to this writer at the time:

> "The Barley House Wolves have had a small contingent of its team missing for about the past year. This small contingent has been deployed to Kuwait in support of Operation New Dawn with varying missions. Some members are in command cells responsible for the various camps in Kuwait while others provide security for convoys in Iraq. The deployed members of the team decided they wanted to keep their hurling skills sharp and started to practice and recruit new members.
>
> On 17 July 2011 the Kuwait Chapter of the Barley House Wolves held the very first hurling match on Kuwaiti soil.

The six a side match was played in the early morning hours in Kuwait, as it reaches 100 degrees by 8am most days in the month of July. The team split itself and formed a green team and a grey team for the match. With six of the players playing in their first match the Wolves anchored both teams with veteran players. The green team was captained by David DeVoy III and the grey team by Eddie Clements.

The grey team struck first sending a point over the bar. The veterans would control the first half of the match with DeVoy scoring a goal to put the green team ahead early in the game. Clements answered in the first half scoring a goal and two more points. Jason Burpee was all over the field making great plays to keep the sliotar away from the grey net. Jeremy Chaisson made several great stops in net for the green side to keep the score close. At the end of the first half the score was Grey 2-3 (9) and Green 1-0 (3).

The second half belonged to the rookies though, the green team charged back to keep the score even closer. DeVoy switched with Chaisson and played goal for the second half making great saves to keep the grey team at bay. With rookie Jon Demers moving up to forward he found the back of the net three times for the green team. With solid defense on both sides of the field from rookies Brandon Dodge and Eric Moore the teams continued to play hard.

Burritt made a save off Chaisson that would make Tim Thomas proud. Mike Ricard and Mike Moranti both moved the ball well up the side of the field to the green team forwards. Rookie Tim McMahon had two goals on the day for the grey team. Chaisson added two points late in the game to go along with his goal earlier in the second half to tie it up.

The last two minutes of the match were hard fought on both sides. The grey team though emerged victorious with a final score of Grey 4-8 (20) and Green 5-3 (18).

It was a great day for the Wolves and for hurling.

Edward L. Clements Jr
SFC, NHARNG
Delta Co. TF 3-197th

Illustration 30. BHW Kuwait Chapter Team July 2011, Kuwait (197 Fires Bde Public Affairs File Photo)

For the rest of the deployment, the Kuwait Chapter tried to get drills in whenever they could. They were also hoping that if all went well, and that meant mission completion and making it home alive, that four of the Kuwait Wolves would get their place in the team back home when the BHW played in their 3rd North American National Finals in San Francisco that September.

Back home meantime, the Barley House Wolves in Concord NH were in another battle, the new Junior C Adult Hurling Championship for mostly American hurlers in the Northwest GAA Division.

The Wolves had been going very well in the three team competition against rookies Worcester and brother club, Portland, and it was the latter two who made it to the final on August 27, 2011. Clements, a good center back and midfielder, was delighted to make it back in time to play in the final and it was the Wolves who took that very first Junior C Championship.

Next stop was San Francisco and the 2011 Nationals.

They had never won a game at the Championships and the Wolves had been determined all summer long to improve and make a better account of themselves this time around. That they had won the inaugural Junior C title was evidence that the team was really beginning to find its feet.

On Labor Day weekend, the Barley House Wolves were primed for battle.

Their first game in the Nationals Junior C Championship was a Quarter Final pairing with newcomers, Benton Brigade from Oregon on the Friday. The

Wolves claimed their first Nationals win with an impressive showing. Things became a little bit more tense as they were now into the semi final on Saturday with opponents, the Indianapolis HC second team. But again the Wolves were victorious when winning almost by double scores.

Meanwhile in the other part of the draw, St. Louis were going strong and they qualified to meet the Barley House Wolves to decide the 2011 Championship.

In the final both clubs competed hard throughout an exciting game. St. Louis started strongly but the BHW fought back and went up by two points at half time. However, the Wolves missed some scorable free hits (penalties) and lost out by a single point in the end. A heart-breaker.

Number 8 Valas, though disappointed after the game took nothing but positives from the experience.

"St. Louis is a great club; nothing but respect for them. We are hungrier than ever now, having tasted victory at this level. It will not slip away again," he told this writer in an email the following day. The final result was St. Louis 1-11 (14) BHW 3-4 (13).

The Barley House Wolves club is still growing with over 50 of a membership in early Spring 2012. The sport and the club means a lot to the National Guard soldiers especially in that transitional period after deployment. Helping them to make that adjustment and feel a sense of continued comradeship, the club and hurling speaks to them personally.

National Guard Capt. Rob Burnham, in September 2011 told National Public Radio's Shannon Mullen about the similarities to a mission. "I've said that stepping off the pitch is something like stepping off the field of battle or coming off a mission."

Though similar the hurling field battle helps the soldiers who had experienced the real thing. "It's something healthy, something physical that allows you to blow off some steam. And something to look forward to that's different than being member of, say, the VFW (Veterans of Foreign Wars)."

When talking with club co-founder LTC Ray Valas, the NPR reporter began to realize that hurling meant more than just keeping fit and staying in touch. Said Valas:

> "I recently had a guy that's played for a few years come up to me and say, 'You know, I never mentioned this to you, but I just wanted to thank you for getting this club started.' I said, 'No sweat.' 'No,' he

said, 'you don't understand. After Afghanistan, I had a really rough time, and this changed my life.'"

That soldier was Sgt. 1st Class Roy Lowes. He told NPR, "When I came up to Ray and told him that, I think that moment was ... it took being on the hurling team for me to understand some of my own, um, psychological — I guess — maybe, needs."

Lowes had deployed to Afghanistan in 2004 as a combat medic and to help train Afghan soldiers. Said NPR:

> "He says that because of the constant danger, he felt safe only with people he knew he could trust.
>
> I wish there was a way I could just go, click, switch it off, you know, as you take your uniform off, that you shed that. But you can't. I'm a lot better now, but when I first got back, I couldn't stand in line in Walmart for more than a couple minutes, and I had to leave."

Lowes says he was jumpy and aggressive for months. Then he heard about the Barley House Wolves.

"'Some part of me really needed that small team environment," he says. "'That player who has the same jersey as I have, I know he's there, I know he has my back, I don't have to think about it, I don't have to second-guess anything.'" Said NPR, "Lowes says now he gets stressed out when he can't make it to practice."

The Barley House Wolves will be looking to defend their Northeast GAA Junior C Hurling Championship title in the summer of 2012 and depending on their mission schedule they hope to make it to the NACB Nationals in Philadelphia on Labor Day Weekend, and perhaps go one better than last year.

The decision that members of 'Charlie Company' took at Shannon Airport in March 2005 was a moment of courage reflecting all that is good in the American spirit. The type of spirit that asks ...'what if..?' and answers ... 'why not!'...

Since that fateful day, the New Hampshire National Guard army soldiers within the backdrop of war, have followed through on their decision. As a unit, as a team, and as Americans, they feel the better for it.

Sgt. 1st Class Clements in speaking to Koladish for his magazine article put it like this. "We look at a hurling game as a battle. So that bond we had in battle over there, we carry onto the pitch."

The Wolves bring that unique passion and spirit to the sport of hurling. Playing the sport has helped forge a stronger bond. The game's unfamiliarity and uniqueness started everyone on an equal footing, and maybe other U.S. military personnel will also reach out to the ancient sport.

Wolves co-founder Lt. Col. Valas told this author in a communication that he thinks the military is a ripe recruiting ground for new hurlers and hopes that other units in time will get hooked on hurling:

> "One of our development plans is to try and get other state's National Guard units to start clubs and develop some good rivalries. If you think about it the military is a good pot of soil to plant a hurling club in.
>
> You have groups of men who are fit and enjoy competitive activities and new challenges."

Hurling is also reaching out to the young generation as the sport is spreading like wildfire across American college campuses.

Chapter 7

College Wildfire

U.S. College hurling had a premature start at the campus of St. Mary's College California. It wasn't given a chance to flourish. Today however, there is a new drive to bring hurling to west coast colleges and such has been its success that the sport is spreading life wildfire on campuses all across America.

The main drive began in 2006 at Stanford University where student John Mulrow was teaching an Irish-American culture student class. Mulrow has Irish ancestry but little did he know that a field trip to San Francisco would herald the arrival of the Irish sport of hurling to the west coast college circuit.

He remembered seeing hurling as a child but had never played and was eager to find out more. So on St. Patrick's Day he took the class on a field trip to San Francisco where he met Irish immigrant and the then San Francisco GAA PRO, Eamonn Gormley – who would go on to become the driving force of college hurling in California and America.

Gormley stands out as one who has reached out to the local community and he went about this in a novel way at the time:

> "When I was PRO for the Western Division San Francisco GAA, one of the things I did was set up an information booth at outdoor events in the San Francisco Bay area. I would go to farmers markets and festivals and basically explain what Gaelic football and hurling is," recalled Gormley in an interview for GaelicSportsCast in March 2010.

One of these events was the St. Patrick's Day Parade in San Francisco and it was here he met John Mulrow:

> "He told me he was interested in hurling and wanted to get involved and [asking] was there a local club he could play in. So I said, you are a student of Stanford, have you thought about setting up a club on campus and this was something that had never been done before to my knowledge."

The student was given some coaching DVD's and Gormley also arranged for donations of hurling equipment from a local club as he also organized the aid of Irish natives who got on board with coaching.

Playing a key role also in getting essential equipment to the new hurlers was Milwaukee's Dave Olson, who was North American GAA hurling development officer at the time. Gormley started a beginners clinic for hurling on the Stanford campus and from there things got moving.

At the start as a means of getting noticed on campus, the initiated took the art of marketing to new levels.

"We started playing on the Sigma Nu lawn ... and our goal would be to try to hit the ball onto the Muwekma lawn, all the way at the other end of the row," Mulrow later told the Stanford Daily college paper.

Illustration 31. Stanford Team 2011 (Photo courtesy of Stanford HC)

However, when Mulrow went abroad, interest faded until students Ben Arevalo and Sam Svoboda, hearing about it through the campus newspaper, decided to take up the challenge.

A fledgling group got going and during practice time, campus heads were beginning to turn. None more so than Irish native and faculty member, Eoin Buckley:

> "I saw some guys playing hurling out on Wilbur field [while driving home one day] and knew I wanted to play again.

I played as a kid till I was sixteen, so I gave them a bit of coaching but they seemed to know what they were doing," Buckley told the college paper.

From there the group grew and by the Spring of 2008, they got recognition as a college sport.

Soon word of Stanford playing hurling made its way to the college's immortal sporting rivals, University of California Berkeley. That fall, Fionnan O'Conner got hurling started on campus at Berkeley.

Fionnan is a first generation Irish American with Irish immigrant parents from Dublin. As a boy he went with his parents for the annual summertime vacation to Ireland and while there his God Father Patrick DeRoe would take him to hurling games. "I remember seeing County Galway beat County Kilkenny in the 2005 All Ireland Championship Semi Final, and being blown away," he recalled to this author in a recent Facebook interview.

His cousins in Ireland played hurling with their local club Scoil Ui Chonnail and often Fionnan used to puck a ball around with them. A seed had been planted and when it came time for him to enter college at Berkeley he found out that hurling had already started at Stanford:

> "When I went to Berkeley, I saw that John Mulrow had started a hurling team at San Francisco and I coaxed my roommates Nick Nordahl (current club president), Zach Streng and Josh Roberts into starting a club of our own.
>
> We got in contact with Sam Svoboda over at Stanford and he put us in touch with Eamonn Gormley and the local GAA who've been tremendously supportive ever since."

No matter where one goes in the world an Irish man is likely to pop up, and as in Stanford with Buckley, so too another was found in Berkeley. "Coincidentally there was a very strong hurler, Liam Ready, getting his PhD at Berkeley and he gave the captaining and expertise to get the whole thing off the ground," O'Conner recalled.

Fionnan O'Connor has since graduated from Berkeley, and interestingly, is currently writing a book on the history of whiskey.

Later in 2008, Gormley in an effort to get things organized founded the California Collegiate Gaelic Athletic Association (CCGAA) as there was increasing interest from students at other California colleges looking to start hurling on their campuses.

Illustration 32. Cal Berkeley Team 2010 (Photo courtesy of Berkeley HC)

So with the two colleges up and running the next thing to do was get them playing each other and that wasn't a tough call as 'Cal' and Stanford's sporting rivalry is legendary. Mulrow returned to campus later that year and once again got involved with the club as an organizer and player.

On Saturday, January 31st, 2009 at Stanford University, the first ever Inter-Collegiate hurling match took place in America.

Faculty as well as students were allowed to line-out, so this lead to the inclusion of two Irish natives on the more inexperienced Cal side, while Stanford had one Irish player.

That first game turned out to be a thriller.

Stanford got off to a good start and it looked like they would go on to victory but Cal came storming back in the second half to take the game by one point, on a final score of three goals and 10 points (3-10 = 19 points total) to 3-9 (18).

Despite losing the opener in an aggregate best of two series, Stanford went on to create history and win the first ever Northern California Collegiate Hurling Championship.

Eamonn Gormley described the importance of that first game both from a historical and cultural perspective:

> "This game has an exciting future on U.S. college campuses. We had a bigger non-playing crowd at this game than we get at some of our championship games in the city.
>
> Inviting the American public to watch a game between a club called Naomh Padraig and a club called Na Fianna would give them a higher standard to look at, but it wouldn't mean anything to them.
>
> Cal v Stanford – that means a lot to them as you could see from the enthusiastic support that came out today," Gormley said in a report on the NACB website.

Suddenly, the sport for the very first time was being presented through an American cultural paradigm. Stanford and Cal were giving hurling an American voice that it never had before. The sport was taking on American cultural norms. No longer was it hidden away within the Irish immigrant population. Hurling now had the fascinating possibility of breaking into mainstream America through the vast college sporting network.

After Stanford administrators gave the hurling group the go-ahead to set up an official club on campus, Berkeley soon followed suit. This now allowed a Freshman on campus at Stanford or Berkeley, when deciding on the multitude of team sports on offer in the Club Sports Program, to choose to play Hurling for the first time in the history of both institutions. This alone is a ground breaking development for the advancement of the sport in the U.S.

Should a fresh faced Stanford student perchance wonder what the heck is hurling anyway, the following is what he will learn when he visits the Hurling Club link:

> "Stanford Hurling is a team dedicated to spreading the sport of hurling throughout the Stanford campus and to other colleges as well. Hurling is an ancient sport that originated in Ireland and is the fastest field sport in the world. The game shares common skills with many other sports and is played like a mix between lacrosse and field hockey.
>
> In 2009 we became the first team to win a collegiate cup competition in U.S. history when we beat Cal in a two-game aggregate series. Almost all of our current players picked up the sport at Stanford, so there is certainly no experience required.

If you're interested in staying active, learning an incredible sport and having a lot of fun, please please contact us or stop by one of our practices!"

Before 2008, this athletic offering did not exist.

John Mulrow points to another advantage of having a new field sport on campus is that a student, who might not cut it at making the regular mainstream team sports, gets a chance through hurling to make a team and take on Cal. "Most students here wouldn't get a chance to play a game for Stanford against Cal. Here is that chance," he explained to the college newspaper, the Stanford Daily.

An important outcome of Hurling's official recognition at Stanford is that like the 23 other sports on offer at the college, the hurling club is eligible to receive college funding, crucial field space and a booth at the activities fare for recruitment.

Stanford Hurling Club founder, Mulrow, after that historic first match, told Eamonn Gormley – who documented the event with unique video footage for You Tube – that the sport had a chance of gaining a foothold:

"I like to think of hurling is just an awesome sport that people haven't found out enough about yet. I know it's pretty popular in Ireland but it's spreading through the college system pretty quickly. This is the first year that we have two teams in the California Collegiate Gaelic Athletic Association an official team, and man, when people see hurling they want to play.

It really speaks to the athlete in a lot of people and it's catching on like wildfire. And, whether you are Irish or not, you are going to love playing this game."

Word about the new series and Championship game also made it onto a local TV network's evening news. Gormley's video recordings of the series and distribution through You Tube helped get the word out about hurling on college campuses in the region.

The following year in 2010, the 2nd in the series took place and this time it was Cal Berkeley who took home the honors. Two Irish natives played with both teams and a change saw the young Northern California Collegiate Hurling Championship played over a three game series.

The second championship began that February with Berkeley – much improved and also pulling from a bigger sporting pool on campus - exacting revenge in taking Game 1 with an easy 21 (4-9) to 13 (3-4) win. Stanford had to win Game 2 to stay alive and they did just that in a narrow 15 to 13 victory.

Game 3 was a high scoring thriller with 11 goals, where Cal this time won by two points 25 (5-10) to 23 (6-5). Cal Berkeley took the series and the second Championship.

Students signing up at both colleges spoke of their excitement for an Eamonn Gormley You Tube video after one of the games.

Chris Stucky from Stanford said, "I love the game. It's fantastic. Ever since I started playing I have just fallen in love with it."

While Berkeley player, Sam Crenshaw wrote in his college newspaper (The Daily Californian) of how, "Hurling is an amazingly exciting and fast-paced game that has already made history on campus."

CCGAA founder Gormley also felt that the second series was a great success with a notable improvement by the young players in their new game:

> "I'm very happy with how the series went. The one thing that everybody is talking about is how the standard of play has greatly improved from last year.
>
> It's a miracle that these games are happening at all. It wasn't so long ago that there was no concept of college hurling. Now it's gone from zero up to a full-fledged championship. The next step is to get others on board and to get them into the championship next year," he told the podcast, GaelicSportsCast.

In late 2009, Gormley formed the first ever national collegiate body to govern Gaelic sports across America, The National Collegiate Gaelic Athletic Association (NCGAA). "We're on the road to something big I think," was Gormley's summation to GaelicSportsCast.

The NCGAA hopes to continue the development of hurling, and even introduce Gaelic football as well to U.S. college campuses.

Other California college students wanted to get in on the act with fledgling hurling teams trying to get off the ground in the University of Southern California, Cal Poly San Luis Obispo, UCLA, UC Davis, San Diego State, Loyola Marymount University in Los Angeles, and University of San Francisco.

Interest in playing hurling has also reached along the northwest to places like Oregon State University and the University of Washington.

Stanford Captain Sam Svoboda thinks the game has a future:

> "When most people try it they like it a lot. You can see in just these past three years when we started it up, there were no other teams in California. Then Cal got started, and then USC started the beginnings of a team.
>
> Then this year it has grown even more as USC is nearly ready, along with University of California (UC Davis), San Diego State University (SDSU) Oregon and Washington State. So you can really tell it's spreading all up and down the west coast," declared the young American hurler in a 2010 email interview.

Illustration 33. UC Davis Hurling Team 2011 (Photo courtesy of UC Davis HC)

UC Davis, located near Sacramento, had been trying to form a club with the help of Cal and Stanford, who occasionally traveled for clinics and practice. Student friends had heard about what was happening with hurling in Stanford and wanted to see if they also could get a club going on campus.

One of those students was first generation Irish American James Daly and he told the podcast GaelicSportsCast about the early efforts to get things off the ground:

> "I transferred into Davis and there was some Freshmen talking about starting the sport there. They had friends who heard about the one in Stanford. So then, I found those guys and pooled my resources with people who were interested and got out training."

Though familiar with Gaelic sports, as his Dad who is from County Cork in Ireland played Gaelic football, James preferred hurling. He had already joined a new all American team, the San Francisco Rovers formed in 2009, and so had some experience of the game.

Daly would became co-chairperson and coach of the new UC Davis club along with fellow student and Rovers player, Mitch Hennessy.

Daly enjoys playing the sport and sees hurling having an equalizing element about it. "I definitely like how it's fast and it's physical. Having a hurl in your hand is not about being the biggest person on the field, it's about using that tool effectively. You know, anything can happen."

Eventually, a solid core of about 15 players began to take root at Davis. During the summer of 2010, the UC Davis college newspaper The Aggie, featured efforts in getting hurling going on campus in an article entitled, "UC Davis Hurling Club brings international sport to Davis." Daly told the paper that the sport, "sells itself."

Sophomore and co-chairman, Mitch Hennessy, felt his background in baseball, tennis, golf and crew has helped him learn the sport of hurling. "It just felt natural to me to play this sport ... I can incorporate skills from every other sport I've played and use them in hurling." He added that to play at the highest level, a hurler not only needs a lot of speed but must also have endurance.

This author has seen video footage of Hennessy's play, and after only two years of the new sport under his belt, it is remarkable how he has developed as a hurler.

Another student to get hooked on hurling is Conner-Collado. He had a background in soccer, basketball, crew, and track and field before taking up hurling. He had recently returned from a trip to Ireland where he had learned about the sport. While walking by practice at Davis one evening, he decided it was time to join the ranks.

In the 2011 championship, newcomer University of California (UC Davis) joined Cal and Stanford for the series. A new format saw teams getting more game time with every team playing the other twice, resulting in four matches for the season.

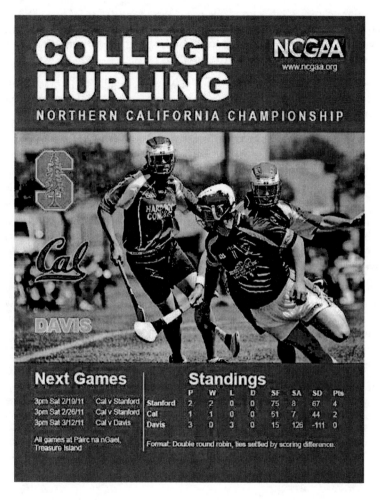

Illustration 34: NCGAA 2011 Championship (Image courtesy of NCGAA).

As to be expected, it turned out to be a baptism of fire for the students from Davis as unfortunately they came out second best in their games with Stanford, and champion's Berkeley.

It was left to Cal and Stanford to fight it out once more for the Championship and in the first game Cal once again did enough and it left

Stanford with a 14 point gap to bridge if they were to take back the title. The final game in the series was played at Stanford and the home side saw a good smattering of campus student support, and South Bay Irish, who over the years had taken a shine to the team.

Stanford started brightly in the final, however as their rivals had done in the past, Berkeley soon got back into the swing of things and went on to retain the 3rd Northern California Championship when winning by 36 to 28.

Meanwhile in Los Angeles, the University of Southern California (USC) – known in sports for their powerful USC Trojans football team - is still trying to get hurling up and running on campus.

Players from San Diego State University (SDSU) joined USC in LA in a scrimmage match against Cal in early 2010 and ever since then USC has been trying to increase awareness of the game. This fledgling group was featured in the college newspaper, the Daily Trojan, in March of 2010 and regular player at practice Pat Sebastian said it can be tough to recruit new players when the sport is not seen:

> "This is the club's first year as a school-sanctioned sport, and recruitment has been slow. That's partly because few people know what hurling is ... in theory it sounds dumb ... I'm trying to explain: 'We have this stick thing.' But you can't equate it to anything in America."

It is difficult to explain a sport that doesn't appear anywhere in the U.S. on mainstream free-to-air TV. Nevertheless, the USC group is trying to get to a stage where they can compete against the other three California colleges.

The steady growth of hurling on California college campuses has also influenced off-campus clubs to take up the sport in the San Francisco Bay Area. The San Francisco Rovers Hurling team are a prime example.

THE ROVERS

The San Francisco Rovers have become something of phenomenon amongst the Irish community in the Bay Area.

The Rovers are a group of young Irish Americans who came together in 2009 to form a Junior C Adult hurling squad. Their success has been an eye-opener.

The club had been in the works for a number of years and consists of mostly local youth, with the majority having an Irish heritage. The growth of college hurling influenced the setting up of the club as another young student, this time from City College of San Francisco (CCSF), Bryan Lynch, founded the club. Once started, players from UC Davis and UC Berkeley were also calling themselves Rovers.

The resident Irish hurling community has supported this team from the start with several of the coaches and resident Irish players, taking an interest in growing the sport locally. The team competes in the Junior (adult lower level) Hurling competitions in the San Francisco GAA leagues at Treasure Island in the city and over the past three years have stunned spectators with their performances.

After forming in April of 2009, the young team got some valuable game-time against both Berkeley and Stanford during the summer. Boosted by two wins, they decided to head to their first National Championship in September and compete in the mostly all American Junior C Adult Hurling Championships in Boston.

The Rovers first Nationals turned out to be a momentous occasion for the young Americans as they went undefeated (4-0) and took home the Junior C Adult Championship.

The following year they came back for more but this time competed in the Junior B adult grade at the Nationals. However, the American side rose to the occasion and won their second National Championship in a row. This was an historic achievement as they were an all American team with no Irish players.

In that Junior B grade, they would have come up against teams with Irish native players and to triumph in such competition was noteworthy and an indicator of what might be possible in the future. Rovers founder Lynch put things into perspective on what the early victories meant to the young American side:

> "When you think that it started out with a bunch of fellas pucking around in the evenings and turned into registering a team, traveling to Boston and winning it [Junior C] was definitely a good feeling at the time. We didn't really have much expectation going there but we had some well fought games to bring us the cup," he recalled in a recent interview with this author.

The Rovers had now earned the right to play at the Junior Adult A level (Senior is top level) in 2011, and on home turf in San Francisco. This meant that they would be up against teams with all Irish players – both resident in San Fran and those drafted from Ireland for the summer. This would be a major step up for the young team whose average age is 19-24. However, they never got a chance to prove themselves in the Nationals at the Junior A level.

The early part of 2011 brought change as a lot of players moved on and when it came to competing in the second highest level at Junior A in the San Francisco GAA Championship, the mostly American side found the going difficult:

> "We lost a lot of players from the first two years and playing in the Junior A Championship was tough having a team made up of 90 percent American born players.
>
> Playing against teams made up completely of Irish born players, both resident and summer players who had been playing all their lives, it was tough to compete at that level but we did come close to winning two games just not close enough."

The Rovers have added more Irish resident players since said Lynch and even have drafted some Irish players over for the summer. They also hope to field Junior A and B teams in the summer of 2012.

What started off as a young American team has now had to draft in Irish players in order to compete at close to the top level. They have had to adopt to the Irish model of doing things, ready or not. A model that has failed repeatedly to grow Gaelic sports in this country and kept things squarely within the Irish ex-pat community.

The 'Rovers try as they did, never made it out of the high level local championships to qualify for the Nationals at home.

Still, Lynch remains positive and feels that there is a good future for the club with players coming through youth ranks. "There's a lot of good players coming up through the youth problem that will be sure to be strong players in a couple years. It's looking good for the future and we're looking forward to this year."

But will those young players stick around to adult level or will they also move on as has been the trend in New York GAA youth circles??

MIDWEST COLLEGE HURLING

In the Midwest meanwhile, hurling is also spreading at an incredible rate in colleges as eager hurlers have sprouted in universities in Indiana, Minnesota, Ohio, and Pennsylvania.

The first ever Midwest collegiate hurling match was held in Indiana on April 4, 2009. This game took place at Lake Sullivan Park, Indianapolis, and featured two of the regions great college sporting rivals, Purdue University and Indiana University. These two colleges have been the driving force in getting hurling started on college campuses in the Midwest. Purdue, with greater playing experience, took honors on the day.

Purdue began playing hurling in 2005 while Indiana got hooked two years later.

The original members of the hurling club at Purdue University were: Matt Schwertfeger, Kit Smith, Zack Hamilton, Burke Eizinger, Andy McHenry, Jon Suhl, Mick Sweeney, David Pinkston, Mike Yurkovich, Matt Suhl, and Bel St. John.

During the research of this book, an email interview was conducted with Matt Schwertfeger where he told of Purdue's learning curve. It by and large replicated what had been going on at colleges on the west coast.

Illustration 35. Purdue Hurling Team 2009 (Courtesy of Purdue HC)

At the start, Purdue weren't sure of where to begin but begin they did:

> "When the club began, we did not really know what to do; exactly what skills there even were, or how to even coach. The internet provided some much needed help, and three fellas [Irish immigrants] from County Wexford, Limerick and Dublin in Ireland were able to help out," Schwertfeger explained.

The fact that new hurling recruits had to surf the web for information on hurling, something that other new adult clubs have had to do as well, points to the failure of the North American GAA and the parent body in Ireland to properly set in motion a marketing plan in promoting the game worldwide.

At a micro level, the North American GAA's recently introduced games development program has been a positive move with coaching and refereeing clinics and officers, made available for new clubs. But the American governing body has neglected planning and promotional strategies in eliminating uncertainty when someone forms a new hurling club.

Putting information and resources links on the NACB website is useful for an American athlete who stumbles upon the site but there is zero mainstream promotion on a nationwide basis to point athletes and potential hurlers in that direction. Money matters may be an issue here but the North American County Board expertise and volunteer nature can also be problematic. We return to the issue of the national promotion of hurling in the concluding chapter.

Schwertfeger attended one of the NACB's coaching clinics and completed a Foundation Level and later a Level One course. This coaching knowledge had the desired effect on practice at the Purdue campus:

> "With more coaching experience and knowledge, we have seen the learning curve lessen. Players are picking up the fundamental skills much more quickly than in previous years. And, I think the general athletic ability of our players hasn't changed all that much from 2005 to now," said Schwertfeger in the interview.

He also pointed out that those who had developed hand-eye coordination, particularly through their lacrosse background, found it easier to learn the basics with baseball players coming in a close second. But he added that pretty much by the end of a semester "most people are generally equal."

Hopes were high after that first Midwest game and the former Purdue student-player, Schwertfeger, thought there was a real chance that the sport would continue to grow:

> "This first Midwest collegiate hurling match complements the matches already taking place on the West Coast. University of California Berkeley and Stanford have been battling in the first American college matches ever.
>
> With more college clubs emerging at colleges in Wisconsin and California and at Ohio State, the future of American collegiate hurling looks promising," he wrote in 2009 on the Indianapolis Hurling Club website.

Schwertfeger also pointed to the help of former North American Hurling Development Officer, Dave Olson, and Tom Sheehy, the Central GAA Division Games Development Administrator, for getting that first game off the ground in the Midwest.

But it hasn't always been plain sailing as one of the biggest problems is that when club founders and organizers graduate or transfer, there tends to be a vacuum. As a result a new college hurling support organization had to be set up in the region. A collection of like minded students felt that it was time to set-up a governing body for college hurling and so in September 2009, the Midwest Collegiate Hurling Association (MCHA) was formed.

Its basic mission: to organize competition schedules, grow the sport and help new clubs get started. Soon students at Penn State PA, University of Michigan were asking the MHCA for advice and help in setting up a club.

Schwertfeger who is the current chairman of the MCHA feels there has been great progress in such a short period of time as the initial two colleges sprang to six with Ohio State, University of Akron OH, University of Pittsburgh, and University of Minnesota, all starting off teams.

In an interview for the podcast GaelicSportsCast in early 2011, he expressed his delight in Midwest growth:

> "I mean it was fantastic, it really was. I expected slow going for a while with maybe having Purdue and IU (Indiana University) and maybe Ohio State, but having six of them and having other people coming out and saying, 'hey, I'm interested in doing this', it kind of made everything worth while. It made it feel like that we were doing something; getting the word out.
>
> People are contacting us and it is fantastic. It's far surpassing what I thought it would be in a year or two."

Spring and fall competitions have taken place over the last two years at various locations in the Midwest with the emphasis on every team getting game-time towards the development of the sport in the regional college circuit. Since the body's foundation there have been regular clinics for coaching and referee courses for the growing student hurling population in the area.

As with the majority of the new adult hurling clubs forming in places with no historic attachment to Irish culture and hurling, so to with U.S. colleges. While the numbers involved at any one college at present are small – this of course without any organized national media promotion drive for the sport, and, no free-to-air viewing (of Irish championship) for students to get a feel for the game – the potential for hurling to gain a solid foothold on colleges campuses clearly exists.

When you consider that the average U.S. college campus population is as high as 50,000 – bigger than some counties in Ireland alone – the potential to spread a new sport is great. Then factor in that there are a lot of young people who are sports minded, fit and looking to keep fit, and who are looking to try out something new when in college, a sport like hurling has the potential to thrive on American campuses.

Schwertfeger has been there from the very start as he is the founder of the hurling club at Purdue. Like other Americans his discovery of hurling was quiet accidental.

He went to Ireland to study at the National University of Ireland in Galway (NUIG) and it was here that he found hurling:

> "I stumbled across the University team at practice one day. I asked what it was and they were more than happy to show me the ropes, show me everything. I even went back a few more times and they gave me a little more instruction. I was there with a friend of mine and we said, 'hey, we should play this when we get back. It's really a good game. We enjoy this.'"

Sure enough when they got back stateside and to IU, they started things off and at their first practice they had about two dozen people – "we kind of hit the ground running," Schwertfeger stated in the GaelicSportsCast interview.

Early summer of 2011 was another momentous occasion for the sport and another first. The month of May heralded the first ever national college championship with the playing of the National Collegiate Hurling Championship in Chicago.

Berkeley traveled as winners on the west coast to play IU and Purdue. There was also an East v West competition that featured a collection of college players from both regions. The tournament was held over two days at Chicago GAA headquarters at Gaelic Park in the city with Indy taking the historic first title over Cal Berkeley.

Illustration 36. 2011 NCGAA Championship inaugural winners, Indiana University (Courtesy of NCGAA

The national college body the NCGAA, then announced that the 2012 College Nationals would move west to Stanford in California. This competition took place over Memorial Day weekend, Saturday May 26 – May 27 at the Palo Alto campus.

Last year Indiana University won the inaugural event – they were unable to make it to California this time – but their state neighbors Purdue did. It turned out to be a worthwhile trip for the Indiana college as they went unbeaten throughout the tournament, taking UC Davis and Berkeley in the early rounds before accounting for host's Stanford in the final on a scoreline of Purdue 30 (5-15) Stanford 12 (2-6). Third place went to Cal Berkeley when defeating UC Davis by 27 to 22.

As well as the rising number of universities taking up hurling in the west and midwest regions, there has also been further growth in the south with a college in Tennessee now starting to play the sport. Over on the east coast meanwhile, the hurling bug is also catching on as recently three new colleges have taken up the sport and in three separate states.

In their innovative November 2011 Newsletter, the MCHA said, the recent "largest movement by far has been on the East Coast. Three clubs have been formed on the campuses of University of Massachusetts, Amherst; University of Connecticut [and] University of New Hampshire."

The newcomers got to taste the action at games in November (2011) when playing at Hartford, Connecticut. This latest development in the East has delighted the MCHA. It is very encouraging for the sport's future in America as the spread to the south and east, allows hurling to define a truly national identity.

Illustration 37. UCONN Huskies with Northeast GDA M.Moynihan (left). (Photo courtesy of Mike Moynihan)

Looking to the South, the new club in Tennessee is another example of the sports growth, especially in states with little or no Irish immigrant population. These southern and latest U.S. college hurlers hail from Middle Tennessee State University (MTSU). They have already joined the growing ranks as they played at home against Purdue in December 2011.

It was a beautiful 60 degrees Fahrenheit at MTSU for the host's first competitive game with a nice crowd gathered for throw-in. Both clubs fielded full teams and the rookies got off to a great start with an early goal, but Purdue fought back and with their more experienced players went on to take the game.

The NCGAA reporting on the game said that the event was a great success. "The match was yet another demonstration of the growth of hurling on college campuses in the United States. MTSU has a promising future and are a welcome addition to the stage of collegiate hurling."

The story of how hurling started at Tennessee State is noteworthy in that it is an exact copy of how things got started seven years ago in Purdue.

Two students from MTSU in May of 2011 went to Ireland to study abroad for one month. Jamie Norris and Ryan Buckley found themselves at the Tipperary Institute and like Schwertfeger, and without prompting from anyone, discovered hurling when stumbling across a group playing one evening:

> "While over there, that's where we saw hurling for the first time in Tipperary. And, we kind of fell in love with it and wanted to bring it back to the states. Once we got back we found out that it was already here and wanted to start our own team because Tennessee didn't have one," said Buckley in a recent telephone interview (2012) with this author.

The MTSU hurling co-founders made friends with the Tipperary college hurlers and got to see their first ever hurling match live when they traveled with the group to see a major championship game – yet another battle between rivals, Tipperary and Cork.

Buckley thought the spectacle was fantastic and really caught the imagination. "I thought it was wonderful. Extremely fast pace. Captivating. I couldn't look away for the entire match. Unlike any other sport I've seen! Even soccer or football have never held my attention like hurling did."

Roone Arledge would already be setting plans in motion.

A few days before the match a few of the Tipperary Institute hurlers showed the Tennessee students a few basic guidelines for playing and understanding the rules of the game. This Hurling 101, "made things a lot easier to watch once we understood what was going on," recounted Norris.

Before that evening the Tennessee students ... Norris, though Irish Amercian, had never heard of hurling before:

> "I hadn't heard anything before [about hurling]. I'm a football fan myself so it was new to me, but again ... it was so much fast paced. You can't turn away from it. Even if you glance away for a few seconds, you'll miss a lot of things that go on, which is something that I really love about the sport.

It's real fast paced. Get's your attention. It's very physical as well as football, and that's something else that made me enjoy the game of hurling," Norris said.

Like his fellow student, Ryan Buckley also plays football and baseball, and has been playing for the past 10 years. But when the two came back to their own campus Middle Tennessee State, they set about starting off a hurling club.

The college had about 25,000 students in 2011 – small by U.S. standards – but it has the highest number of undergraduates for any third level institution in the state of Tennessee.

Norris and Buckley began their efforts by gathering interest from athletes looking to learn a new sport. The two did the best they could trying to do some coaching on what they learned and saw in Ireland and also by reaching out to coaches with hurling clubs in the region and beyond.

The regional hurling community in Atlanta, GA, Indianapolis and Orlando, Florida, helped out as much as possible. Weekend coaching camps were held as well as watching videos on You Tube, which helped to advance skill levels, and soon the numbers grew to about 15 regular players at practice.

Illustration 38. MTSU scoop drill session with GDA Colm Egan (Courtesy of Jamie Norris, MTSU HC)

Help also came from the direction of Indiana University where later in 2011, after only about seven months of starting off the sport, Middle Tennessee State University got to play that first competitive game against Purdue.

As in Purdue and elsewhere, it's not just Irish Americans who are discovering the sport as a look at the Roster at practice in MTSU shows that "every athlete" is up for the game with names like: Kammerzell, Hayman, Solomon, Nowotarski, Thomas, Biggs, and Weidman.

Jamie Norris believes that hurling has a real chance to increase in popularity on American college campuses. "A lot of people grow up playing different sports. This is something new. A lot of people are looking for something new, something exciting. And, I think this is something like the new hot sport that's going to come through."

Like new hurlers on Western and Midwest campuses, the Southern students – who have a solid history of playing football and baseball – are blown away by hurling. Students are telling similar stories all across America. They are describing similar experiences. Hurling is speaking directly to them – Hurling is selling itself.

If the sport gets the proper national marketing support, then there is every reason to believe that more and more students will get hooked.

Norris and Buckley are building a solid core of players and with continuing local hurling network support they hope the sport can blossom at Middle Tennessee State. They are also keen to get things started in other colleges in the area. They are looking to Nashville, which is just 30 miles north of the campus at Freesboro, in order that local competition can begin.

In late 2011 on the East Coast meanwhile, the rookie hurlers at University of New Hampshire (UNH) are on a mission to promote their new sport at the college as they have set-up the 'Students for the Advancement of Collegiate Hurling'.

The aim is to teach students about the sport of hurling and the young group has already started skill workshops on campus. The new student body got official recognition from UNH as a student organization in April 2012 and is to later apply for sports club status.

Meanwhile, at the University of Connecticut (UConn) hurling with a solid core of players has also taken its first tentative steps. UConn took part in their first ever hurling tournament in Rockland, New York on Saturday, October 25, 2011 and did extremely well.

The event was put together by American John Wilkinson, President of the UConn hurlers, Fulbright Scholar, Cuan O Flathartha (son of Tomas O Flathartha, well known Gaelic football manager in Ireland) and UConn team mentor, Alex Whitney.

UConn did very well in the Group stages of the tournament as they beat Rockland in their opening game, then just lost to Allentown Hibernians PA, before triumphing over Baltimore in their final group game. In the semi-final a Washington DC side just shaded the young student team by a single point. It was a fantastic start for UConn and a good beginning for college hurling competition in the east.

Another historic first for U.S. college hurling took place at Hartford, Connecticut on Saturday November 12, 2011. This event saw the three new hurling teams in the east, UNH, UConn and University of Massachusetts (UMass) take part in 7 a side Hurling Tournament. This competition saw games between college and new club teams from Pennsylvania, Massachusetts, New York and Connecticut. Host, Hartford Hurling Club, were playing for the first time in their very first tournament.

Some of the club teams paired up with the college sides, and it was a side from Worcester, MA who came out on top at the end of a successful tournament. The event was put together by the Hartford GAA Club along with the colleges, New York GDO Simon Gillespie and North East GDA, Mike Moynihan, who was referee throughout the tournament.

Illustration 39: University of New Hampshire Wildcats HC & members of the Barley House Wolves at the College Sevens Tournament, Nov 2011 (Courtesy of BHW HC Facebook).

The rise of hurling on campuses on the West Coast, the Midwest, in the South and now the East, along with the foundation of the California Collegiate Gaelic Athletic Association (CCGAA), the Midwest Collegiate Hurling Association (MCHA) and the National Collegiate Gaelic Athletic Association (NCGAA), sees a real chance that hurling can make a breakthrough into the American mainstream sporting landscape.

The U.S. college sporting system is already well established and structured as in the National College Athletic Association (NCAA) and as such makes it easier for a new field sport like hurling to carve a niche in the sporting arena.

The demographic is huge with college enrollment according to the U.S. Dept of Education at 20.4 million for 2009. This is five times the population of Ireland and with an average of 20 sports per college. The number of athletes that participate in NCAA's programs for 2011 be it football, baseball, field hockey, rowing, tennis, basketball, ice hockey, track & field and others was put at 430,000.

There is a large number of college students who do not participate in sports for whatever reason, so from purely a numbers perspective, there is plenty of scope for growth for a new field sport. If a student wasn't able to make the cut on the High School team be it at football or baseball, he or she might like to try a field sport at college. Currently there is far less competition for places in hurling, and game-time is practically guaranteed. And, even students who play baseball and football, are too finding hurling attractive.

College sports also play a huge role in community and state life in America. The number of U.S. states that don't have any professional Big Four sports side is almost at 50% with the vacuum filled by the town, city or state supporting the local college team. Attendances at college football games are huge with some crowds exceeding 100,000 and this is the sporting landscape that the game of hurling is now just beginning to enter.

When you consider, that American Football, got its start on college campuses, there is no reason to believe the same formula – though the historic contexts are different – can't be worked and followed for hurling.

Football evolved from the game of rugby, and saw its early game-state introduction in the U.S. on college campuses on November 6, 1869 in New Brunswick, NJ, when Rutgers University took on Princeton in the first intercollegiate football type game. Rules were modified over the next decade and soon the sport flourished on the college circuit taking hold of the American imagination in the process. Collegiate football was popular up to the early stages of the NFL in the 1920s and beyond, and has stayed popular ever since. Could hurling follow a similar historic road?

In many respects, the clock is being switched back almost 150 years, with the sport of hurling having to start all over again but this time, crucially, not solely confined within the Irish immigrant community.

Today we see growth in a growing network of hurling clubs in local communities and throughout colleges campuses across the United States. What does it all mean? Will hurling's new journey of discovery, find a genuine home in America?

Chapter 8

The Big Picture

There is every reason to believe that hurling can become a staple diet for U.S. college students, and that it can also blend further into America's mainstream sporting landscape. Based on the experiences of the past, in order to lead hurling's discovery in a land of promise, certain paths have to be followed. Principally, it is a matter of approach.

The foundation of the recent U.S. college hurling body, the National Collegiate Gaelic Athletic Association (NCGAA), points things in the right direction at college level as it is modeled similarly to the NCAA. The body aims to promote and help grow hurling (and Gaelic football) clubs at colleges with a goal of organizing an annual national championship, which it has already realized.

This is a good beginning as a governing body as it is able to co-ordinate regional schedule making and implement decision making on a national level. Though this organization, in only its third year, is very much in its infancy, the grounds for solid foundation have already been laid. With more U.S. colleges taking up the sport, audiences, financial backing and sponsorship will allow for national promotional campaigns.

The NCGAA has also started off from a point whereby all officers except its chairman, Eamonn Gormley, are American. This makes a difference in that the organization culturally and structurally is American centric by nature and as such looks to American models and values.

In contrast, founded in 1959, the NACB has had 53 years of governance with only one native chairman, Irish American Joe Lydon, the current head. This factor alone points to how the organization stayed within the Irish born immigrant enclave. It described an Irish centric worldview within America. Though becoming American citizens and supporters of America, organizations like the NACB and the NY GAA, described a country within a country.

However, it is more a case of philosophy than country of origin that makes the body other than American centric. The main focus of the NACB over the years has been on keeping the games "alive" within a confined space. They achieved this through a two fold approach. 1) Irish immigrant player living in America long-term. 2) Supplementation via short term but annual Irish summer players.

This can be seen as Irish dependent, Irish centric approach presented by organizations based in America and 3000 miles away from the homeland.

Today, this thinking appears to be changing as there is an understanding for the most part that the future road the NACB must take is towards Gaelic sports development in America. After 53 years there appears to be a consensus that the future of American Gaelic sports lies not in Irish summer players and Irish immigrants but in growing American players. However, while this new attitude is currently in vogue it is often difficult to ascertain the degree to which it is followed and trusted.

At the NACB's 2006 AGM - where this writer was present – the secretary in his report wondered with low levels of Irish immigration, how the sports would last in America:

> "The 2006 season followed very closely in the footsteps of the 2005 season in being one of the most challenging in the history of the North American County Board.
>
> Attempting to deal with rapid changes [player migration] over the last couple of years has been crucial to the survival of our games in North America. An almost non-existent level of immigration from Ireland, and in many cases reverse emigration, in addition to extremely tough U.S. emigration laws, are placing a tremendous strain on clubs to stay alive," stated secretary, Eamonn Kelly.

Kelly, a longtime secretary and later PRO of the NACB, has done a tremendous amount of good work within the organization. He has often plowed a lone furrow, especially in his genuine efforts to issue timely divisional competition summaries.

His 2006 report was reflective of the organization as a body that thought of itself as carrying the torch and keeping the likes of hurling alive in America. But could you really say that anymore given that at the time the all American born club, the Milwaukee HC, was growing at a phenomenal rate and growing also were Indy HC, St. Louis, Denver, and Seattle? Would it have been more precise to state that hurling and Gaelic sports were in trouble only in the areas where the Irish immigrant/summer player dependent model was in place?

Keeping such a model as your staple diet when in reality it should have been replaced 30 years ago is contrary to recent development efforts.

Ironically, given the move towards greater emphasis on development, things haven't changed all that much in 'real terms' as the 2011 NACB AGM called for an increase in the number of Irish summer players that can play at top level in certain Gaelic sports codes in the traditional Irish leagues in Boston, Chicago, San Francisco and Philadelphia for the 2012 season.

As in the past, allowing for such increases is a short-term solution for hemorrhaging traditional Irish clubs whose long-term prognosis is not good. Facilitating such models flies in the face of efforts by the new all American clubs like Milwaukee, St. Louis, Benton Brigade, DC Gaels, Denver, and the Portland Marauders, who in promoting locally, grow hurling from scratch just like a certain Michael Cusack did at the very beginnings of the GAA in Ireland.

Presently, those players who do come over to play for a summer for an Irish traditional club get royal treatment.

Former Northeast GAA Division PRO, Connie Kelly, who is attached to the Boston Kerry Gaelic football club, paints a picture of events which take place to this day. "We pick them up at the airport. We put them up in an apartment. We get them a good job," Kelly told the Boston Globe's Jeremy Miller for an article in 2007.

Competition among clubs to recruit summer players from Ireland is intense. In reality, the Irish model is suffocating a sport like hurling in America. Over the years emphasis on the Irish import model superseded all resulting in adult and youth development being neglected. "We've spent too much time feeding the head while letting the body starve," youth coach Martin Bannon, of Hyde Park told the Globe.

With the focus Ireland centered, a game like hurling became hidden away within the Irish immigrant community where corralled it couldn't break free to fulfill its destiny.

Every time an American picks up a hurley something clicks. Something instinctual takes over as the game itself speaks to the player. Americans who take up the sport feel somehow that the game was made for them and these same Americans on public parks across the U.S. have been in the front trenches of bringing about changing attitudes.

GREATEST GAME, BUT WORST PROMOTION

For hurling to make the breakthrough into the American sporting landscape the sport needs marketing. Up to now the sport has had practically zero orchestrated national marketing.

When the Midwest College hurling chairman American Matt Schwertfeger spoke with GaelicSportsCast in 2011, he talked about how students cannot figure out why they hadn't heard about the sport before. They also wondered why they hadn't heard of the NACB's annual National Championships in America.

> "A lot of students don't know that there is even adult teams and they think it's only colleges and we say no, no ... When you tell them about Labor Day weekend and the North American [Nationals] and all that stuff, they're kind of blown away by it and say well 'why haven't I heard of it.'
>
> And this brings up a big point, yes, why haven't we heard of it? Why hasn't it been promoted you know more than it is ... and I don't have the answer for it."

Meanwhile in Ireland, the Gaelic Athletic Association (GAA) in Ireland, the body responsible for marketing hurling, is basking in the romance of it all claiming it's a sport that's second to none, yet American students new to the game know next to nothing about it.

Former President of the GAA Christy Cooney, after the Super Bowl of hurling – the All Ireland Hurling Final – repeated (as GAA President at the time) a familiar mantra on Irish radio in September 2011.

He said, 'We have the greatest game in the world'.

But, the 'greatest game' hasn't been promoted as such. In fact, the 'greatest game' has the worst promotion in the world. The sport has never been allowed to fulfill such a destiny because of lack of efficient organization and promotion.

Now creating marketing packages within a cultural environment that already has certain notions about a sport and its players, can be problematic and this is especially so in America. Unlike in the past, when U.S. newspapers in major urban centers sent reporters to cover weekly hurling and other Gaelic sports, information today is largely found second hand.

Commenting on the ancient game's health, newspapers can paint a picture to America and Irish America that is ever-so blurred. This is often not helped when influenced by an Irish immigrant perspective that is prone to subjectivity and generalization, as well as American romanticism of Irish culture.

Newspapers in New York, Boston, Chicago, and San Francisco, for generations have been writing the same kind of stories – Gaelic sports declining with migration to Ireland – or – growth for Gaelic sports as immigration rises in America. An endless cycle of newspaper inches reflecting the endless ebb and flow tied to Gaelic sports and Irish migration/immigration cycles.

The Wall Street Journal in a 2007 piece repeated history one more time when writing on the plight of hurling in the New York metropolitan area on account of dwindling Irish immigration and hurlers to the city.

The headline of 'Hurling in America Has a Problem – Too Few Irishmen,' paints a one-sided point of view, in fact the header should read: 'Hurling in America Has a Problem – Too Many Irishmen!'

In the article, one former hurler in New York says that "hurling is becoming extinct" and that, "the way it's going now ... we will be lucky to get two more years out of hurling in New York." The latter comment was correct as the club New Jersey/Kilkenny [referenced by the hurler], which ironically had won the last two NY championships at the time, folded in the past few years.

The comment is subjective as hurling is only becoming extinct within the Irish immigrant and summer player type club/league, while at the same time is flourishing in places like Milwaukee, Madison, Denver, St. Louis, DC and Indy where clubs reach out to Americans to play. Today there are four new hurling clubs in New York brought about largely by Americans wanting to get involved and play. Becoming extinct in that Irish immigrant imagined 'country' but growing in the 'real' country.

The Wall Street Journal in their piece also queried the promise for a game like hurling. They thought that promoting the sport in America would be difficult and naturally enough were basing such notions on conceptions that no one had ever bothered to put right:

> "Turning Americans on to hurling will be tough. To many Americans, hurling is just a slang term for vomiting. Once they learn that it's a sport, they often confuse it with curling, the winter Olympic sport played with brooms," the Journal wrote.

Has the New York GAA, or the NACB, or the GAA in Ireland, addressed such confusion? No, they haven't.

Where is the promotion campaign to clear confused minds? Where is the savvy video advertisement that informs about the sport in clear and unambiguous terms?

And, it's not a case that the GAA in Ireland could not afford monetarily to organize such promotion efforts as during that same period it drew in extra revenue on account of opening Croke Park temporally to 'foreign' games. While such monies were "recycled" to clubs (in Ireland) and some to overseas development, could not the GAA have spent just a few more dollars to promote hurling in America, after all doesn't 'the greatest game in the world', deserve it?

For sure, Ireland has never been a political and economic world powerhouse. It has a small population of 4.5 million living on a small island across the Atlantic Ocean. At present, it is suffering greatly at the hands of an economy gone woefully wrong. Given that economic and social-cultural context, it is understandable to a degree, that influence and large scale finance has never been readily available to the likes of one of its largest organizations, the GAA.

The GAA as a voluntary and sporting organization, has been very successful since its foundation in 1884 and is the largest entity of its kind in Ireland, and indeed, the world. For a small island nation to have the largest amateur sporting body in the world with some 1 million members is no mean feat. It is tremendous.

However, the GAA does have the fourth largest stadium in Croke Park, in Europe, but surprisingly its sports are unheard of on that continent too. If you were to stop a person on the street in Rome, Berlin or Paris, and ask if they had heard about hurling or Gaelic football, a shrug of the shoulders would be the most likely response. And yes, while it does take planning, time and money to invest in the promotion of world sporting organization's game/s one feels the will and the vision has been lacking. Hurling deserves better.

Yet, the realization that things have to change has been taking hold of late and this has come from inside the Irish GAA community.

Sean Kelly, a former President of the GAA in Ireland, who held office from 2005 to 2007, and is currently a Member of the European Parliament (MEP), has called for change when he addressed the Belgium GAA Annual General Meeting (he is the Honorary President) in early 2010.

The Hogan Stand Website (writes on Gaelic sports) carried a report on the address where Kelly said that the GAA organization had no world standing as a sporting body and this placed a heavy burden on local clubs to develop:

> "As it stands, our games have no international status and therefore no legal status in countries such as Belgium, France or Germany. This means in practical terms that clubs based in these countries cannot

apply to local authorities for free use of public sports facilities, as our games are not seen as sports per se."

Likewise when an American hurling club seeks to find a location to play, explanations about the sport to local parks departments must be lengthy if trying.

Seattle Gaels is an American club that finds acquiring field space an issue which former ice hockey player and club hurling manager Matt Everett puts into perspective when answering an email query in late 2010.

> "We rent fields from the Seattle Parks and Recreation Department. This has been the single biggest headache for the club, as space in Seattle is limited and there is a huge population of adult and youth field-sport leagues."

When a new hurling club goes to local government offices in the U.S. to acquire playing time on public parks, the fledgling entity is already at a disadvantage as the sport's profile is but a blip on America's sporting radar.

> "The lack of recognition is hobbling the development of our games on the ground. Our clubs in Units such as Europe have to go to great expense to hire private pitches, while other sports can access public facilities for free," Kelly told that AGM, which ironically was held at the European Parliament in Brussels, Belgium.

He went on to call as a way forward for an International GAA Federation and to affiliate "to the European and International Olympic Committee, the gold standard for recognition of Sports." Kelly also said that if the GAA was recognized globally then funding for clubs (in Europe at any rate) would be possible.

You would think that the former president's comments would spark interest at the GAA Congress four months later in the Spring of 2010 but such is the structure of the annual AGM that such topics are discussed privately and not on the main floor with all the counties' representatives present.

Overseas motions will get discussed but generally delegates from abroad get shepherded behind closed doors despite the fact that each of the seven unit's are deemed to be 'County's' of Ireland as in the North American County Board (NACB).

In the U.S. if there was an Olympic alignment, it could mean lenient tax structures and exemptions from paying tax on land, facilities, and gear. Apart from Olympic affiliations new hurling clubs on the ground have to consider their type of legal body and impending benefits.

Non-Profit Status for a club, can mean you can pay lower incorporation fees and keep more of your money in the club. A situation can also arise whereby a club can pay less for something like public event tents. Rules may vary according to locality and state.

Then there is the situation where an Amateur Athletic Organization can organize as a charity/tax exempt body. Tax exempt status 501(c)(3) is the most expensive to apply for and maintain.

There are two types of amateur athletic organization that can qualify for tax-exempt status in the U.S. The first type is an organization that fosters national or international amateur sports competition but only if none of its activities involve providing athletic facilities or equipment. The second type is a 'Qualified' amateur sports organization. The difference is that a qualified amateur sports organization can provide athletic facilities and equipment.

An important element that applies to either status is one of facilitating attractive donations and sponsorship in that according to the U.S. Internal Revenue Service (IRS), "either type of amateur athletic organizations are deductible as charitable contributions on the donor's federal income tax return. However, no deduction is allowed if there is a direct personal benefit to the donor or any other person other than the organization."

In the eyes of the U.S. Internal Revenue Service (IRS) an organization is a qualified amateur sports organization if it is organized and operated:

> "Exclusively to foster national or international amateur sports competition, and primarily to conduct national or international competition in sports or to support and develop amateur athletes for that competition. The organization's membership can be local or regional in nature."

It is unclear as to the NACB legal status but it appears it is a non profit N60 Amateur Sports Clubs/Leagues type body.

The operational structure of the GAA organizes its sports worldwide based largely on the county board system employed in Ireland. Like Europe, America is one of seven worldwide 'county' boards affiliated to the GAA in Ireland. This approach sees the parent body looking through an Irish prism when it views the organization of Gaelic Sports on a global scale.

From a purely structural standpoint, the American GAA organization (NACB) is somehow similar to that of Ireland even though the U.S. with 50 states and a population of some 313 million is supposed to fit the one system fits all county club system of Ireland.

The NACB does have its own unique structures as in its separate divisions, but its designation in the eyes of the parent body as a 'County' board, appears problematic. Ireland and America share similar western traits but there are also many differences – social, cultural, political, or sporting organization models. Developing a sport in a country requires plenty of thinking and planning. Like anything else, it usually means taking account of and respecting social and cultural traits.

On a worldwide basis the Irish diaspora has always been playing hurling and Gaelic sports within their own migrant networks. Down through the years, the GAA though insisting they had the best games in the world – especially deeming hurling so – surprisingly never thought of itself as a world sporting organization. The Gaelic Athletic Association could be described as a quasi socio-cultural national organization that happens to play sports.

Looking back to the organizations foundation in the 1880s, when Ireland was under the reign of Britain – and, a time when lots of other sporting bodies were formed in order to codify games – the GAA, in its Official Guide, saw its function as "a National Organization which has as its basic aim the strengthening of the National Identity in a 32 County Ireland through the preservation and promotion of Gaelic Games and pastimes."

The people of Ireland, at the time of the organization's foundation, deeply supported the cause of preservation and promotion of the ancient pastimes. Additional aims of the association followed cultural norms in wanting to:

> "Actively support the Irish language, traditional Irish dancing, music, song, and other aspects of Irish culture. It shall foster an awareness and love of the national ideals in the people of Ireland, and assist in promoting a community spirit through its clubs."

Such aims clearly go beyond the playing of sport alone.

In another part of the association's Official Guide 1.7, it demands that the Irish language be used in official documents and correspondence. The connection to culture be it in the form of song, dance, language or sport describes a very national perspective.

The early leaders of the organization had a clear vision of what they wanted to achieve and with new GAA clubs forming in every county in Ireland – the organization became a great success.

In danger of being assimilated into imperial norms, the GAA had given the Irish people back its cultural identity. With each new club - renewed spirit, pride and a sense of Irish identity grew. The Irish rallied around a new flag. The GAA had become a country. To a large extent it still is.

And, every time an Irish immigrant in America or Europe, or anywhere else, plays hurling or Gaelic football, ladies football or Camogie (hurling for ladies), a sense of identity and belonging is recreated.

For an Irish person going each week to Gaelic Park in the Bronx, or to the sports ground at Canton outside Boston, the sense of being transported back to Ireland when witnessing games is palpable.

This author having reported for over four years on the Gaelic sports scene in Boston (living 18 years in America in total) experienced first hand how the sports connect one to that country far across the sea. You surely felt you were in Ireland for the day.

Perhaps Americans or Britain's when they play baseball or soccer on foreign shores, feel something similar. But for most Irish, the act of playing Gaelic sports abroad reinforces deep connections to people and place.

The GAA in Ireland has succeeded in its basic aim to preserve and promote the sports nationally but the advent, for example, of Americans taking up the game of hurling (Gaelic football too, and also the French taking up football), sets in motion a new dynamic. Now the organization is forced to look beyond a one size Ireland-centered approach and consider how best to proceed.

U.S. YOUTH DEVELOPMENT

The initiation of six part time Games Development Officers in America (and 10 in the UK - time of writing) sees the parent body in Ireland taking some of the first tentative steps, on-the-ground at a micro level, to develop Gaelic sports in the U.S.

Nine years ago in New York, another step was taken when the GAA in Ireland in co-operation with America GAA or NACB, New York GAA and Canada GAA, started off a North American youth championship to compliment the work being done on the ground when forming youth leagues.

The event called the 'Continental Youth Championships' (CYC) has been a tremendous success and is seen as an early blueprint of sorts towards games development in the United States. The championships are growing each year and regularly see over 2,000 young Americans playing hurling and Gaelic football at different locations annually.

The CYC began with the playing of Gaelic football principally and it is unclear as to why hurling also didn't make a start at the time. Perhaps it was due to the fact that there was more Irish traditional clubs in America that played Gaelic football and as such coaching and development was easier to facilitate. Or, that football's influence and organization was greater than that of hurling at the time.

In a letter to the North American GAA in 2005 from the then GAA President in Ireland, the aforementioned Sean Kelly, on the eve of the second CYC championships in San Francisco, sees the event as a possible means for Gaelic sports to progress in America:

> "We would hope that initiatives such as this will encourage young players to progress to play our games at adult level and thus ensure the future of Gaelic Football on the continent ... I am confident that this festival of football will become an integral part of the GAA calendar and will prove a valuable foundation stone for the future development and expansion of Gaelic Games on the continent."

The CYC is proving to be success, at least in the short-term but as to its long-term effectiveness is another matter.

For instance young Americans, who have come up through the NY GAA Gaelic football development program (New York GAA Minor Board founded in 1970) over the past 10 years, see that sport as their third or fourth choice.

Their sporting preferences are mainstream American sports like football and baseball and there is no guarantee they will continue on playing Gaelic when reaching adulthood. In fact many of them have dropped out of Gaelic football because of getting a college scholarship playing sports like American football.

Let's take a closer look at one of the underage GAA clubs, the NY Celtics GFC (Gaelic Football Club) out of the Fordham/Yonkers area of the Bronx.

Started in 1970 as the Fordham Irish American Football Club - three years later incorporated as the NY Celtics - it is one of the oldest and most successful underage clubs in New York and America with 43 Championships. The organization competes at U8-U21 and in 1985 it won five underage NY Gaelic Football Championships which is a record up to this year (2012).

The club has largely an Irish American player profile and in 1983 started its first adult team at Junior B Adult level. It won that championship in 1987 with a mix of Irish and American players, and followed that with a Junior A level win in 1997. Last year in 2011 with some 10 Americans out of a team of 15, the Celtics went to the final of the NY GAA Junior A Championship once more. They lost 18 to 16 to a mostly Irish-born NY Monaghan team.

NY Celtics Chairman, American and former player John McCarthy, has nurtured winning underage American teams down through the years. In a recent interview (2012) with the podcast GaelicSportsCast, he was asked if the reason for not making it to the higher grades of Intermediate and Senior is because of having to play Irish born teams. "I would certainly say that does have a factor. It is very hard to take."

Players from underage clubs also get a chance to hook up or be drafted as individuals into the more senior teams which may feature summer Irish Inter County players. But often many young Americans find a higher grade of Gaelic football in New York an intimidating environment and the San Francisco Rovers hurlers have experienced this difficulty as a team when playing against mostly Irish born players.

In New York, a lot of American born players do get to play in the five team Junior B Championship (football) but once they rise to Junior A status, they will be competing against mostly Irish players. While there are those that will say that this is a normal upward progression, one could ask is it wise to try and fit an American into an Irish immigrant sporting model where most clubs place priority on winning local championships?

The NY Celtics have put in the time and effort in developing champion underage sides to adult level. But when it comes to competing at a higher grade they are beaten by clubs who haven't put in the time and effort to develop locally - one can see how 'it is hard to take'.

If New York Junior A, Intermediate and Senior clubs had to put in the same effort at development as the likes of the Celtics then perhaps you could truly say that an upward curve could be realized. Under such a system equity is championed and competition flourishes.

But keeping young American players interested in Gaelic sports is a real issue. They have progressed through the NY GAA underage program but American sports stay priority. "There's a lot more American sports and they hope to get scholarships to college. It's been a battle for all the clubs here at the NY Minor Board level to keep it going. It is an ongoing problem over the years," says McCarthy.

If the Continental GAA Youth Championships is to see real progress this issue must be fully addressed.

And, what if the underage player in New York, Boston or San Francisco wanted to play one day not just for club and city but for his own country ...? Well, he'd have a problem because as things stand with the separation of America into two entities, NACB and NY GAA, he wouldn't be able to have such an opportunity.

If those same young American players coming through youth development ranks were channeled into structures that viewed them as priority where evolving Junior B and C took center stage and not contrived and inequitable intermediate and senior grades, then a more sustainable future might be realized. Coupled with a phasing out of the summer player, genuine club and city teams can emerge. Gaelic sports like Hurling can then gain a foothold on-the-ground similar to what's taking place at colleges.

It is not so much about improving hurling standards, that surely will come with time, but more about increasing American player numbers and competition as in Milwaukee or St. Louis so as to build a community of players, a city of players, and a country of players.

But the likes of NY Celtic's John McCarthy also understands that in order for the numbers to increase development must reach beyond cultural boundaries. "To get it to the next level, I do feel that we do need to branch out and get into the community more to make it a bigger and better organization."

Meanwhile, where will the likes of Milwaukee, Denver, Indianapolis, Washington DC Gaels, and St. Louis hurling clubs be in 40 years time? Judging by the growing numbers of Americans getting involved with these clubs, the chances are that they will have thriving home grown leagues and perhaps even genuine inter-city team leagues. There is also the distinct possibility that Americans will find a route through the current Irish roadblock to form a USA Hurling Team in their own country.

The fundamental philosophy for developing a sport like hurling in America should not be based on reaching a certain standard but on growing numbers of people who enjoy the sport. From there like any other, the sport will evolve beyond the Irish community, and more importantly, beyond Irish norms and existing systems. Sport in America, often hindered historically by racial consideration, has inevitably risen above ideological boundary to find its own way forward. Hurling USA can follow suit.

STYLE

There is a realization that things have to change. The North American County Board (NACB) in October of 2010 started off an interesting hurling program, when forming a Hurling Development Committee (HDC). This body reports back to the parent body in Ireland as a further on-the-ground initiative.

Their short term goals as outlined to the 2011 North American GAA Convention consist of working to help existing local and regional tournaments, more hurling clinics, equipment grants, the compilation of a national schedule of games and to have hurling clubs in each major city as a long-term ambition. There are several American players from American clubs on this committee. This is a positive development.

But if the parent body, the GAA in Ireland, want to continue its idea of Gaelic sports development in the Unites States should the structure of the NACB change to a more American style operation?

The NACB in conjunction with its partner the Munster GAA Council in Ireland – a branch of the parent body – in April 2012 finalized a Five Year Strategic Action Plan (2012 -2016) for Gaelic sports in the U.S. Without doubt, this Strategic Action Plan is a watershed moment for American Gaelic sports as it represents the first real effort to organize the sports from a developmental perspective. Such a plan and its successful execution could influence the kind of NACB that might eventually appear.

At the plan launch NACB Chairman, Joe Lydon spoke of its importance and how the Action Plan provides a road-map for the future. He said it was another milestone for the association and that it will enhance the organization at all levels in the NACB area:

> "Our challenge is to not only to reach our targets and goals but to exceed them and develop our organization to a level not envisaged when it was first set up. Truly then the GAA can boast of being an international Association underpinned by strong and vibrant units outside of Ireland." (GAA Press Release: North American County Board Strategic Plan Launch, April 12, 2012).

The scope of the plan is broad but its focus is squarely on games development as outlined in its opening paragraphs. "We will ensure that the development of our games remains the key objective of the NACB."

The main areas addressed in the Five Year Action Plan is on administrative structures and operations, communications, sponsorship, finance as well club excellence, player welfare, facilities, scheduling and games development.

The latter theme is the primary focus and is to be delivered via introduction to games, the GDA program, coach and referee education, development camps and clinics, amongst other approaches.

There are several interesting initiatives such as introducing Gaelic sports like hurling to parents and school teachers via coaching courses, starting a Gaelic sports Scholarship Program for students and expanding the Games Development Administrator (GDA) program to all Divisions by 2017.

On marketing, Gaelic Sports in North America are to be included in information packages for students on 'Study Abroad' programs by 2013; the advertisement and promotion of all Introduction Programs in conjunction with PRO's & NACB marketing; all divisions and clubs to have Facebook and Twitter representation and a call for "work towards having Gaelic Games shown on National TV in North America by 2016."

Divisions and clubs are also given the responsibility "to develop a relationship with local media outlets/sources in order to better promote local GAA activities," while a committee is to be setup to, "look at an overall national sponsorship and increasing exposure of GAA brand within the USA."

From an operational perspective, a further committee will evaluate the current divisional alignment and make recommendations (where necessary) for restructuring divisions and clarifying the functional purpose of a division.

The idea of information packs for students on 'Student Abroad' programs is progressive and could help generate further interest about Gaelic sports on U.S. campuses. Having PRO's reach out to local media is another positive, as is setting a time-frame for getting games like hurling on mainstream U.S. TV.

How the plan is executed and evolves remains to be seen. Whether the structures and operations have a more American feel over time remains to be seen.

While it is natural for any international organization to want its individual country units to duplicate its systems and doctrines, respecting local traditions and norms is paramount for local success. One of the themes in the plan focuses on 'Fixtures'. In America this translates to Schedules. Fixtures is an Irish term and its use can lead to misunderstandings within a Gaelic sports environment in America.

What degree of marketing and branding strategies is employed in the Five Year Plan will play a vital role in deciding the effectiveness and success of developing and promoting sports like hurling in America.

The early phase of the plan in the guise of the Games Development Administrator initiative points to how development and coaching models might eventually take shape. The idea of self sufficiency for America in relation to games coaching and refereeing is paramount but what style will the coaching model follow. The NACB website at the time referenced this in saying, "When first putting this long term plan in place it was the NACB's objective to become self sufficient in the two specialized areas of coaching and refereeing development. The key element in the plan was replicating the structures developed and in place in Ireland."

Coaching level courses within the GAA in Ireland have come about in roughly the last 25 years or so. The GAA has arrived late to the world of camps, coaching and clinics and it could be fair to say that in principle, the GAA followed international guidelines for coaching and development standards and then applied them to Gaelic sports. Will the coaching structures and courses be suitable for non-Irish beginners who are used to the ice-hockey and baseball grip? Will coaching take into account the local sporting cultures and norms?

The coaching of sports in America has had a long history going back to the very start of college football with the first paid coach in 1890 at Williston Northampton School, one Amos Alonzo Stagg.

Throughout the 20th century coaches at U.S. colleges have been standard practice for developing young athletes. Football coaching in the High School system is particularly well established. The sport's coach in America holds a special place in the social and cultural landscape. The word 'Coach' is synonymous with American sport.

Historically in Europe, be it in Ireland or the UK, coaching development as with the American college and high school coach, is not as pervasive and systematic.

Author John Lyle in his book, 'Sports Coaching Concepts. A Framework for Coaches Behavior' says, "The career coach to be found in U.S. high schools, colleges, and universities (within a structured and hierarchical competition programme) is not matched in the UK [and Ireland] and differs in almost all respects from the traditional club."

Lyle adds that the effect of all this is that job opportunities, infrastructure, career pathways, educational requirements, and a body of literature and research has been gathered through this American sports coaching system.

No doubt it is a positive step for the GAA to introduce the basics of coaching into the Gaelic sports system in America but when you consider the historic time-line, together with the competition from other sports with comparable systems in place for generations, it clearly paints a picture of neglect.

In the past the lack of urgency by the parent body in Ireland placed Overseas GAA Units like the North American and NY GAA in difficult positions. Clubs tended to fall back on the immigration model as a means of staying afloat when no help from Ireland was forthcoming. Unfortunately that model has became a crutch for far too many clubs. Yet, some of these are beginning to look for change in the long-term as well.

The NY Tyrone Gaelic football club, who went to the final of the NY GAA Senior Football Championship in 2011 (heavy reliance on Irish summer players), is such a club.

Secretary of the Bronx based club is Irish and County Tyrone native, Seamus McNabb, and he told the podcast GaelicSportsCast in late 2011 of the need to move away from the summer players and concentrate more on the resident Irish and young American players.

> "The key is to concentrate on your home base if possible. I know that there is all these students coming here and it's nice to give them the opportunity to play. But you know personally speaking and for Tyrone club as well, we'd rather get away from the whole reliance on the sanctions [summer player].
>
> I don't think it's good overall for the game. The whole season evolves around that and I don't think it's good. The financial element is also a burden on all the clubs; the whole aspect of getting them work and accommodation and that. In the long-term somebody should be looking at that as something to get away from."

In the new North American GAA plan, though asserting the importance for the future, there is no direct reference in the strategy as yet for a complete overhaul or modification of the summer player model for the long-term. However, the Five Year Plan is a very positive development for hurling and Gaelic sports in general. In the past things suffered because there was no plan. There was no road-map for the future. Now there is.

A lot of good work has been done by the NACB over the years and the latest generation of officers like American born and recent PRO (since 2010), Tim Flanagan, in reflecting the changing philosophy within the organization, talks about an exciting future for Gaelic sports and for hurling.

Prior to publication of this book, Flanagan spoke to the Orlando Weekly on today's exciting times for hurling and Gaelic sports. He said that over the last several years membership of the NACB has grown to double what it was just five years ago. "We're starting to get to the point where it's really going to take off."

The Orlando paper told of Flanagan's perspective on the growth of hurling clubs in America as due to "to a lot of 'little fires,' as opposed to one big moment." The paper continued, "Flanagan thinks hurling has enormous potential in the North American market. His association is throwing its resources behind developing the sport. 'We are putting in place a strategic plan for the next five years on how to promote and grow this game," he says. Ideally, he says, national television channels would broadcast hurling games.'"

But those 'little fires' that have taken place across America be they in Milwaukee, Indianapolis or St. Louis have in their own right been much bigger and brighter than any the NACB has ever attempted to light.

It's a delicate matter introducing a new sport like hurling (though older when thinking it was historically hidden away within the Irish immigrant community) into the American coach dominated world. However, on its own merit, hurling is strong enough to stand in any cultural environment.

The Games Development Administrators (GDA) are doing a great job at grassroots level with coaching, camp developments, games scheduling and approaching schools. But is an Irish hurling coaching course going to work for a young American at High School, already familiar and coached in American sports basics, and no doubt playing at least four American sports? In this regard, the five year plan's 'Introduction to Games' will have to eventually evolve into a best practice scenario for America.

Games Development Officers and youth club members feedback will play a crucial role in paving the way forward in any newly introduced system. But doing nothing and keeping the status quo is no longer an option for the NACB and its parent body in Ireland. That realization is progress and can only be positive moving forward.

The folks involved with the Milwaukee Hurling Club have been successful because they are developing and marketing the sport after an American fashion – fully fledged draft for competitive competitions (adult), two referees on field and modifying Irish drills to suit both adults and kids.

Yet, the familiarity aspect for American kids is not there as they don't see the sport on TV and have no knowledge or context for how to play. This is where the macro approach to developing hurling has to come in if efforts at a micro level as in GDA coaching is to be effective. A macro approach involves a marketing and promotion campaign run in conjunction with the micro approach. What might a macro approach look like?

MACRO PROMOTION

This author believes a two-fold approach to promotion can evolve in both local and national campaigns. There is also the possibility that local can turn into national.

The Indianapolis Hurling Club recruit and promote locally. They recently got noticed locally by such folks as the 2012 Super Bowl Village Committee who invited them as a local sporting club in the city to exhibit in the lead-up to the big game. In Indy HC's case local became national.

Take also the case of all those American player clubs who reach out to the local community for recruitment, they get noticed by their local TV stations and next thing you know the club is featured in the local TV news. Often the same clubs will contact the TV stations to come out and do a story on them. This type of local marketing could benefit every single hurling club especially the more traditional Irish immigrant club if forced to recruit American adults. And, if that means starting from scratch – as did Milwaukee 17 years ago and now the largest hurling club in America – then that is what development locally should be all about.

At the Indy Hurling Club Super Bowl gig, the Indy club displayed the sport of hurling on the street in downtown Indianapolis to thousands of onlookers. One of the club officials, an American, talked over the PA about the drills, the history of the sport, the local club, and their competitions. People were invited to try-out the various hurling skills. This type of promotion had never been done before by the American GAA.

The NFL has handed the GAA in Ireland the blueprint for urban promotion in America.

The local hurling clubs are already in place in the various cities around America and with planning – as in acquiring public entertainment licenses and strategy in building a sporting exhibit – around an Urban Promotion session - the sport puts itself out there to be seen and heard. Couple this with smart videos of such events into marketing packages mixed with Irish Championship clips, local leagues, and you have something that can be sold to TV networks for promotion purposes and also as teasers for local and corporate sponsors.

Now also, you have something that can be shown to High School students from an American cultural standpoint. Will the NACB Plan eventually role out similar marketing strategies and follow the lead of clubs like Indianapolis?

While the NACB has recently upgraded its website coupled with new You Tube and Facebook platforms, communication problems have been known in the past when divisions failed to give game reports on a timely basis and ongoing problems still persist with communications.

The divisional and NACB officers are there on a voluntary basis and that can bring its own efficiency and management issues. This is a crucial issue that may affect the new plan's success.

At present the North American GAA County Board (NACB) is a volunteer based run organization. Meetings and phone conferences are held regularly but there isn't anyone working 24/7 to run the affairs of the association. A lot of selfless good work has been put in by volunteer officers over the years, but does the structure of the organization need to change? Compare it with the likes of USA Rugby who have a dedicated CEO and full time staff.

Founded in 1975, a full 24 years after the NACB got going, USA Rugby today is growing from strength to strength with 90,000 members. It oversees amateur rugby teams and is responsible for the development of youth, high school, collegiate and club rugby programs, as well as the national teams representing the U.S. in international competitions.

This is in comparison to the NACB (though growing) with reportedly 10,000 player membership (NY separate membership).

A case may be made that rugby enjoys a more global and national profile than the likes of hurling and the GAA, but given that hurling and Gaelic football have been played in America for well over 100 years, you would expect a much greater membership pool. Yet, this is to be expected if members are constantly coming and going following the immigration-migration tide.

USA Rugby is a member of the United States Olympic Committee (USOC) and the International Rugby Board (IRB), whose headquarters ironically are in Dublin, Ireland.

According to a report by the Center for the International Business of Sport (CIBS), entitled the 'Economic Impact Report on Global Rugby' (2010) and commissioned by Mastercard Worldwide, since the Rugby World Cup 2007 rugby has enjoyed Global participation increase of 19%. Towards such growth the IRB says it has invested in development programmes some $248 million from 2009 to 2012 made possible due to the commercial success of Rugby World Cup.

Apart from the World Cup tournaments success, another factor helping such growth is rugby's affiliation to the International Olympic Committee where it will see Rugby Sevens featured for the first time in Rio de Janeiro 2016.

Said the IRB Chairman Bernard Lapasset in the IRB website on rugby's inclusion in the Olympics:

> "We are also noticing the boost that Olympic Games inclusion has given Rugby and we are excited by the opportunities that are now being presented to our Member Unions through National Olympic Committees as we count down to Rio 2016. We are working in partnership with the International Olympic Committee and the Olympic family to ensure that Rugby Sevens' Olympic debut is both memorable and successful."

The report also cites huge advances in America where a whopping 350% participation increase has been experienced since 2004. Along with IRB grants, growth has come from the showing of the U.S. College Sevens championships and the World Cup 2011 on NBC TV as well as the live broadcast of the USA leg of the 2010/11 HSBC Sevens World Series.

Other American TV channels to broadcast rugby are Fox Soccer Plus, and ESPN (College). USA Rugby meanwhile, earned more than $6 million in revenue in 2010 through memberships, IRB grants and sponsorship ($1 million). The GAA in Ireland whose own revenue in 2010 amounted to almost $76 million, spent in that year approximately $1,354,629 on the International Rules Series a hybrid Australian Rules and Gaelic Football game played twice every three years with Australia.

Developed to facilitate international representative matches between both codes, the game has no club representation worldwide with occasional once-off friendly club tests taking place in Australia. It is largely accepted that the game itself doesn't have a future and if anything has helped the Australian Rules (AFL) over Gaelic in that AFL scouts recruit Irish players away from Gaelic football.

The recent 2011 International Rules Series in Australia saw poor attendances yet crowd numbers in Ireland in the 2010 series were relatively healthy. Ireland, unlike Australia the prior year, showcased their best players.

There have been many critics of the series none more so than respected County Tyrone All Ireland winning Gaelic Football manager, Mickey Harte. He is adamant that the series should be ended. He says that instead of supporting the series, the GAA should invest the same energy and resources in promoting Gaelic sports internationally. He conveyed this sentiment to the Irish News newspaper ahead of last year's (2011) event in Australia:

"The so-called International Rules series is about to be embarked upon yet again. Formerly known as Aussie Rules and then adjusted to the Compromise Rules, this package has long outlived its usefulness - if indeed it ever did have any.

As you are probably by now well aware, I have had - and continue to have - huge reservations regarding this project which, in my opinion, does a total disservice to the development of Gaelic games on the international stage ...

The GAA should end this engagement immediately, and go to work on augmenting the endeavors of true Gaels in many parts of the world who operate without compromise."

Some years expenses are significantly more than others (home and away) but if the higher costs associated with playing this series were diverted into say a core full time staff in America, the chances of the U.S. GAA plan's future could be greatly enhanced.

The GAA in Ireland if they are serious about the development of hurling and Gaelic sports in America, need to invest greater resources and perhaps think about putting a small team led by a CEO or Director General (as in Ireland) in charge.

The NACB with its volunteer officer base will always have problems in performing in an efficient and timely manner even with the best intentions and plans.

There might be a body of thought in Ireland that think it's too soon to make such an investment in America but that thinking is short sighted. The efforts being put in at local level by clubs such as Milwaukee and Indy Hurling need to be complimented by a more professional approach.

In its current format, the NACB is unable to attract any local sponsor of GAA sports in America (at time of writing) with only the one Irish company as a partner. Even though this is an area to be targeted in the new NACB Strategic Plan, this performance is very poor by any standard. Meanwhile, USA Rugby has nine sponsors, three of which are major U.S. brands.

At present the North American GAA does not have any professional promotion videos for the American market on their website. They do have a link to amateur videos of various Gaelic sports in America on their new You Tube Channel. The new website is a major improvement on past efforts in style and overall quality.

The recently founded Greenville Gaels Hurling Club from Greenville, South Carolina, in early 2012, produced one of the most professional promotional videos ever created in American Gaelic sports circles. It is top quality.

The NACB itself, though recognizing its quality and appeal has placed it on their Home Page. Yet, there is no similar specific NACB short promotional video currently available as an advert for Gaelic sports in America.

While the Five Year Plan calls for comprehensive marketing strategy to be put in place, clubs like Greenville are already ahead in the game.

Contrast this with the Australian Rules sporting body in South Africa, the AFL South Africa. Over the past 10 years this organization has been developing and aggressively promoting Australian Rules in South Africa through a Youth Program. On their website home page there is a professional video promotion for the sport. There are also local news clips on 'Australian Rules' in South Africa on the home page.

Can a volunteer led organization manage the affairs of a growing hurling and Gaelic sports community in such a large and populated country as America? Over the years, the GAA in Ireland realized that a full time staff was needed to run the Irish organization. There is a 64 member administration staff employed at present and while they organize principally for over 2,300 clubs in Ireland, the time is fast approaching that in the interests of efficiency, stability and growth, a small scale staff may have to be employed in America.

GETTING ON AMERICAN TV.

The most effective method of utilizing a macro approach for the promotion of a sport like hurling is through the medium of free-to-air TV.

The NACB, in fairness to them and as noted by PRO, Tim Flanagan, have been at pains to communicate to the parent body in Ireland that the Irish hurling championship has to be shown to the mass American audience if real growth is to be realized (the same applies for Gaelic Football).

Flanagan in an interview with the Irish Examiner newspaper in May 2011 about the growth of GAA in the U.S. talks of American's efforts to grow the sport of hurling and how it could be jeopardized by the parent body coming up short in getting games on American TV:

> The "driving force behind this [hurling club growth] seems to be Americans and Irish-Americans, as opposed to native Irish.

"However, the failure of Croke Park to allow the free-to-air showing of Gaelic games in the USA has hindered our ability to promote and expand the games and the GAA beyond the Irish and Irish-American communities.

"As long as people have to pay $20 per person each week (man, woman, and child) to see one GAA match broadcast from Ireland, we will not see any significant gains in the promotion of the GAA in North America. We must have free, live viewing access to Gaelic games as the people of Ireland and the UK do."

The $20 viewing payment is for entrance to pubs in the U.S. who have the specific pay per view channel to show the Irish championship each summer from Ireland.

At present Premium Sports, has the rights to show Irish Gaelic sports like hurling to an American audience via pay-per view to commercial premises, Internet Streaming and through MHZ Networks – an independent non-commercial television broadcaster.

It is unclear as yet how a recent March 2012 ruling in a New York District Court, where Premium Sports took a NY bar to court over an allegation of piracy will affect Gaelic sports and viewership in America. The owner used Slingbox technology to show an International soccer game, and without charging the viewing fee.

Slingbox technology allows a person watch their home television from anywhere in the world. The court said it wasn't piracy of a simultaneous satellite signal but a delayed signal.

New York Irish Central media outlet, reporting on the ruling in early March said, "Judge Katherine Forrest ruled that the 'transmission that was shown from an apartment in Dublin, Ireland was not the initial transmission and that defendants had not "intercepted" the transmission'. In effect, she stated it was a rebroadcast, not an interception of a live signal and that the initial live signal had been legally acquired in Dublin."

Premium Sports are to appeal the decision (at time of writing) but if it stands it could mean Irish bars in America can show Gaelic sports from Ireland via Slingbox without having to charge customers a viewing fee. This could mean greater exposure for sport's like hurling. It is unclear how such an eventuality might alter GAA and Premium Sports contracts.

It is understood that the GAA in Ireland has made numerous representations to the various large commercial Free-to-Air TV outlets over the years (when out of contract) and as yet has had no takers. Whether that representation was face-to-face or communication sent from Ireland is not clear but one suspects the latter mode of inquiry has been the preferred route.

Looking at the approach of another – not organization but individual, Russell Crowe, the actor – we see things can get done.

An Australian is Russell and he loves his sport. Rugby League is the movie star's particular sporting passion. Such is his zeal that in 2011 he successfully negotiated face-to-face with Fox Sports in America to show his beloved Rugby League on American TV.

Crowe happens to co-own a South Sydney rugby league team (time of writing), and in May 2011 the Courier Mail in Australia, reported that NRL (National Rugby League, Australia) chief executive, David Gallop stated:

> "This new United States agreement significantly adds to the mainstream exposure of two of our biggest events ... It sees more than 40 million homes across the United States now able to experience live the passion and rivalry of the 2011 Harvey Norman State of Origin Series and the Telstra Premiership Grand Final."

The power of persuasion can be a very useful thing from time to time, and apparently, Mr. Crowe has it.

One might think that people in Ireland, or for that matter Irish movie stars like Liam Neeson, Colin Farrell or Gabriel Byrne, might be able to bend some ears but of course none of the trio might be sport's owners, or hurling enthusiasts. But then, given the fact that some 36 million people in America call themselves Irish American, you'd think the Irish might have more bargaining power when it comes to showcasing the likes of hurling.

Rugby League, let alone Rugby Union [IRB game], is little known and understood by the American population. Yet, somehow in one fell swoop Mr. Crowe is able to convince a U.S. TV network to carry a largely unknown sport to a country. The same country that according to the U.S. Census Bureau (2009) boasts some 81,100 Australian residents and a mere 95,000 who claim Australia as their ancestral home.

But yet, with all their tireless trying, the GAA in Ireland haven't been able to sell a sport like hurling to American TV executives.

Being nice you could say that some British residents might also be interested in viewing Rugby League from Australia ... and so the audience is increased. But if you were selling hurling to an audience in the U.S. one would surely start by talking up the potential appeal of a 36 million Irish ancestry base who – know little or nothing about hurling but on discovery love it – might still be interested. Add in roughly 122,000 Irish-born residents of the U.S. (2009) and some 50,000 undocumented – the recent Irish influx increases the former figure further – and perhaps one could strike a deal.

Selling travel Ireland ad spots would be doable, as could selling Irish cultural and sports tourism packages.

In 2010, the GAA in Ireland received a whopping state grant from the Irish Department of Tourism, Culture & Sport of $674,427, and perhaps a portion of such monies could be channeled in improving awareness of the likes of hurling via tourist outlets in America.

Overall, TV exposure could greatly benefit the Irish economy and be a boon for hurling clubs, and the NACB and NY GAA into the bargain.

In growing a sport like hurling and raising the profile of the GAA, European County Board (ECB) GAA Secretary, Tony Bass in an interview for an Irish newspaper in July 2011, followed up on Sean Kelly's call for an affiliation with a body like the International Olympic Council.

> "The ECB has brought this matter to the attention of GAA Annual Congress on a number of occasions. However because of the practice of confining Congress debates to rule changes, they have not been debated and are referred to Central Council which has referred them to the Overseas Committee.
>
> Most of the international units especially Europe and Asia have expressed similar views. Our latest attempt this year was referred to a new high-level group charged with developing an International Strategy and we have strenuously pushed our arguments when we met them."

Bass added that, "Worldwide recognition and development would enable Gaelic games to become one of the premier international field sports with considerable potential for promoting Ireland, the games and our culture."

Over the past two years, the association has been meeting with its 'Overseas Units' (name changed in April 2012 to 'International' units) like North America GAA or NACB, and New York GAA, to plan such a world strategy in relation to Gaelic sports like hurling. Two years of feedback from the various 'units' including America, has yielded a further process paper from the parent body in Ireland with no world plan as yet.

Opportunity for growth of the organization in America and on a global level is taking root but how such opportunities are used to suit individual countries awaits to be seen. One suspects that, the GAA in Ireland dipping its collective toe into the American and international sporting arena, is full of trepidation in what might await.

Another former GAA president, Peter Quinn, believes that the organization must be more assured, business like and leave the romance of the past behind or get left behind.

Quinn as president in the early 1990s played a major role in the redevelopment of Croke Park Stadium to its current world class status, but warned that the congratulatory ceremonious are over and that it's time to move on. "We've done the lap of honor around Croke Park [reference to succesful refurbishement of stadium]. It's time to go outside now and face the serious tests that are presenting themselves in a rapidly-changing sporting world."

In an interview for the Irish Examiner in 2007, Quinn adds:

> "Everybody in Croke Park [GAA Headquarters] is working hard, but in terms of effectiveness it should be more streamlined. Strategy is more important than day-to-day administration. We have become an administrative rather than a strategic organization."

Quinn also says the organization must be more pro-active and assured going forward:

> "Our greatest strength is the weakness of our competitors in real terms. But will it always remain so? I believed prior to 2002 that we had spent the previous 10 years building up a huge level of confidence in the GAA through the redevelopment of Croke Park, but when we suggested some changes, we got defensiveness.
>
> That's not the hallmark of a progressive organization or one that's full of confidence and that worries me as we look towards the next 20 years in a rapidly changing world, both locally and globally."

The arrival of American hurlers on the scene forces that global perspective, ready or not.

Eamonn Gormley has shown how practice and simple PR work-on-the-ground at fairs and festivals, can start the ball rolling in the setting-up of regional and national college sporting bodies. Gormley has also played a major part in introducing rookie hurlers to the game when creating promotional videos on You Tube. One of those videos, which has received more than half a million views since March 2009, uses a collage of edits of major televised hurling games in Ireland and results in a basic 101 of the skills of the game.

In many ways it has become the gold standard for introducing rookies to the game in the U.S.

Gormley believes that if the like of hurling is to make an impact on the American mainstream population it is necessary that proper media advertising strategies be created.

In an innovative and insightful paper in 2006 to the North American GAA Congress, outlining a 10-year plan for development and promotion in America, Gormley the then NACB PRO, laid it down in black and white what really needs to be done.

> "While the low-budget marketing activities of grassroots GAA members will get some results for recruitment purposes, they will never make a noticeable dent in the dominance of other sports. Television remains the most effective medium and is the only one that is going to get our games anywhere near mainstream consciousness," he told the conference.
>
> "Since free airtime is hard to come by, the only surefire way we can get on air on popular networks is to use paid advertising in the form of a professionally produced TV commercial. It should get to the point quickly and immediately sell the benefits of the game. One could be made for hurling, one for football ... The commercial[/s] should be played repetitively at prime viewing time for a fixed period."

Gormley realizes that there are obvious costs involved but feels that these can be met through re-investment of media rights into America along with investment by private companies like Guinness marketing products in the U.S. and the Irish tourism lobby with an eye on the lucrative Irish American market. In his paper he adds that media advertising must work in tandem with existing clubs, divisional and national structures so as to get the maximum return from a dedicated marketing campaign.

Gormley's paper in many ways is a Blueprint for progress as regards the development and promotion of sports like hurling in America. To the extent it was fully adopted by the GAA powers in America over the intervening years is unclear, however, from a marketing perspective, it certainly was not. Will the new Five Year Plan reflect a similar marketing strategy for American TV?

The sport of hurling has been played in America for well over a century but because of the vagaries of the lack of proper and united organization, infighting, immigrant assimilation, economic woe, war, ebb and flow of immigration, limited sports model, and above all, a mind-set to wrap oneself in the comfort of an insular culture, hurling failed to make it onto the American sporting landscape.

However, with the growth of all-American clubs, Irish and American mixed clubs, there is a new awareness that the summer immigrant model is not sustainable. The first steps in introducing grass roots development and the execution of a meaningful strategy to grow awareness about hurling, means that the future for the ancient sport can still be very bright in America.

That the sport is hooking young and adult Americans at an ever increasing number is evident and surely rates hurling as an exciting new sport in the U.S.

Sports TV God, Arlene Rutledge, would have taken one look at the sport of hurling and seen its potential, to thrill and excite. To bring agony, yet ecstasy. To unite in the face of battle. To transcend time and place.

Will another Rutledge step forward and see hurling's potential to entertain? To tell a story? This author believes that if he were alive today he would jump at the chance of making hurling an American TV sport.

One of the historic and philosophical cornerstones of the GAA in Ireland had been to frown on outside cultural norms and to pursue national ideology. In the preamble to the Official Guide Part 1, initial aims following on from 'promotion and preservation' are clearly stated, "the overall result is the expression of a people's preference for native ways as opposed to imported ones."

Could the GAA in Ireland now be strategically importing its own ways into America? Or, should those same 'ways' that Americans have recently discovered in the game of hurling, be allowed the freedom to develop the sport according to the country's own cultural norms?

Isn't it time the game itself decided the answer to that question?!

The high scoring element alone has the potential to attract a lot more Americans to the sport and that includes those at home watching in a potentially huge U.S. TV market.

It's not rocket science as to how any sport gets to be popular within a culture. People come together to participate in playing a particular sport as in the early days of baseball, American football, or basketball. Michael Cusack founder of the GAA in Ireland began to revitalize hurling when playing with his friends in the Phoenix Park in Dublin. As a sport evolves, player numbers increase. Teams and clubs are formed. The sport spreads to different cities and regions. The sport develops a following and gets more popular. The sport is introduced to schools and colleges and starts to further ignite the imagination. Potential sponsors see revenue opportunities. They in turn are followed by media folk eager to sell papers and airtime back to followers of the new sport. Before you know it a country has a new sport on its hands.

Building anything from grassroots isn't easy and takes time. However, the likes of Milwaukee, St. Louis and Indianapolis clubs and others, are building real numbers, real clubs and real communities. A new reality for hurling is being created.

When we look at things in life we tend to view them with a short-term lens. Did we ever think we'd see the day when water wasn't free? That imports would challenge and supersede the American big-car industry? Everything changes. When considering life in the long-term, we gain a sense that things are not set in stone. Sport is no different. Hurling's mainstream popularity won't happen over night - though it will happen much faster than before on account of modern technology - the sport nevertheless will make the breakthrough into the American sporting landscape, if nurtured properly. It can certainly become more popular as another sport to play in America but does this mean it could ever hope to challenge the big four. The answer to that question is unknown at this moment.

There are those who say that could never happen, as the big four are rooted in America's culture. Even a world game like soccer can't really make the breakthrough in America, they might say – though public soccer fields are sprouting everywhere. So, how can hurling, they say?

They, always say a lot.

Hurling is spreading beyond the Irish immigrant communities and is finally speaking for and selling itself. From there it will grow and expand.

One day Irish Americans in celebrating St. Patrick's Day might look forward to participating and watching a major hurling event at the festive time. Already, the ones who are lighting the 'little fires', are making this happen.

Today most old sports have faded to extinction but hurling is very much alive. This ancient game is still with us and in America it is breathing new life. And, could any sport in the world ask for a better country than the United States in which to make a fresh start?

A country where sentiments such as can't, never, or won't are cast aside and replaced with 'what if', 'fix' and 'let's do it'.

Hurling has discovered a promised land.

References

Arledge. Roone, ABC Memo to Edgar Scherick , as quoted in, Ronald A. Smith. Play-by-Play: Radio, Television, and Big-Time College Sport. (Baltimore MD, John Hopkins University Press, 2001), 16.

Baker. William Joseph, 'Sports in the Western World' (Illini Books edition, 1988) p 113.

Baran, Stanley J. The Industrial Benefits of Televised Sports, SPORTS AND TELEVISION, Museum of Broadcast Communications (MBC), http://www.museum.tv/eotvsection.php?entrycode=sportsandte

Brennan. Cathal, The Tailteann Games, 1924-1936 <http://theirishstory.com> (Feb, 2011).

Crowther. Nigel B, 'Sport in Ancient times' (Westport CT: Praeger Publishers) 2007

Darby. Paul. 'Gaelic Games, Nationalism, and the Irish Diaspora in the United States' (University College Dublin Press, 2009), p34-35.

Darby. Paul (2009) "Without the Aid of a Sporting Safety Net?': the Gaelic Athletic Association and the Irish Émigré in San Francisco (1888-c.1938)', International Journal of the History of Sport, 26:1, p68.

Gould, Joe, 'Hurling: in Ireland's oldest, roughest, fastest sport, the stars of the game give it their all-and then go back to their day jobs,' Men's Fitness Magazine 22.10 (Dec 2006): 99(3). General One File. Gale. Boston Public Library. 4 Sept. 2009

Hardy. Stephen, Polo at the Rink: Shaping Markets for Ice Hockey in America, 1880-1900. Department of Kinesiology, University of New Hampshire.

Hall, S. C. On Irish Society before the Famine. Encyclopedia of Irish History and Culture. Ed. James S. Donnelly, Jr.. Vol. 2. Detroit: Macmillan Reference USA, 2004. 893-896. Gale Virtual Reference Library. Gale. Boston Public Library. 16 Sept. 2009.

Hurley, John W. Shillelagh: The Irish Fighting Stick, (Pipersville PA, USA: Caravat Press 2007) 78.

Journal of Sport History. 2006 Vol. 33 No. 2 p. 156-174

Keenan. Donal, The Ultimate Encyclopedia of Gaelic Football & Hurling. 2nd ed. (Cork : Mercier Press, 2007) 11.

Kevin Whelan, The Cultural Effects of the Famine.. in Joseph N. Cleary, Claire Connolly, eds., The Cambridge Companion to Modern Irish culture, p 146.

King. Seamus J. A History of Hurling (Gill & McMillan 1996) p6-8.

Kirk Session Records of Glasgow. The Club of True Highlanders, as quoted in Hugh Dan MacLennan. 'SHINTY'S PLACE AND SPACE IN WORLD SPORT', The Sports Historian (became Sport in History in 2003) 1998 May Vol. 18 No. 1 p. 1-23.

Kirsch. George B, Othello Harris, Claire E. Nolte, eds. Encyclopedia of ethnicity and sports in the United States. (USA-Greenword Press CT) p 235.

Koch. John T, Celtic culture: a historical encyclopedia (ABC-CLIO 2009)

Leibs. Andrew, 'Sports and Games of the Renaissance' (Westport CT: Greenwood Press 2004)

Levy, Nat, 'Irish Festival highlights game of hurling', The Register-Guard, Eugene OR, March 8, 2009.

Lyle. John, Sports Coaching Concepts. A Framework for Coaches Behaviour. (Rutledge 2002).

MacLennan. Hugh Dan. (Aberdeen University, Scotland.) 'SHINTY'S PLACE AND SPACE IN WORLD SPORT'. The Sports Historian (became Sport in History in 2003) 1998 May Vol. 18 No. 1 p, 1-23.

Marjorie Levy. Patricia, Cultures of the World, Ireland, (USA, Marshall Cavendish , 1993.)

Megan Gwynne Mullen, 'Television in the multichannel age: A brief history of cable television.' p131, (Blackwell Pub., 15 Feb 2008).

Mic Mac History – Population, 1999. http://www.dickshovel.com/mic.html

Moynihan. Daniel Patrick, 'Making the Irish American: history and heritage of the Irish in the United ...' in reprinted study of the Irish in New York City eds., Joseph Lee, Marion R. Casey, p (2006) p 467

Moriarty. Colm, 'Irish Archeology blog. Hurling, its ancient history'. Sept 3, 2011.<http://irisharchaeology.ie/2011/09/hurling-its-ancient-history/>.
Mullan. Michael L. Ethnicity and Sport:The Wapato Nippons and Pre-World

War II Japanese American Baseball. DEPARTMENT OF SOCIOLOGY AND ANTHROPOLOGY SWARTHMORE COLLEGE. Journal of Sport History, 26.1:82-114.

North American Society For Sport History. Proceedings And Newsletter. (Dalhousie University, 1989).

O'Flynn. John, The History of the Gaelic Athletic Association in Canada. (Bloomington,IN: Trafford Publishing, 2008) px.

O'Flynn. John, The History of the Gaelic Athletic Association in Canada. (Bloomington,IN: Trafford Publishing, 2008)) p1.

O'Sullivan. 1998, p34, quoted in Colm Moriarty. Irish Archeology blog.'Hurling, its ancient history'. Sept 3, 2011 <irisharchaeology.ie/2011/09/hurling-its-ancient-history/>

Paddy Dolan & John Connolly Dublin City University, Civilizing processes and hurling in Ireland: 1884-2000 Ireland in Lennon, 1997, 11, 46, 99. Local Sport in Europe Conference - (4th eass Conference European Association for the Sociology of Sport, 31 May - 3 June 2007, Münster, Germany).

Rader. Benjamin G. Baseball, a history of America's game. Illinois History of Sports. (University of Illinois Press, 2008, 3rd Edition.) p9.

Riess. Steven A, City Games: The Evolution of American Urban Society and the Rise of Sports, (Illini Books, 1991).

Robert T. Walsh. THE SPORTS OF AN IRISH FAIR. Some Reminiscences of This Extinct Custom—A Game Resembling Baseball a Thousand Years Ago, Outing Magazine 1891 March Vol. XVII No. 6 p. 432-435.

Rolleston, TW, Celtic Myths and Legends. (New York: Dover Publications) p183

'The Day of Days,' Pro Quest Historical Newspapers Boston Globe (1872 – 1926) Boston Globe, (July 6, 1880) p1.

Newspapers, Magazines & Websites

About USA Rugby, USA Rugby,
http://www.usarugby.org/#goto/About_USA_Rugby

Australia Matters for America, http://www.australiamattersforamerica.org/2011/10/95000-americans-are-of-australian-ancestry/

Boston Daily Globe, Sept 30, 1888.

Boston Daily Globe, Oct 4, 1888.

Boston Daily Globe, Oct 4, 1888.

Boston Daily Globe, Oct 5, 1888.

Boston Daily Globe, Feb 17, 1889.

Boston Daily Globe, July 5, 1893.

Boston Daily Globe, Sept 2, 1895.

'Cardinal and Cal make history'. The Stanford Daily, Jan 2009.

Carroll, Joseph T, 'The Gentle Irish.'THE SLASHING, COLORFUL SPORT OF HURLING IS MUCH MORE THAN A GAME TO FERVENT PATRIOTS—IN THE U.S. AS WELL AS IN IRELAND,' Sports Illustrated, Aug 28, 1967.

Kaitlyn Joseph. The Fastest Growing Sports in America. Yahoo Voices: http://voices.yahoo.com/the-fastest-growing-sports-America-3383378.html?cat=14 (June 5, 2009).

Cusack. Ian, 'Is GAA ready to take on the world?' Irish Examiner, July 25, 2011.

Dougherty. Conor, 'Hurling in America Has a Problem -- Too Few Irishmen,' The Wall Street Journal, July 26, 2007.

Freeman. Joe, 'Hurley men. The Orlando Hurling Club celebrates a true Irish pastime,' Orlando Weekly, March 15, 2012.

History Page. New Haven Irish Festival & Feis, Connecticut Irish Festival. http://www.ctirishfestival.com/History.html

'Hurling: That's a sport,' athleticgals.com. June 27, 2009.

'Irish Allow US game'. New York Times, Oct 3, 1953.

'Irish American Baseball Hall of Fame Inducts Walter O'Malley, O'Neill, Garvey, Sculley, Joyce And Lucas,' Irish Examiner USA, Tuesday July 15, 2009. p 34.

Irish Festival List, http://www.azirishmusic.com/fest_irish.htm

James O Shea, 'Landmark ruling in favor of Irish pub sued for showing soccer game live,' Irish Central March 8, 2012. *http://www.irishcentral.com/news/Landmark-ruling-in-favor-of-Irish-pub-sued-for-showing-soccer-game-live-141885283.html*

Krag-Arnold, Kelly, 'UC Davis Hurling Club brings international sport to Davis'. The California Aggie. May 2010.

Miller. Jeremy, 'THE LACK OF THE IRISH', Boston Globe, June 3, 2007.

New York Times. Sept 26, 1888.

New York Times, Dec 19, 1892.

New York Times, Nov 24, 1892, p5.

New York Sun, March 12, 1893, p9.

NFL, Chronology of Professional Football. NFL History 2012. http://static.nfl.com/static/content/public/image/history/pdfs/History/Chronology_2011.pdf

O'Conner. Colm, 'Far away fields are greener as GAA goes global', Irish Examiner, May 30, 2011. http://www.irishexaminer.com/sport/gaa/far-away-fields-are-greener-as-gaa-goes-global-156161.html#ixzz1pZNWX6Hh

'Pluck of the Irish,' The Insider, Milwaukee Magazine. July 1, 2009.

'Report shows Rugby's growth in new markets'. IRB April 2011, http://www.irb.com/newsmedia/mediazone/pressrelease/newsid=2042293.html

Simcoe. John, Hurling should be fun first, Hurley to Rise. April 8, 2011. http://www.ydtalk.com/hurley/2011/04/08/hurling-should-be-fun-first/

Smith. Ronald A. Play-by-Play: Radio, Television, and Big-Time College Sport. (Baltimore MD, John Hopkins University Press, 2001).

Summers. Brian, 'Hurling club finds a niche with odd sport'. The Daily Trojan, March 2010.

'The Boys of Sliotar. They make you want to hurl,' Street Smart Chicago, Newcity Communications Inc, April 2011.'Tipperary takes hurling game': 37 to 8', New York Times, May 31, 1926. p 12.

The Irish Herald, San Francisco. December, 2009.

'Tipperary takes hurling game': 37 to 8', New York Times, May 31, 1926. p 12.

US Lacrosse, Players Post College,
http://www.uslacrosse.org/TopNav2Left/Players/PostCollege.aspx

US Internal Revenue Service, Exempt Purposes - Internal Revenue Code Section 501(c)(3)
http://www.irs.gov/charities/charitable/article/0,,id=175418,00.html

US Internal Revenue Service, Section 501(c)(3) Organizations Amateur Athletic Organizations.
http://www.irs.gov/publications/p557/ch03.html#en_US_2011_publink1000200111)

Variations of Stickball, University of Georgia,
http://toli.uga.edu/information/variations.html

Young. A.J. 'Sandy', The Continuing Saga of Ice Hockey's Origins. p. 47-48.

Club & GAA Websites

'About STLGAC', St Louis GAC, http://www.stlgac.com/

'2nd Annual Hibernian Hurling Invitational', 2009. Indianapolis Hurling Club, http://www.indyhurling.com/article.aspx?id=21258000_fp5tziei9u

Benton Brigade HC website. <http://www.bentonbrigade.com>

'Cal Make it Two in a Row'. California Collegiate Gaelic Athletic Association (CCGAA) http://www.cacollegesgaa.org/

Club History. Portland Hurling Club.
http://www.portlandhurling.com/history.htm

'Harte: Rules does nothing for Gaelic games',
http://hoganstand.com/ArticleForm.aspx?ID=156861 (October 21, 2011).

'Irish Fest - A Festivus for All of Us', Indianapolis Hurling Club.
http://www.indyhurling.com/article.aspx?id=21174177_ke14lvamjy

Kelly calls for International GAA federation, Hogan Stand Website. January 26, 2011.

Milwaukee HC Website, http://www.hurling.net

Twin Cities Robert Emmet's HC, http://www.**twincities**hurling.com

Madison HC Website, http://www.madisonhurling.com

Fox River HC Website, http://www.foxriverhurlingclub.com

Mathew Schwertfeger. 'First Ever Midwest College Hurling Match'. Indianapolis hosts match between Indiana and Purdue,' Indy Hurling Club Website, 2009.

'Middle Tennessee State University Plays First Match.' NCGAA. <www.ncgaa.com> (Jan 2012)

'Promoting Gaelic Football and Hurling in the US'. GAA – Continental Youth 2005. Letter from Sean Kelly President. NACB Website 2004.

'Spring 2012 hurling season.' St Louis GAC, http://www.stlgac.com/

Podcasts

GaelicSportsCast, '#14 Progress on and off the field – Washington DC Gaels,' January 22, 2010: http://www.gaelicsportscast.com/2010/01/22/14-progress-on-and-off-the-field-washing-ton-dc-gales/

GaelicSportsCast., '#15 US National Guard Soldiers playing hurling, ' Jan 2010: http://www.gaelicsportscast.com/2010/01/26/15-us-national-guard-soldiers-playing-hurling-the-barley-house-wolves/

GaelicSportsCast, "# 17 Hurling will take off says American Hurling Officer – Dave Olson,' Feb 2, 2010 http://www.gaelicsportscast.com/2010/02/02/17-hurling-will-take-off-says-American-hurling-officer-dave-olson/

GaelicSportsCast, '#26 Stanford oust Berkeley in Game 2 of California Collegiate Hurling Championship,' March 2010: http://www.gaelicsportscast.com/2010/03/02/26-standford-oust-berkeley-in-game-2-of-california-collegiate-hurling-championship/

GaelicSportsCast, '#35 – Stanford and Berkeley set for hurling final,' April 2010: http://www.gaelicsportscast.com/2010/04/09/35-stanford-and-berkeley-set-for-hurling-final/?preview=true&preview_id=494&preview_nonce=8b45d8e5f4>

GaelicSportsCast, "#121 Orange groves, palm trees and hurling," August 11, 2010: http://www.gaelicsportscast.com/?s=orlando+hurling+club+.

References

GaelicSportsCast, "#160 Madison Hurling Club – proud of their new sport," October 19, 2010: http://www.gaelicsportscast.com/?s=madison+hurling+club+proud+of+.

GaelicSportsCast, '#180 Cork captain sees 'Wolves as shining example for hurling,' Jan 2011: http://www.gaelicsportscast.com/2011/01/10/180-cork-captain-sees-wolves-as-shining-example-for-hurling/

GaelicSportsCast, '#182 UC Davis join California college hurling circuit,' Jan 2011: http://www.gaelicsportscast.com/2011/01/15/182-uc-davis-join-california-college-hurling-circuit

GaelicSportsCast, '#209 Midwest College hurling opener,' March 31, 2011: http://www.gaelicsportscast.com/2011/03/31/209-midwest-college-hurling-opener/

GaelicSportsCast, '#229 Midwest College 1, March 2011: www.gaelicsportscast.com/2011/05/29/229-thrilling-college-nationals-day-1/

GaelicSportsCast, "#274 'Macs and Galway lead Boston charge," Sept, 2011: http://www.gaelicsportscast.com/2011/09/01/macs-and-galway-lead-boston-charge/

GaelicSportsCast, "#309 New York Celtics brilliant underage success," Dec 2011: http://www.gaelicsportscast.com/2011/12/20/309-new-york-celtics-brilliant-underage-success/

GaelicSportsCast, "#320 Portland Maine kids learning hurling," February 2012: http://www.gaelicsportscast.com/2012/02/17/320-port-land-maine-kids-learning-hurling/

You Tube

eamonnca1, 'Hurling- An American Perspective', You Tube, April 12, 2009 http://www.youtube.com/watchv=AiuzYvScbnY&feature=related eamonnca1

wisn.com, 'Irish Game Makes Its Way To Milwaukee,' You Tube, wisn2news, May 18, 2008, http://www.youtube.com/watch?v=ttSbj9tNwmE&feature=endscreen&NR=1

ajvarelas1, 2011 MILWAUKEE HURLING CLUB FOOTAGE ...MCH,' You Tube Sept 12, 2011. http://www.youtube.com/watch?v=XjiGghj0InAWCSH6.com

'Ancient Sport Played In Portland,' You Tube, WCSH TV Portland, ME, June 27, 2010.

http://origin.wcsh6.com/life/community/who_care_recognitions/story.aspx?storyid=119480&catid=2

Facebook

Indianapolis Hurling Facebook Page, 'Indy Hurling Chosen as a super sport'. http://www.facebook.com/IndyHurlingClub> (Jan 25, 2011).

Reports & Email Interviews

Karen Fink, Interview email 2009.

Matt Schwertfeger, Interview email 2010.

Ray Valas, Interview email 2010 & 2011.

Matt Everett, Survey email 2010.

GAA, 'UConn Huskies First Hurling Game!', http://www.gaa.ie/about-the-gaa/gaa-overseas/news/2510111354-uconn-huskies-first-hurling-game/

'A Century of Boston GAA. Boston and North East Gaelic Athletic Association 1884 –2000'. North East GAA, Aug 2000.

'ANNUAL SURVEY OF FOOTBALL INJURY RESEARCH 1931 – 2008'. Prepared for American Football Coaches Association, National Collegiate Athletic Association, and The National Federation of State High School Associations. February 2009

Eamonn Kelly. *Historic Collegiate Hurling Game.* NACB Website 2009.

Eamonn Gormley. *Games For Life. Ten-Year Strategic Plan for GAA Games Development and Promotion in North America,* (NACB 2006).

Fast Facts. National Center for Education Statistics. US Dept of Ed.

'*MCHA Newsletter, Vol 3. Issue 1.*' MCHA, November 2011.

NACB, 'Development and Promotion in North America,' NACB 2006.

National Collegiate Athletic Association. NCAA, 2011.

Official Guide Part 1. Gaelic Athletic Association (GAA) 2011.

NACB, 'Report on the Activities of the Hurling Development Committee in 2011', NACB 2011 Convention.

About the Author

Denis O'Brien

Denis O'Brien is a Freelance Journalist based in the North West of Ireland, in the town of Ballinamore, in the County of Leitrim.

He is writer, producer and publisher of the popular podcast, GaelicSportsCast.

GaelicSportsCast reports on Gaelic Sports news around the globe via daily and weekly podcasts as well as written reports.

Mr. O'Brien is a former emigrant himself as he spent almost 20 years in America, where he lived in New York and more recently in Boston.

Since returning to Ireland in the past few years, he has worked as a Freelance Reporter and later as a Staff Reporter for the former Leitrim Post newspaper.

While in America Mr. O'Brien reported Gaelic Sports news from Boston with weekly blog and local newspapers publications.

He has written for the Boston Irish Reporter, the New York Irish Examiner, and contributed to the Irish Examiner, Leitrim Observer, Anglo Celt, The Sligo Champion, Sligo Weekender, Donegal News, Shannonside Radio and Ocean FM Radio.

The Rules of Hurling

Rules of Fair Play

RULE 1 - THE PLAY

1.1 The ball is in play once it has been thrown in or pucked, after the referee has given a signal to start or restart play, and it remains in play until:

  (a) The referee signals a stop;
  (b) The ball has passed completely over any boundary line or strikes any flag marking the boundary lines;
  (c) The ball has been prevented from going over any boundary line or is touched in play by anyone other than a player.

1.2 The ball may be struck with the hurley when it is on the ground, in the air, released from the hand or lifted with the hurley.

1.3 A player may run with the ball balanced on or hopping on his hurley.

1.4 A player may catch the ball, play it on his hurley, and bring it back into his hand once. A player who has not caught the ball may play it from the hurley into his hand twice.

1.5 The ball may be struck with the hand, kicked, or lifted off the ground with the feet.

1.6 The ball may not be touched on the ground with the hand(s), except when a player is knocked down or falls and the ball in his hand touches the ground.

1.7 When a player is in possession of the ball it may be:

  (a) Carried in the hand for a maximum of four consecutive steps or held in the hand for no longer than the time needed to take four steps.
  (b) Released and struck with a definite striking action of a hand.

1.8 Player(s) may tackle an opponent for the ball.

1.9 Provided that he has at least one foot on the ground, a player may make a shoulder to shoulder charge on an opponent-

  (a) Who is in possession of the ball, or
  (b) Who is playing the ball, or
  (c) When both players are moving in the direction of the ball to play it.

When he is within the small rectangle, the goalkeeper may not be charged but he may be challenged for possession of the ball, and his puck, kick or pass may be blocked. Incidental contact with the goalkeeper while playing the ball is permitted.

1.10 For a run-up to a free puck, sideline puck, or puck-out, a player may go outside the boundary lines, but otherwise players shall remain within the field of play.

1.11 A player may hold up his hurley or hand(s) to intercept a free puck.

RULE 2 - SET PLAY

2.1 The referee, facing the players, starts the game and restarts it after half-time by throwing in the ball between two players from each team, who shall stand one behind the other in their own defensive sides of the half-way line.

All other players shall be in their respective positions behind the 65m lines.

2.2 After a foul, play is restarted by a free puck or a throw-in where the foul(s) occurred.

Exceptions

(i) In the case of fouls by defending players within the rectangles, the following shall apply:

A penalty puck shall be awarded for an Aggressive Foul within the large rectangle. The penalty puck shall be taken from the centre point of the 20m line.

A free puck from the centre of the 20m line shall be awarded for a Technical Foul within the large rectangle.

(ii) A free puck, awarded for a foul by a defending player inside his own 20m line but outside the large rectangle, shall be taken from the 20m line opposite where the foul occurred.

(iii) When a player is fouled immediately after he plays the ball away, and a score results, it shall stand. Otherwise, the referee shall award a free puck from where the foul occurred or, if more advantageous, from where the ball lands or crosses the sideline. With the option of a free being awarded from where the foul occurred being retained, the rule shall apply in the following circumstances as outlined:-

    (a) If the ball lands over the endline, a free shall be given on the 20m line opposite the place where the ball crossed the endline;
    (b) If the ball lands inside the opponents' 20m line, a free shall be given from the 20m line at the point where the ball crossed this line.

(iv) Where otherwise specified in the penalties listed in Rule 4, Sections 14, 15, 16, 17, 18, 19, 27, 28, 29, 30, 34; Rule 5, Sections 16, 36; Rule 6.4.

(v) When play is restarted by throwing in the ball after a foul(s) within 13m of the sideline, the throw in shall be given 13m from the sideline and directly infield from where the foul(s) occurred.

(vi) When play is restarted by throwing in the ball after a foul(s) between the endline and the 20m line, the throw-in shall be given on the 20m line, opposite where the foul(s) occurred, subject to the Provisions stated in (v) above.

All players, except the player taking the free puck (excluding penalties), shall be 20m from where the free puck is being taken or all players, except those two contesting the throw-in, shall be 13m from where the throw-in is awarded.

2.3 A penalty puck shall be taken at the centre point of the 20m line and the semi-circular arc, and only three defending players may stand on the goal-line. All other players, with the exception of the player taking the puck, shall be outside the 20m line, and shall not cross the 20m line or the arc until the ball has been struck. If a defending player(s) fouls before the ball is struck and a goal does not result, the referee shall allow the penalty puck to be retaken.

2.4 When opposing players foul simultaneously, play is restarted by throwing in the ball.

2.5 For all free pucks, including penalties, the ball may be struck with the hurley in either of two ways:

>**(a)** Lift the ball with the hurley at the first attempt and strike it with the hurley.
>**(b)** Strike the ball on the ground. If a player taking a free puck or penalty fails to lift the ball at the first attempt, or fails to strike it with the hurley, he must strike it on the ground without delay. Only when he delays, may a player of either side approach nearer than 20m. except in the case of penalties.

2.6 When the ball is played over the endline by the team attacking that end or after a score, play is restarted by a puck-out from within the small rectangle. The player taking a puck-out shall take the ball into his hand, but should he miss his stroke, the ball may be struck on the ground or may be raised with and struck with the hurley, but not taken into his hand again before striking it. The player taking the puck-out may strike the ball more than once before another player touches it. All players shall be outside the 20m line until the ball has been struck except the goalkeeper and the player taking the puck-out - if other than the goalkeeper. The ball shall travel 13m before being played by another player of the defending team.

2.7 When the ball is played over the endline and outside the goalposts by the team defending that end, a free puck shall be awarded to the opposing team on the 65m line opposite where the ball crossed the endline.

2.8 When a team plays the ball over the sideline, a free puck from the ground shall be awarded to the opposing team at the place where the ball crossed the sideline. If opposing players play the ball simultaneously over the sideline, or if the officials are not sure which team played the ball last, the Referee, facing the players, shall throw in the ball between one player from each team, 13m from the sideline and directly infield from where ball crossed the sideline. A ball that strikes a sideline or corner flag shall be treated as having crossed the sideline. A player on the team awarded a sideline puck shall place the ball on the sideline at the place indicated by the linesman. All players except the player taking the sideline puck, or the two players contesting the throw-in, shall be at least 13m from the ball until it is struck or thrown in. If a player taking a sideline puck fails to strike the ball at the first attempt, he shall not delay in making a second attempt. Only when the player delays his second attempt to strike the ball may a player from either side approach nearer than 13m.

2.9 If in exceptional circumstances play is stopped by the Referee to enable a seriously injured player to be treated on the field or removed from the field of play, play shall resume in one of the following manners:-

(i) If a Team is in possession when the play is stopped, the play shall resume with a free puck to that Team from the position at which the play was stopped, unless the play was stopped inside the opponents' 20m line in which case the free shall be awarded from the 20m line opposite the point where the play was stopped. A score may not be made directly from such free.

(ii) If neither Team is in possession when the play is stopped, a throw-in shall be given at the position where the play was stopped, subject to the provisions in Exceptions (v) and (vi) of Rule 2.2

2.10 If the ball touches any non-player during play, play is restarted by throwing in the ball at the place concerned, but if the ball touches any non-player from a free puck, the free shall be retaken.

Exceptions

(i) As provided in Rule 3.3(a).

(ii) If the ball has been prevented from going over a boundary line by a non-player other than the referee, it shall be treated as having crossed the line, and the referee shall make the appropriate award.

RULE 3 - SCORES

3.1 A **goal** is scored when the ball is played over the goal-line between the posts and under the crossbar by either team. A **point** is scored when the ball is played over the crossbar between the posts by either team. A goal is equivalent to three points. The team with the greater final total of points is the winner.

Exceptions

A player on the team attacking a goal who is in possession of the ball may not score;

(i) By carrying the ball over his opponents' goal-line, or

(ii) With his hand(s).

3.2 A score may be made by striking the ball in flight with the hand(s).

3.3
    (a) A score shall be allowed if, in the opinion of the referee, the ball was prevented from crossing the goal-line by anyone other than a player or the referee.
    (b) If part of the goal-posts or crossbar is displaced during play, the referee shall award the score which he considers would have resulted had a part not been displaced.

3.4 If a defending player plays the ball through his own scoring space in any manner, this shall count as a score.

Rules of Foul Play

RULE 4 - TECHNICAL FOULS

4.1 To overcarry or overhold the ball.

4.2
    (a) To throw the ball.
    (b) To handpass the ball without it being released and struck with a definite striking action of a hand.

4.3 To lift the ball off the ground with the knees.

4.4 To lie on the ball.

4.5 To touch the ball on the ground with the hand(s), except when a player falls or is knocked down and the ball in his hand touches the ground.

4.6 To catch the ball more than twice before playing it away.

4.7 To release the ball with the hand and catch it without playing it with the hurley.

4.8 To drop the hurley intentionally, or to throw the hurley in a manner which does not constitute a danger to another player.

4.9 To tip an opponent's hurley in the air or to tip it up with hurley or foot, for the purpose of allowing the ball to pass through.

4.10 For an attacking player to enter opponents' small rectangle before the ball enters it during the play.

Exceptions

(i) If an attacking player legally enters the small rectangle, and the ball is played from that area but is returned before the attacking player has time to leave the area, provided that he does not play the ball or interfere with the defence, a foul is not committed.

(ii) When a point is scored from outside the small rectangle and the ball is sufficiently high to be out of reach of all players, the score shall be allowed even though an attacking player may have been within the small rectangle before the ball – provided that the player in question does not interfere with the defence.

4.11
   (a) For a player on the team awarded a free puck to stand or move nearer than 20m to the ball before it is struck.
   (b) For a player on the team awarded a sideline puck to stand or move nearer than 13m to the ball before it is struck.
   (c) For a player on the team awarded a penalty puck to be inside the 20m line or the arc before the ball is struck.

4.12 For a player attacking a goal to carry the ball over opponents' goal-line.

4.13 For a player on the team attacking a goal, who is in possession of the ball, to score with the hand(s).

PENALTY FOR ABOVE FOULS - Free puck from where the foul occurred, except as provided under Exceptions of Rule 2.2.

4.14 To be inside opponents' 20m line before a puck-out is taken after a wide.

PENALTY - Free puck from the defenders' 20m line opposite where the foul occurred.

4.15 To take the puck-out from outside the small rectangle.

PENALTY -

(i) Cancel Puck-Out

(ii) Throw-in ball on the defenders' 20m line opposite the scoring space

4.16
   (a) For a player on the team defending a penalty puck, with the exception of the three defending players on the goal-line, to be inside the 20m line or the semi-circle before the ball is struck.
   (b) For any of the three players defending a penalty on the goal-line to move nearer than 20m to the ball before the ball is struck.

PENALTY - If a goal is not scored, the referee shall allow the penalty puck to be retaken.

4.17
   (a) For an opposing player to be nearer than 20m to the ball before a free puck is struck.
   (b) For an opposing player to be nearer than 13m to the ball before a sideline puck is struck.

PENALTY FOR THE ABOVE FOULS – Free puck 13m more advantageous than the place of original puck - up to opponents' 20m line.

4.18 To delay an opponent taking a free puck or sideline puck by hitting or kicking the ball away, not releasing the ball to the opposition, or by deliberately not moving back to allow the puck to be taken.

4.19 To interfere with a player taking a free puck or sideline puck by jumping up and down, waving hands or hurley, or any other physical or verbal interference considered by the referee to be aimed at distracting the player taking the puck.

Exception

A player holding his hands or hurley upright shall not constitute an interference.

PENALTY - Free puck 13m more advantageous than the place of original puck - up to opponents' 20m line.

4.20 To reset the ball for a free/penalty/sideline puck without the referee's permission after the whistle has been blown for the free/penalty/sideline puck to be taken.

4.21 To play the ball again after taking a free/penalty/sideline puck before another player has played it, unless the ball rebounds off the goal-posts or crossbar.

4.22 To foul a free puck by making a second attempt to lift the ball, to hop the ball on the hurley, or to take the ball in the hand.

4.23 For the player taking a sideline puck to attempt to lift the ball with his hurley.

4.24 To make a divot for the purpose of teeing up the ball for a free puck or sideline puck.

4.25 To advance the ball deliberately from the place at which a free puck or sideline puck is to be taken.

4.26 To waste time by delaying a free puck or sideline puck awarded to own team.

PENALTY FOR THE ABOVE FOULS -

(i) Cancel free puck or sideline puck.

(ii) Throw in the ball where the foul occurred, except as provided under Exceptions (v) and (vi) of Rule 2.2.

4.27 For the player taking the puck-out and, having missed a stroke, to take the ball into his hand a second time before striking.

4.28 To be inside own 20m line when one's team is taking a puck-out except as provided in Rule 2.6.

4.29 For another player on the team taking the puck-out to play the ball before it has travelled 13m.

4.30 To waste time by delaying own puck-out.

PENALTY FOR ABOVE FOULS -

(i) Cancel puck-out.

(ii) Throw in the ball on defenders' 20m line opposite the scoring space.

4.31 For a player(s) from each team to foul simultaneously.

Penalty - Throw in the ball where the foul(s) occurred, except as provided under Exceptions (v) and (vi) of Rule 2.2.

4.32 To deliberately go outside the boundary lines to gain an advantage except as permitted by Rule 1.10.

Penalty-Free puck from where the foul occurred.

4.33 To interfere with the goalposts to distract opponents or to gain an advantage.

PENALTY FOR THE ABOVE FOULS Caution offender; order off for second cautionable offence.

4.34 When a team commits a Technical Foul, the referee may allow the play to continue if he considers it to be to the advantage of the opposing team. He shall signal that advantage is being played by raising an extended arm upright. Once he allows play to continue, he may not subsequently award a free for that foul. He shall apply any relevant disciplinary action.

RULE 5 - AGGRESSIVE FOULS

Category II Infractions

5.1 To strike or to attempt to strike an opponent with arm, elbow, hand or knee.

5.2 To strike or to attempt to strike an opponent with a hurley, with minimal force.

5.3 To kick or to attempt to kick an opponent, with minimal force .

5.4 To behave in any way which is dangerous to an opponent.

5.5 To spit at an opponent.

5.6 To contribute to a melee.

5.7 To use abusive language to a Referee, Umpire, Linesman or Sideline Official.

Category III Infractions

5.8 To strike or to attempt to strike an opponent with the head.

5.9 To strike an opponent with a hurley, either with force or causing injury.

5.10 To attempt to strike an opponent with a hurley, with force.

5.11 To kick an opponent either with force or causing injury.

5.12 To attempt to kick an opponent with force.

5.13 To stamp on an opponent.

5.14 To inflict an injury recklessly on an opponent by means other than those stated above.

5.15 To assault an opposing Team Official

Category IV Infractions

5.16 To interfere with a Referee, Umpire, Linesman or Sideline Official - minor physical interference e.g. laying a hand on, pushing, pulling or jostling.

5.17 To use threatening language to a Referee, Umpire, Linesman or Sideline Official.

5.18 To use threatening or abusive conduct towards a Referee, Umpire, Linesman or Sideline Official.

Category V Infractions

5.19 To strike or attempt to strike, or any type of assault on, a Referee, Umpire, Linesman or Sideline Official.

PENALTY FOR ABOVE FOULS -

(i) Order offender off.

(ii) Free puck from where Foul occurred, except as provided under Exceptions of Rule 2.2.

5.20 To commit any of the fouls listed in Rule 5.1,5.2, 5.3, 5.4, 5.5, 5.8, 5.9, 5.10, 5.11, 5.12,5.13 and 5.14 against a team-mate.

PENALTY -

(i) Order offender off.

(ii) Throw in the ball where the Foul occurred, except as provided under Exceptions (v) and (vi) of Rule 2.2

5.21 To commit any of the fouls listed in Rule 5.1,5.2, 5.3, 5.4, 5.5, 5.8, 5.9, 5.10, 5.11, 5.12,5.13 and 5.14 on an opponent on the field prior to the start of a game or at half time.

PENALTY - Offender shall be treated as ordered off and shall not participate (or further participate) in the game.

Note- Once the Referee has received the list of players, or a substitution/temporary replacement slip which includes the offender's name, the player may not be substituted.

5.22 To pull down an opponent.

5.23 To trip an opponent with hand(s), foot, or hurley.

5.24 To threaten or to use abusive or provocative language or gestures to an opponent.

5.25 To engage in any form of rough play.

5.26 To make 'a pull' with the hurley from behind and around the body of an opponent that is not consistent with an attempt to play the ball.

5.27 To use the hurley in a careless manner.

5.28 To throw a hurley in a manner which constitutes a danger to another player(s).

PENALTY FOR ABOVE FOULS -

(i) Caution offender; order off for second cautionable foul.

(ii) Free puck from where the foul occurred except as provided under Exceptions of Rule 2.2.

5.29 To pull or take hold of a faceguard or any other part of an opponent's helmet.

5.30 To attempt to achieve an advantage by feigning a foul or injury.

PENALTY FOR ABOVE FOULS -

(i) Caution offender; order off for second cautionable foul.

(ii) If play has been stopped for the foul, a free puck from where play was stopped, except as provided under Exceptions of Rule 2.2.

5.31 To threaten or to use abusive or provocative language or gestures to a team-mate.

PENALTY FOR ABOVE FOULS -

(i) Caution offender; order off for second cautionable foul.

(ii) Throw in the ball where the foul occurred, except as provided under Exceptions (v) and (vi) of Rule 2.2.

5.32 To hold an opponent with the hand(s)

5.33
    (a) To charge an opponent in the back or to the front.
    (b) To charge an opponent unless:-
        (i) He is in possession of the ball, or
        (ii) He is playing the ball, or
        (iii) Both players are moving in the direction of the ball to play it.
    (c) To charge an opponent for the purpose of giving an advantage to a team-mate.

PENALTY FOR THE ABOVE FOULS -

(i) Free puck from where foul occurred, except as provided under Exceptions of Rule 2.2.

(ii) Caution offender for committing any of the above fouls a second time; order off for a further repetition or for other cautionable foul.

5.34
    (a) To push an opponent with the hand(s) or hurley.
    (b) To hold an opponent's hurley or pull it from his hands.

5.35
    (a) To charge (in a manner otherwise permissible on an opponent) the goalkeeper in his small rectangle.
    (b) For a player in possession of the ball to charge an opponent.

5.36 To use the hurley to obstruct an opponent

5.37 To strike an opponent's hurley unless both players are in the act of playing the ball.

Penalty for the above Fouls –

(i) Free Puck from where Foul occurred, except as provided under Exceptions of Rule 2.2.

(ii) Caution offender for persistently committing such Fouls. Order off for further repetition or for other Cautionable Foul.

5.38 For a player to retaliate between the award of a free to his team and the free puck being taken.

PENALTY -

(i) Cancel free puck.

(ii) Throw in the ball where the original foul occurred, except as provided under Exceptions (v) and (vi) of Rule 2.2.

(iii) Apply any other relevant penalty of Rule 5.

5.39 For a player(s) from each team to foul simultaneously.

PENALTY -

(i) Throw in the ball where the fouls occurred, except as provided under Exceptions (v) and (vi) of Rule 2.2.

(ii) Apply any other relevant penalty of Rule 5.

5.40 When an Aggressive Foul is drawn to the referee's attention by an umpire or linesman, the referee may apply the appropriate penalty as per Rule 5, and shall restart play as per Rule 2.

5.41 When a team commits an Aggressive Foul, the referee may allow play to continue if he considers it to be to the advantage of the offended team. He shall signal that advantage is being played by raising an extended arm upright. Once the referee allows the play to continue, he may not subsequently award a free for that foul. He shall apply the relevant penalty.

RULE 6 - DISSENT

6.1 To challenge the authority of a Referee, Umpire, Linesman or Sideline Official.

PENALTY - Caution the offender; order off for second cautionable foul.

6.2 To fail to comply with a Referee's instruction to wear a helmet with a facial guard.

Penalty - Caution the offender; order off if he persists.

6.3 To refuse to leave the field of play, on the instruction of the Referee, for attention, after an injury involving bleeding.

Penalty - Caution the offender; order off if he continues to refuse.

6.4 To show dissent with the referee's decision to award a free puck to the opposing team.

PENALTY - The free puck already awarded shall be taken 13m more advantageous than the place of original free puck, up to the opponents' 20m line.

Further dissent on an occasion shall be considered as a breach of Rule 6.1 and shall be penalised accordingly.

6.5
   (a) To refuse to leave the field of play when ordered off.
   (b) To rejoin the game after being ordered off.

PROCEDURE - First give a three minute warning to the team captain or the official in charge of the team, or the player(s) involved, and then, if the player(s) refuse(s) to comply, terminate the game.

6.6 A team or a player(s) leaving the field without the referee's permission or refusing to continue playing.

PROCEDURE - as in Rule 6.5 Any player willing to continue shall give his name to the referee.

Map of Ireland

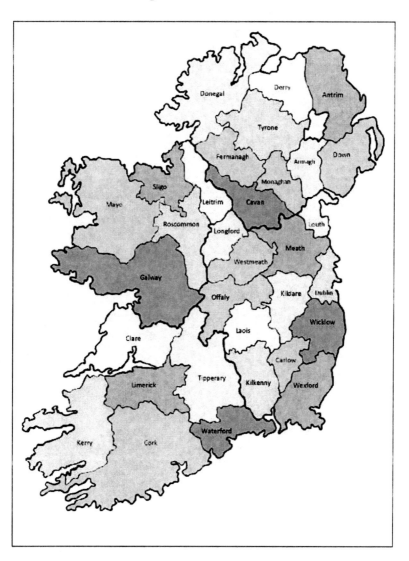

CPSIA information can be obtained
at www.ICGtesting.com
Printed in the USA
FFOW02n1611141215
19650FF